Testimonials for *Inner Journ*

Imagine having REAL historical per perspective that goes beyond one's life story and even family history. Imagine having the big, big, big picture that begins long before we were born, and continues long after our current life ends. Stephen Poplin has written an eye-opening, paradigm-breaking and mind-bending book about his 40 years working as a transpersonal hypnotherapist, regressing his clients back not just to previous lifetimes, but "life-between-life". Whether or not you "believe in" karma and reincarnation, the accounts you read in *Inner Journeys, Cosmic Sojourns* will change your perspective forever. I guarantee, this book will expand your awareness, and your compassion for others -- and yourself.

— Steve Bhaerman aka Swami Beyondananda, comedian and co-author of *Spontaneous Evolution: Our Positive Future and a Way to Get There From Here* (with Bruce Lipton)

Stephen Poplin is so much more than a hypnotherapist or counselor. He is a spiritual warrior who uses stories from his encounters with clients to take us deep into the life beyond this one, showing us both the long history we each carry with us as well as the reflective time between lifetimes necessary to grow and continue the evolutionary journey. I loved the stories interspersed with commentary and humor, and the deep humility and appreciation that Stephen shows for the mystery called life.

— Thom Markham, Ph.D., teacher, author, activist; author of "Redefining Smart" - 21st Century skills, innovation, and high performance cultures

Θ

I've had a lifelong interest in the soul's journey and the works of those that attempt to illuminate it (from Edgar Cayce, Rudolph Steiner, Brian Weiss, Roger Woolger, Michael Newton to Sylvia Brown). Stephen Poplin's book is a welcome addition to my library. Drawing on his decades of research and work as a transpersonal hypnotherapist, he shares stories that weave together spirituality, healing, past life therapy, and metaphysical philosophy. His book thoroughly engaged me and I enjoyed it.

— Ro Loughran, MFT, psychotherapist

"☾,☽"

"Inner Journeys, Cosmic Sojourns" is an excellent cover-all of a broad field of topics. Expertly crafted, Stephen shows us of his vast experience in what can be a very debatable subject. Clear examples are given on how people internalize past-life issues. One gets a sense from reading this of a complex, and caring universe. After reading of so many individual stories, one gets a clear sense of the omniscient intelligence behind it all. This is not a field that can be faked. You either know where you are and where you are going or you just don't. This book is on the mark when it comes to showing us all about how much help is always available to each of us. And for that, I am very grateful. It is easy to miss the point with Stephen's book. Yes, the book is highly recommended. But, the story is Stephen himself. So relaxed, so informed, so experienced. He takes you through a complex set of worlds so effortlessly and with mastery. Seldom have I seen an author live his work; not 9-5, but 24/7. Stephen is a model spiritual citizen, and in this age of glib hype, I don't say that easily. He's right on track and therefore so is his work.

— Rick DiClemente, author of "The Exquisite Zodiac" and host of the online spirituality exploration program, *Astrology Unplugged.*

Θ

Inner Journeys, Cosmic Sojourns is a masterful blend of scholarly research and clinical experience. Drawing on his lifelong study of metaphysics and three decades of private practice, Stephen Poplin provides a concise overview of the history of hypnosis, followed by observations and excerpts of actual client sessions, which illustrate the profound healing power of past life regressions. Some of the topics covered include: reincarnation, death and dying, suicide, soulmates, and life lessons. His clear and descriptive writing style makes these fascinating explorations of "trance-personal" states of consciousness accessible and relevant to both the layman and professional.

— Stephanie Austin, M.A., astrological counselor, teacher, and writer, author of *EcoAstrology: Finding Our Way Home*, and the *EcoAstrology New and Full Moon Updates,* an e-newsletter covering current astrological alignments and how to work with them.

Inner Journeys, Cosmic Sojourns

Volume II

Stephen Poplin

Book cover design expanded by Evan Harrison

Photographs by Stephen Poplin

www.stephen-poplin.com

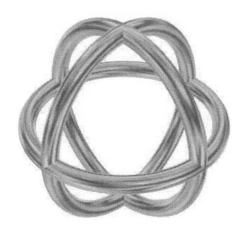

DEDICATION

I offer my heart-felt gratitude to many friends and well-wishers who have advised me along the way. I wish to acknowledge Jürgen Torunsky, Vitae Bergman, Ursula Demarmels, Jim Nourse, Dorothea Fuckert, and Michael Newton for their encouragement and insights.

A special thanks to my many clients who freely shared their stories and lives, and who gave me permission to tell their tales, knowing others may benefit from the telling.

I dedicate this book to my wife, Dr Alenka Poplin.

Inner Journeys, Cosmic Sojourns

II

Life transforming stories, adventures and messages from a spiritual hypnotherapist's casebook

by Stephen Poplin, M.A., CHT

Inner Journeys, Cosmic Sojourns 2

"In the womb before the world began, I was a child among other gods and children who were, or may be, or might have been. There in the dark when we could not see each other's faces, we agreed with one mind to be born, to separate, to forget the pact we made that we might learn the secrets of our fraternity. We agreed to know sorrow in exchange for joy, to know death in exchange for life. We were dark seeds of possibility whispering. Then one by one we entered alone. We walked on our legs, and as we had said, we passed in well-lit streets without recognizing each other; yet we were gods sheathed in flesh, the multitude of a single spirit. Gods live even in darkness, in the world above your heads, in the crevices of rocks, in the open palms of strangers."

Becoming the Child, from "Awakening Osiris: The Egyptian Book of The Dead"- chapter 45, by Normandi Ellis

Preface

Perspectives – Point of Views

We are gods in the body of god, truth and love our destinies.
Go then and make of the world something beautiful,
set up a light in the darkness.

Hymn to Hathor, from "Awakening Osiris"
- chapter 68, by Normandi Ellis [1]

This will be interesting. I have worked with this client several times, and it is a pleasure. He can quickly connect to his higher self, plus his descriptions are rich and colorful. He is now stretched out on my therapist's couch, and we are contemplating plans for the future. He is almost ecstatic. There is a powerful and even wise energy in the room. We continue the sojourn ...

"I'm on a ship, as it were ... this life, this experience we live. We, my partner and I, will travel more; and yet I need to care for this oasis, this garden, our home. Both are wished, both need tending. I want to attract like-minded people. Like you.

The 'crew' here has changed several times. (business employees, who are like extended family) I need more focused people. I'm active. I want to change, to travel. My partner and I both want to dance, move, share and care. This community ... it is a balance, and time is in the quotient."

SP: I hear many desires and motivations. Is this a dilemma, a paradox?

- smiles, and then he channels! -

---

[1] "Awakening Osiris: The Egyptian Book of The Dead", compiled from Egyptian funerary texts and religious hymns from 3000 BCE - 300 CE, translated by Normandi Ellis; pub. 1988.

"Yes. Slow down. Take more time for you. You forget that. Remember, it is just you and me. Let's create more intimacy. *I am your higher self.* Enjoy this encounter. It will nourish everything. Please … come visit me regularly. I'm here, in your breath. Come to the sanctuary – anytime.

Your imagined future will come true. Imagine it first, picture it, then live it, feel it! – Think back ... Life has always brought you to the right place and time; True? *Watch the miracle. Live it.*

Talk about You, - your real you. Your light, and ideals. Share it. You don't have to hide it anymore. Shine your light. This is the Time. It is *your* time. The greatest time. What you have dreamt – is here now! So my earth friend, don't worry, be happy. - He starts to sing. -

Ha ha. I make me laugh. … Thank you Spirit, thank you Life."

Thank you!

Nice to get some clarity from up above! People have been seeking that wisdom for eons. The eternal questions of the soul and spirit are common to all cultures. This curiosity is widespread; people are searching, and asking the great questions. What happens after we die? Is there a soul? Does the soul continue after death? Is there an afterlife, a heaven? Are we reincarnated? How does karma work? Are we destined to meet that someone special? Is this earth life all planned? If it is all planned, then why the suffering?

These and many other important and profound questions have occupied the thoughts of people from all walks of life and have preoccupied wise and learned people throughout history. As one delves into the literature, as well as diving into one's own inner sanctum – the unconscious, the subtle truths make themselves known … *if* we can find ways to cut out the excess noise and narrow opinions handed down to us. To do so we need to question most of our assumptions, redirect our focus, and attune to the source of wisdom, to our animating spirits, our eternal souls. This can be called the journey of personal discovery, and it is well worth the conscious effort.

In the end, we each must take that journey.

There are fascinating and expansive views about how we are all part of a greater divine process that constitutes a wide-ranging and breath-taking journey of souls. This will bring us to past lives. The word "reincarnation" derives from Latin, meaning, literally "entering the flesh again". This concept of the continuity of life is ancient and widespread.

My desire is to add to that accumulated knowledge, my own contribution to the perennial philosophy. This is an eclectic perspective within the philosophy of religion which views each belief or religion as sharing a core, and that inspiration is there to inspire and to share. What do many faiths and religions have in common? This *well of wisdom* has many observers and thus interpreters, but the complexity of God and the Universe can be viewed as the essence of the divine Order. If one takes off the trappings of religious traditions, are we not each perceiving the same (cosmic) God, a universe alive? Some of these perspectives are mysterious and hidden, or hard to understand, which is the definition of the word occult. Many seekers and mystics have gazed into the dimly lit arenas of the Divine, and have re-discovered ideas and truths found in ancient scriptures. The mysteries awaken. A relatively common mystery is of déjà vu, that feeling that we have been here before. [2]

I wish to spark that curiosity. Philosophy means the love of wisdom; searchers and practitioners make the effort and may make the journey to the divine well, the source. And so old knowledge is reviewed, weighed and compared with our present notions and ideas. Things come around. May we come around.

---

[2] For your intuitive pleasure I will include a few passages and phrases in this book that is meant to instill that feeling of déjà vu. Enjoy!

I was nourished at the Well, and in the last decades I found the Source of many springs. Refreshing and profound; the waters quench the main thirst, and it keeps the grail seekers busy. Today there are millions of cup bearers incarnated, and it seems not enough for the task; the thirst is desperate at times, for there are droughts and (un)natural disasters present in our precious lands. The Light shines in the dark. Nevertheless, ignorance takes hold in households poor and rich, for prejudice and knee-jerk reactions are everywhere. Take heart … All in all, whether on a therapist's couch or a charity program in Africa or on an intellectual battlefield in a strange land, there are opportunities to discover, to learn and to awaken. The road less traveled is being trod by millions. There are light-bearers. You may be among them.

I have had the pleasure of gathering information/inspiration from the source – as elusive as it seems at times. Through my work I have "sat in on" thousands of journeys, pilgrimages, battles and births, and the stories are endlessly fascinating. I have been conducting these spiritual sessions for more than thirty years; I will offer many stories and views in this book, volume two of Inner Journeys, Cosmic Sojourns.

A special thanks to my many clients who freely shared their stories and lives, and who gave me permission to tell their tales, knowing others may benefit from the telling. I have changed the names and personal information to honor privacy, and I have sought to keep the individual stories pertinent and illustrative, true to the actual events and sessions. Who are these clients? They are students, lawyers, psychics, activists, doctors, housewives, psychologists, businessmen, nurses, technicians and writers and more.

In these pages you will hear many voices, views and perspectives – not all views are mine. This is a collection of stories, sessions and anecdotes from a hypnotherapist's casebook. The variety of views creates a rich tapestry. By striving to keep to the original sources, views and styles, I aim to maintain the authenticity found in the fresh recordings and transcriptions. There have been revelations, surprises, dreams and tears – and so much more. The background is as big as life itself, and when one incorporates the transcendent aspects gleaned from other lives and spiritual experiences *beyond* the earth plane, the vision is vast indeed. It is quite a trip, and You signed up for it.

How did I get this information? I coax my clients into hypnotic states in order to access this material from the super-conscious. Hypnosis is endlessly interesting in and of itself. I sincerely thank the many trail-blazers of this art. In the addenda I also include a few pages on Edgar Cayce and planetary influences, for the famous psychic told of our sojourns on planets and stars *in-between* incarnations. You will also find references, sources and a bibliography of books as well as movies. Help yourself!

Welcome to Inner Journeys, Cosmic Sojourns

~ 1 ~

Introduction to the Material

Inner Journeys, Cosmic Sojourns

Much of my information comes from reading and research, and from my various spiritual journeys, dreams and intuitions, and for the purpose of this book, from clients who I hypnotize into an altered state of awareness and help to attune to their higher selves, essentially to that famous and mysterious "still small voice" within. And so I *interview* personalities from the past and far away (and a few apparitions); and they communicate and describe their tales, adding pieces to the cosmic puzzles. One can say that I talk to dead people. No need for alarm. I meet spirits, ghosts and the occasional angel. Awesome and humbling. I love this work.

Stay open and be observant, I tell my sojourners. Please follow the divine promptings, which will show us the way, both internally and externally. Allow dreams, intuitions and positive feelings to guide you. Watch for signs, I say. Really. I encourage my travelers to notice actual signs in the street, on a wall, or a conspicuous event, or a passing conversation at just the right moment. Through these signs and events may come divine messages. These events (once we rule out hallucinations and mental disorders) introduces us to the fascinating phenomenon of *synchronicity*, a word coined by the Swiss psychologist and author Carl Jung. [3] The word "coincidence" now emerges in a mysterious and even a mystical form ... syn = with + chronos = time, and events and coincidences take on a more important

---

[3] Carl Gustav Jung (26 July 1875 – 1961) Swiss pioneer psychiatrist who founded analytical psychology and inspired thoughtful mystics and metaphysicians

role. One becomes more aware of the divine communication found in the everyday. The Cosmos will communicate. Spirit is speaking. [4]

I often tell my clients to be on the lookout for synchronicities before and after our sessions, for they could confirm and expand the stories and lessons they have received. There are many fascinating examples of this phenomenon. Very likely you too have experienced this, dear reader/ listener.

Beyond these external events, spirit communicates "internally" via symbols and signs through dreams, hunches and impressions. Think of the light-bulb when one has a brilliant idea. Symbolic language, like music, is universal and crosses beyond the limitations of verbal and written languages. It is a divine communication. Essentially, Spirit is using All means necessary to inspire us and to get our attention – not an easy task in the material world of sights, sounds, online messages, TV and movies - and commercialism! Our senses are oftentimes over-loaded! Where there is a Will there is a Way, however, and Spirit often communicates when the external commotion is turned down, … like through daydreams or night visions, which are not always clear or rational, but could be symbolic, and even prophetic. We are "being spoken to" in so many ways! For those who pay attention, new doors open. Look, and you will see. Listen, and you will hear.

My Own Story

I have been reading about and contemplating spiritual phenomena, ideal places and philosophical possibilities for decades. Although I guide people to past lives and calculate horoscopes, I call myself a practical mystic, for I feel comfortable in the real world and I enjoy using power tools and fixing things. Understanding the subtleties of mass hypnosis, I have learned to read between the lines of political speeches and the misguided prognostications from

---

[4] I use Spirit, capital S, to refer to the Great Spirit, All That Is, and also the realm of the divine, Heaven. When using the small s, spirit refers to individual souls or spirits, as well as the spirit of things and times.

economists, TV experts, and other diviners. Via a multi-year circumspection I can say that I possess a fortunate blend of helpful intuition and common sense, which is not that common. This evolved over time from my observations while working in several hospitals as an operating room technician while serving in the US Army. Amid the sprains and breaks, the emergencies and triage, it dawned on me that there was and is a biological order to the body. A scalpel will cut through the skin, and the body will bleed. A vein cut open can be tied off with suture, and the bleeding will stop. There is a biological/ mechanical consistency about how things work in the body. This seemingly obvious but important awareness helped me to see Order in the body – and by extension the world, which became a basis to think about how things operate (excuse the pun). This Order I perceived in medicine expanded into other areas, which was gratifying to perceive and to realize. From carpentry to electricity, horticulture to astronomy, there is a "cause and effect" understandable set of regulations and other observable physical laws. There is a comforting security that comes from comprehending this orderly design, and the various sciences that are founded on discovering and studying this Order are essentially putting the pieces of the grand puzzle together. This inspired the scientific revolution and the Enlightenment and more. Humanity benefits from this collected knowledge. I was pleased that I perceived this truth relatively early; it helps one to navigate, to figure things out in our world. Grounded in this orderly understanding, one can sidestep the glitzy flash from sly salesmen and preachers who too often lead people down false alleys. As I clean my glasses, I see that the emperor has no clothes, and that PR is oftentimes propaganda. There, in my early experiences in the medical world, the pieces of the puzzle fell into place. Things made sense.

I thought, as did many a researcher, doctor or scientist, that I was figuring things out quite nicely. But my apprenticeship was only beginning. While still working in the surgery department, around age twenty-one, there was a salient event I witnessed that expanded my new-found awareness. A young doctor used hypnosis as anesthesia. The medical staff gathered around to view the hypnotized woman, who apparently was feeling no pain during the surgery. She was awake enough to talk during the procedure, and it was a revelation to me when the doctor told her to stop the bleeding. Stop the bleeding? She did so, somehow, to my amazement (with suggestions to her unconscious mind I was to learn later). The bleeding slowed down to a trickle, then stopped. And so it happened.

But what happened?

This was outside of my frame of reference. This seemed to defy the biological, natural functions. I had to re-order my thinking. I was beginning to learn that there was yet another deeper level to this Order in Life. The seeds of inquiry were planted, and the arena of the unseen, the mysterious, was the next fertile ground of discovery. Common sense had now expanded into the unconscious, and eventually into the paranormal (not clearly understandable in terms of known scientific laws and phenomena) or the super-natural. I was on my Way. [5]

Once I left the Army medical hospital, and the military, I studied philosophy for several years, and in several universities and countries. As I read texts from ancient Greece, India and China (translated into English I must admit), I came across world-views that included mysteries, revelations, oracles, divination and prophecy. Such things were commonplace to these ancient peoples, and they spoke of signs and omens as we do of the weather. Temples were dedicated to Spirit, nature, gods and goddesses. They wanted to dialog with the Divine. They read signs. Some ancient prophecies came to pass and were recorded and discussed. So I looked into the supernatural and paranormal. Fascinating, to say the least. I have been a devotee of things mysterious, arcane, and occult ever since.

---

[5] "The way is not the Way" wrote Lao Tzu, the Chinese sage, in the *Tao Te Ching*. The path you see is not the great path of life.

Peek behind the curtain ... There is an Order behind the order. Pythagoras, Solomon, Heraclitus, Plato and Lao Tzu knew of this, as did many wise ones of the past, West and East. And so I came to study that which is observable, and then strove to perceive beyond it. With an appreciation of physics, I stared into metaphysics, from psychology to parapsychology, from math to numerology, from astronomy to astrology, from present lives to past lives. The Mysteries: That which is unseen and intuited, just beyond our reach and yet knowable, continually intrigues me. I could say that I figured this out myself, but perhaps it was destined; I was born on All Souls Day, a mystery loving Scorpio. Go figure. It has been a rich and rewarding journey. This Order in the seen and unseen world helps to explain the big story, and our spiritual journeys.

Fast forward to today. I have been engrossed in spirituality, metaphysics and religious studies for more than four decades now. As a transpersonal hypnotherapist, I have been lucky enough to actively work with the fascinating topics of peak experiences, higher states of consciousness, and mysticism personally and professionally. Along the way I have uncovered gems of wisdom and inspired visions of spiritual journeys. For instance, the Asian philosophy of Yin-Yang, the balance of opposites such as day and night or light and dark, is a constant source of inspiration. This ancient oriental concept points towards Dualism, polarities and even dichotomies: heat and cold, dry and wet are part of the scheme of things. We find this in relationships too. Furthermore, one could also say that the subjective and objective realms both contribute to our world views. Perceive and compare, use the tools to discover, and keep questioning.

"The truth is not always beautiful, nor beautiful words the truth."
— Lao Tzu (6th Cen BCE) *Tao Te Ching*

One of the benefits of being in this business for a long while is that I have heard and seen a lot. It is very hard to surprise me. Serendipity is my ally, I watch for portents and trends, and I am in touch with my soul guide. Fortuitously I have been focused upon souls and consciousness development for years. I have come to appreciate paradox, irony and humor. I appreciate seriousness and silliness, wisdom and humor. I wrote a satire a few years back, and performed it at a few spiritual gatherings here and there. "New Age Blues" has circulated through the internet since then. A sense of humor is definitely a jolly companion along the metaphysical trail. When I'm not laughing, I'm quite serious. I'm committed to idealism, ecology, and a better world, and I have little patience for short-sighted moralists nor for con-artists on the make, whether they be Bible-thumpers, online scammers or opportunistic executives and politicians. With my spiritual worldview, I recognize that these difficult people may be playing roles, and they too may be teachers in disguise, but we also have free will and must make a stand for the good of all sentient life. This takes discretion and courage and a certain circumspection – for appearances can deceive. One must beware of reactive judgment and hubris. Who knows what the back-story is? May I, may we, have the wisdom to discern and the intuition to see beyond what the Hindus call Maya, the veil of illusions. In the meantime, can't we just learn to live together in peace and respect? There must be better living options, greener pastures, sustainable procedures, and wiser ways of living together. Can we make sense of this complex world that is the teaching ground between matter and spirit, bodies and souls, misery and inspiration, want and plenty? It is not always easy down here. Then I hear my guide … "Let us strive, nonetheless."

Getting Clear Information

I wish to quickly address the procedure of trance sojourns, for this is where I receive so much inspired information – presented here in these book. It is the source of unending fascination, but things can become tricky too. Looks can deceive, and a good story might be a tall tale. Many of my clients go fairly easily into a trance state, but they sometimes expect it to be different – hoping for some techno-cinema show – and thus sometimes miss the fact that they have arrived! Wait! This is it! These sessions sometimes feel like a daydream, and almost all my subjects are still cognizant of sounds and stimuli in the room. Shouldn't this feel differently, ask my sojourners. Part of my job is to re-educate my passengers on the actual possibilities of trance and how one might perceive these recollections. One could say that I help people to *snap out of it*. What is It? Why, the things that get in the way. Like the conditioning found in familial, social and religious traditions. There are inspiring parents, clever communities and gems of wisdom found in many families and faiths, but I am referring to negative, fear-based conditioning or teaching here. Eyes open. Bells go off, my bullshit meter is activated, when I hear, "Don't question it, just have faith." There are consequences to blind faith. In the addenda I include a Public Service Announcement. I present there some sinister issues to unconscious states and hidden motives. *FYI*

In life and living one can pick up a bad habit or idea, or come to expect something … that may not happen. Although I have been impressed with what transpired and what was transformed with these soul-led spiritual and transpersonal journeys, some clients, due to their expectations of exploring some past life, may be disappointed. I remember a client, an elderly lady who sent an unhappy email after a "failed regression" while simultaneously describing a sense of well-being after the session. Furthermore, she had more physical energy to climb the stairs in her apartment building, something she had not experienced in years – but she was unhappy because her recollections were not so clear!? Expectations! What can I say?

I can say this: if one's expectations urge us into other areas or negative thinking, we cannot perceive that which is right before us. In fact, we can get lost along the path we are treading. Like the zen story of the young fish asking the older one "Where is this wondrous thing called Water? I hear it is the Source of all Life!"

"Why, all around you", was the answer. Hmm, answered the young impatient fish, "This is water? But all this is normal, not special."

And so it is. Wonder may be found in the little things of life. Our souls are just behind that intuition. Spirit is behind our breath, as near as our heart-beat, and often subtle. And so I coach my clients, "Let us set aside our conscious minds and open up to the divine. Trust and trance out, and dive in." We go in and out of trance all the time, by the way. In fact, some people go quickly and easily into trance. You may be one of them.

Off we go? Not so fast. Even after I encourage my sojourners to trust more, some may still ask, *Is it true?*

From time to time someone asks me how do I know that my client is telling the truth. Aren't some people making this stuff up? Some are, yes. False memory syndrome is described as memories which are factually incorrect but are strongly believed, sometimes distorting memories, actions and relationships. Related to this are false ideas which are believed to be true. History books are full of such believers and fanatics, who sometimes unleash their misperceptions like viruses or plagues, some of which created fools' quests, great misdirections and even calamities such as persecutions, feuds, genocide and wars. As for individual memories during a regression, some perceptions may be ungrounded or even untrue. From my experience, such false memories would be a sham in our session – and I am on the lookout for authenticity. I rely on getting in touch with wise and honest souls. If the story seems contrived, then something would seem odd, and the inner Self would intuitively know this. There would not be a logical consistency, or maybe the "voice" would be off. By that I mean the one presently speaking is not the wise authority. The Ego is quite clever and ingenious, and self-important fantasies may crop up too. I recall not believing a client who, in his own trance, told me that he was Alexander the Great.

However, this macho guy brought in his secretary to take notes, and I think he just wanted to impress her. I cut the session short. Maybe we can try later, I suggested. Outside of such Lotharios trying to sway, I recognize that the trick is to get past the imaginative unconscious mind and connect to the wise soul within. Finding that authentic voice can be like detective work, but that is my aim.

It is good to be skeptical, to ask questions. We are seeking answers here. I am on the lookout for voices and personalities that I can trust. There are many voices. And so an important part of this job is to separate the voices. Who is speaking? Which perspective? Who am I communicating with? This will keep me busy. I will use my perceptions, and filter the words, stories and voices to get to the truth – well, as close to the truth as I can in this mysterious realm of ghosts, spirits and reincarnation. The tools of hypnosis come in handy in this work. I guide my sojourners past the conscious mind and deep into the psyche. Sometimes the sky opens and the light floods in; sometimes it is like a maze in dark foliage. It is complex, and fascinating.

Let us now dive deeper into the subconscious and the unconscious ways that we all take in or perceive our world.

"What a mother sings to the cradle
goes all the way down to the coffin."

- Henry Ward Beecher (24 June 1813 – 1887)
American clergyman, social reformer, and speaker

Ω

Varieties of Trance/ Hypnosis or "The 9 doors of suggestion"

I give lectures on this topic concerning the ways we learn, or can be imprinted, but here are the crib notes. I feel it is important for each and every person to know about these "doors" of hypnotic suggestions, these Gateways to the unconscious, for they influence us every day and our whole life long. As you read of these various ways that ideas and notions can be given or "planted", think about our families, churches, synagogues, classrooms, news stations and media. We are being bombarded with "lessons" and rules and helpful advice. Recognize that these doors are not nefarious or misleading. They are simply the doors or gateways of suggestion and thus through them ideas can be planted. - Good ones and not so good ones. Be aware.

The gateway to the unconscious is open, or can be opened, in the following ways and situations.

The Varieties of Hypnosis or "The 9 doors of suggestion"...

* **authority** - a person, expert, boss, superior, or the Law. This first begins with parents, and then the "baton" is passed on to babysitters, teachers, principals, policemen, bosses, doctors and nurses, and to politicians! For the most part ordinary citizens just go along with authorities, but remember, this is an automatic response and we are letting our guard down, or not using our own powers of choice and discrimination when we just *obey and follow* the authorities. Am I advocating not listening to authorities? Please don't get distracted. I am describing how suggestions are implanted in the sub-conscious mind.

* **repetition** ... let me repeat that. Ideas, notions, beliefs and even languages are "imprinted" when we hear things over and over again. From nursery rhymes to catchy jingles to memorizing things "by heart" or by rote, ideas and notions go deep. When we hear something enough times, and from many persons repeating the same lines, we just *take it in* as normal, if not reasonable. Advertisers and political

campaigners know about this, as does the military. "Theirs not to reason why, Theirs but to do and die." (from the poem *Charge of the Light Brigade*, Alfred, Lord Tennyson 1854)

* **emotion** - When emotions are strong, thinking is not. - "He was overcome with his feelings." ... "A crime of passion" is usually comprehended, understood or sympathized, and even a legal excuse in court cases (temporary insanity), ... "She was not in her right mind" - uh, *which* mind was she in? ... "Cool down and think about it." Emotions can temporarily shut off the logical or circumspective abilities. Wily salesmen and aggressive leaders are on to this one. Obviously one way to get support for a war is to elicit strong feelings of patriotism, fear, anger, revenge and battle excitement, among other emotions. "Mission accomplished."

* **peers** - conformity, peer pressure; "fitting in" "being cool or hip"; we are all aware of this dynamic when we look back upon our school daze. This is an innate survival mechanism and part of social systems: perhaps we are instinctively inclined to act in a pack. This would certainly make sense when we consider our evolutionary history of defending ourselves from stronger creatures or warring tribes. This *group-think* doesn't end with cavemen, nor with adolescence. Take the case of Dr. Barry J. Marshall and Dr. J. Robin Warren, who won the 2005 Nobel Prize for Physiology/ Medicine. Their discoveries of bacteria in the stomach were supposedly impossible (everyone knew that nothing could live in the acid stomach). Their research was ignored for a long time by the medical establishment, their peers. Besides, they were from Perth, Australia. This is a backwoods, out of the way, area. Yes, prejudice is carried by peer groups and the conformity principle; even scientists and medical doctors are guilty of this (who are authorities by the way). The pressure of peers, oftentimes led by a vocal minority, is paradoxically the glue that bonds us in communities and can be a uniting principle; it is also holding back progress in all levels of society when groups

are stuck in recalcitrant and narrow-minded constructs and unexamined ideas. (See my "public service announcement" in the addenda!)

* **tradition**: "Because it's always been done that way!" and "This is the way it is." I am editing this section right after Easter, the time of remembrance of Jesus, the resurrection, and the Easter Bunny. Where did the bunny come from? Carrying eggs in a basket? History, of course, will explain it to us, but that is not the point – and the majority of people with children who delight in Easter baskets don't care: its tradition! "If it has been around this long, there must be something to it." And "It has withstood the test of time." This is sometimes true, such as great pieces of art or music. But *war* has been around longer. Should we honor it too? Logic doesn't always play a part in establishing and following traditions. In America, the natives are called Indians, because Christopher Columbus got lost and thought he had arrived in the Indies. The mistake stuck. Perhaps it is time to reconsider traditions ... keep the best, and out with the rest.

* **linking** – A complex, unconscious association with a person or group. This occurs when there is a "link", or invisible threads of connection, to others. "You are just like your Dad!" "That's how *we* do it." (See how this fits in with tradition?) "A chip off the old block." or "You are a Jew - Catholic - Muslim," etc., or "You remind me of your mother, grandfather, dead aunt, etc." You are a Mexican, Russian, whatever sub-group or nationality - *and now think about what this implies...* Those connections that our quick, facile minds make could *link* the person, group, religion or national character to emotions and associations like pride, suffering, guilt, persecution, neuroses, ingenuity, creativity, and so forth. It is all linked together in these "innocent" associations, sometimes by a casual reference. For instance, one could say to a child "you remind me of your Uncle George." This could be merely seeing a physical resemblance. However, the child knows George likes to drink and then becomes

violent. "Am I like that?" asks the child to himself. He looks in the mirror, "Maybe I am."

* **imagination** ... All things are possible! The mind instantly sets its analytical abilities aside in order to stretch, imagine and soar! Great! Visualization and stories and music and dreams all "arrest" our minds and allow us to imagine the possibilities! Here is a quick induction, or hypnotic opening, for children: "Let's pretend!" The next thing we know, the child is talking to the butterfly and making plans for the fairy ball in the magic garden. How fun. Similarly the word *suppose* means to take for granted without proof; this is a workable definition and a clear description of imagination and how this is one way to by-pass our conscious gateway. New and imaginative suggestions create different possibilities. This helped us, in ancient times, to "picture" the enemy, or an untried approach or design, or a new group endeavor, I suppose.

* **role** - The position creates the notions and attitudes, such as "in the line of duty", a doctor's oath, or a self-righteous leader... "I'm the decider." Those who are married or have been married know that there are even palpable roles in the institution of marriage! "The wife belongs in the kitchen" is not sounding too proper these days. Who was convinced by the US President who declared I'm *a very stable genius*? Some people are fooled by their own importance or role. There are those who get caught in the power or trappings of their positions. With this in mind, just think about the implications of "It comes with the job." "It was my duty!" or "My job was just to follow orders." As we turn the pages of history, however, and view duty and roles at the Nuremberg trials in Germany after WWII, this "just following orders" excuse was not acceptable. The citizens of the world declared that there are higher authorities and laws to follow (which brings us back to making our own decisions, and making up our own minds!).

And Number 9 ...

» **Hypnosis** - using direct or known communication agreements - not unconscious or *just given* as a matter of course in our lives, but agreed upon by the hypnotherapist and the subject. When one seeks therapy, this agreement to allow suggestions from another is one of the most honest forms of influence. Hypnosis may use all of the above ways to open up the sub-consciousness mind. The hypnotist is asked to use these skills for specific purposes. This is a contract to change or improve something that is more than likely unconscious, like a habit or fear, and to aid the client to find peace, resolution and freedom – and to explore past lives.

There are various approaches, methods and *inductions* to open the gateway hypnotically. An induction is the process, usually through words, that lowers the conscious mind's defensive autonomy. There are three main types of hypnotic inductions, and they are connected to the natural and ubiquitous list I have just given:

> ➢ father/yang approach – this combines authority, role, emotion, linking and repetition (direct commands, emotional directives)

> ➢ mother/yin approach – combines emotion, imagination and linking (invitations to go along and take it in)

> ➢ indirect approach - linking, peers, emotions, roles, authority and/or imagination (don't think of the pink elephant). The psychiatrist and hypnotist Milton Erickson was a master of this form of induction. He ably used metaphor, stories and confusion techniques and, on occasion, included others in his therapy - actors (peers) playing parts or roles for the therapeutic process.

Note that all of these ways by-pass the critical or conscious mind, moving us a little closer to that *automatic pilot*. Also note that drama therapy, psycho-drama and expressive arts therapies utilize most all of these listed dynamics *plus* role playing and group dynamics, or the power of peers. When these techniques are constructively and consciously used, people can have amazing breakthroughs, revelations and healing. Imagine how effective education could be, consciously utilizing these methods! One could write a book or two on the varieties of hypnosis and its methodology and many uses. This is beyond the scope of this book, but I did feel inclined to share these 9 doors of suggestions and how we are being influenced.

Now, putting it all together to get those past life recollections? Somewhere between sleep and wakefulness is that state called hypnagogia, another word associated with hypnosis, which means sleep. Although we all experience hypnagogia, just for a few moments before and after sleep, the hypnotist can guide us into this resourceful state, accessing the unconscious and the creative genius within. We spiritual hypnotherapists use our skills of inducing trances (a process to re-direct the consciousness to a point termed an altered state of awareness) to help people to get past the every-day, conditioned mind in order to aid them to contact their higher selves, that divine part that is cognizant of past lives, soul lessons and life purposes. In the realms of speculative philosophy and spiritual cosmology, we ultimately will fall back upon our intuitive awarenesses, that *feeling of rightness* or being in the *cosmic zone.* Knowledge is where it's at, and the original meaning of **gnosis** was "the intuitive knowledge of spiritual truths." The origin of words opens up understanding; for instance, the actual meaning of *educate* [educare] is "to develop the *innate* capacities within". Yes, the answers are within. That's what I'm striving for!

"This concept of rebirth necessarily implies the continuity of personality... (that) one is able, at least potentially, to remember that one has lived through previous existences, and that these existences were one's own...."

- Carl G Jung, Swiss philosopher, psychotherapist

The Method

How can we access these greater revelations? We need good methods, and sometimes wily ways, to get there. At times we need to overcome preconceptions. Clients come to me with suppositions, hopes and expectations. They often come with baggage from families, school and religions too. By the time they book an appointment with me, however, there is an openness to the ideas of reincarnation, life after physical death, and a spiritual world. When a past life regression or a "life between lives integration" session is sought, one's belief system at this stage is fairly open, curious and expansive. This makes my job easier. My clients are usually very interesting people and a pleasure to work with. I am a lucky fellow. Although many of them have never tried meditation, nor participated in a group trance experience (like guided reveries or imaginative guided journeys), or attended a self hypnosis class, the one factor of *openness* is very important — and may be enough to open the inner doors to meta-memories, or memories from the in-between. However, an expectation that a spiritual session will unfold like an illustrative case from a best-seller, or like a TV reproduction, or even like a Hollywood blockbuster (quadrophonic sound, of course), is setting oneself up for disappointment. Some people are subjectively prone to receive clear visual memories, but there are other senses that are valid – as well as emotional recollections and body sensations that could be quite profound. It is difficult to avoid expectations, but usually it is more reasonable to just allow whatever comes.

I do not often ask my client "What do you see?" for I do not really know that my tranced subject is seeing anything. Perhaps this person has a stronger intuition, or senses body feelings or may hear things instead. In our intake discussion I coach my sojourners to be aware of what they perceive – which means what do you feel, sense, see, hear, touch etc. Perceptions and impressions. There are many ways that we receive information and perceive things inwardly and outwardly. Many may experience mere parts of memories, for instance; perhaps just an old photograph sort of memory, or a conversation in the background. We are looking for important and relevant past life and in-between life memories and lessons, however, so we now ask our higher selves to please give us as clear and as relevant material as possible! I remind my clients, "as you receive these perceptions, please turn up the volume, expand to the clarity and insights." Along the way, or during the spiritual session, I will then ask ... what meaning is here for you today? I am urging the wisdom within ... we wish to integrate the spiritual information, and inspiration, into one's life – as well as open the door to future revelations.

Basically I urge my sojourners to Commune with their divine selves, for it is the soul that has the greater meta-memories and it is my intention to get in touch with that wisdom. This wise Self is just behind the conscious veil, and undoubtedly inspired the seeker to read the books, watch the appropriate shows and programs, and even escorted the personality to just the right time and place to hear a significant conversation that seems to be speaking especially to her. A message, a light-bulb. Ahh. And so they hear about me, or another hypnotherapist, and book a session. No coincidence. We are divinely led, if we listen and see and follow. Keeping with this sense of significance, I many times begin my spiritual exploration with my sojourners by suggesting "Go to your most *relevant* past life." I do not ask the unconscious to take us to their *last* life, which might not be the best place to start the exploration. Rather, what, when and where shall we begin a relevant or significant search for meaning, connection and truth – that have meaning for us today? What have we lived through; what have we learned?

We experience an important past life, learn the lessons, come to the end and die, and move on from there. In Spirit/Heaven we revue, distill and plan. Based upon our past life Karma, our desires for growth and knowledge, and the complex dynamic of working with our soul groups, we are advised by the Wise Ones about possible life choices. Then we incarnate, again.

The result is the life you see in the mirror.

∞

In volume one I introduced various themes such as Time, Ghosts, Bleed-Throughs, the bardo, entities, Karma, partners and Soul-mates, etc. In this volume I introduce the various ways we can be imprinted and affected by past lives, from birthmarks to left-over issues to gripes and rages. We will be discussing ghosts, aliens, spirit guides, soul partners and angelic help. There is much to explore in the unseen worlds. As we peer into past incarnations, the lessons and dramas from events long ago oftentimes accompany us this time around. There are the dynamics of cause and effect, actions and reactions. I now introduce one of those reactions, namely that "planted" as a result of our own past wishes and vows. Our declarations and conclusions may sometimes set the stage for the future – even beyond the grave. We continue the explorations in the next chapter with the question, What have we set in motion?

~ 2 ~

Oaths and Promises – Binding Contracts

> Truth lies on the hearts and tongues of men. Speak and live. You are creator and creation. Your life is craft, your supple body molded by word, sculpted by desire, fired by deed. You poise yourself between life and fate, the will of men and the will of gods. In the beat of a heart, the suck of breath, you are the universe. Making. Making. Making.
>
> *Becoming the Craftsman*, from "Awakening Osiris"- chapter 44, by Normandi Ellis

Someone asked the psychic Edgar Cayce, [6] "From which side of my family do I inherit most?"

Cayce replied, "You have inherited most from yourself, not from family! The family is only a river through which it (the entity, soul) flows!" This interesting answer from Cayce certainly gives one pause to reflect. In this chapter we will explore the intriguing "contracts" that we ourselves signed and sealed.

A simple and even funny example was a lady in a big US city who, though white, was thoroughly mixed with the urban black sub-culture. She was a round, laid back white woman surrounded by mostly African Americans and some dark skinned Latinos. She was a Scorpio who was fascinated by the occult, Tarot cards and reincarnation; so she came to me. We regressed back to the 1840s to a

---

[6] Edgar Cayce (18 Mar 1877 – 1945), called the sleeping prophet, gave inspired readings for decades. Part of his legacy is found at the Association of Research and Enlightenment (ARE) in Virginia Beach, VA. I am a big fan of his, and studied the Readings for years.

life on a southern plantation in Alabama, where she was picking cotton. It was a hot day and she was tired. She wiped the sweat off her brow and looked at the Masta and his family, having tea under a shade tree. "I sure wish I was white," she declared. Then she looked around her. She loved her family and friends, going to church and singing gospels, eating hominy grits, and the laughter. She was essentially content with her being black but ... those whites had it better. So every now and then she would utter her wish of being white. And so it came to be … in her present life she indeed was born white. In her teens she started hanging out with the black kids, mixing in, picking up their slang and fitting in. She loved soul food, Motown music, rhythm and blues, and worked as a nursing aid in a predominantly black community clinic. She even married a black man. I looked at her anew. Basically she had a thin veneer of white skin on a totally black and happy frame. That past life cotton picker got what she wanted, and kept what she loved. She was a white skinned black woman. Oh, and one last funny addition – her husband was named Mr. White, so she is Mrs. White!

I think about my past life in Moorish Andalusia, Spain, which I described in volume one. Muslims did not eat pork. I have a certain aversion to this meat. It dawned on me, once I was aware of that past life in the 14th Century, that I swore off pork in old Andalusia, and the inclination follows me still. I avoid it.

><

I have come across several women over the years with a similar pain, and a pattern – at issue with "the other woman". One lady in particular comes to mind. She was unhappy with her ex, who she left because he was unfaithful. She was quite angry with the woman too; my client really berated that lady (she actually said tramp) for breaking up her marriage. She blamed her and brooded about her. She moved on, however, and met a new man. Oddly, her new partner had the same name as her ex-husband, and guess what? He is married, so now *she* is the other woman! Her vow, her anger and her righteousness was looking her in the face. She soon saw the irony and came to forgive the other woman in her own past. She now knew what it was like. She vowed, furthermore, that she would not be a home wrecker. Did she then leave this married man? No. She has a "separate arrangement" with this partner,.... they have a child together, and she does not want him to leave his wife (and the other four kids!) for her. She will manage. She made her vow.

A friend of mine described his conflict ... he wanted love and a relationship, but he could not commit, especially because he had revolutionary ideas. Are these aims mutually exclusive, I asked? He regressed to a past life in Scotland when he was fighting against the English for independence. He had a wife and two children. When he was out on a skirmish he returned home to a burning pyre, and his wife and two children were burned to death. He was enraged, and full of remorse and sorrow. He told himself that a fighter for justice had no business having a family, for he was putting them in jeopardy. He should not have done that – it was selfish. He swore that as a freedom fighter he would never marry and have children. We found his dilemma. The Scotsman had made his vow, a fiery declaration.

What other vows were made in past lives?
For many years I have guided spiritually inclined people, and a sub-group of seekers include peaceful hippies, New Agers, folk musicians, vegetarian nutritionists, wholistic health professionals, organic gardeners and idealistic teachers. These are often thoughtful people with strong convictions and ethics. Working with them, some common themes emerged, such as past lives as monks and nuns, from Christian to Buddhist, many of whom lived in convents and monasteries. They all took vows of their faith, practicing discipline, prayer and devotion. Almost all took the classic vows, and the most

significant I found were 1) obedience, 2) chastity, and 3) poverty. These vows, uttered and promised so many centuries before, still echo in the behavior and consciousness of these sincere people today. Are they still keeping those vows? Yes and No. Most are in rebellion, caught up in a moral struggle to do the right thing, fighting with themselves over these very themes, and not quite understanding the dilemma, and debate, of oaths they don't even remember.

"The LORD bless you! I have carried out the LORD's instructions."
    - The Bible, 1 Samuel 15:13

Let's take a deeper look. Obedience? These people are oftentimes anti-authoritarian, contrary and independent thinkers. They are not going to follow the crowd, and definitely not the institutions. Been there, done that. However, there is often an undercurrent of guilt, "shoulds," and a certain social pressure that they should keep quiet and be a good boy or girl. Many rebel, pointing out the fallacy of blind obedience and the importance of an informed and consenting citizenry. One should make informed decisions! On the negative side, some just are reactive to perceived repression, from advice kindly given to laws not worth following, and there is often stress and tension – unless they are left to their own projects, hobbies, beliefs, crafts and gardens. Some of these folks may be quick to say "You can't tell me what to do!" You see, as obedient ex-monks and nuns they quietly followed too many rules, regulations and traditions in the past. Today they declare, Enough of that! On the positive side, past lives spent in discipline and obedience have developed self-regulating individuals who have a sound inner compass, a moral consciousness, and so these people can be positive role models in their families and communities. They are the recyclers, ecologists, activists and organizers. They can become (just) authority figures, the lay equivalent of abbots or mother superiors, worth listening to, as they intuitively know the Way. They are the calm ones with good advice and a ready ear. They are the meek, who may inherit the earth. One more thing ...

They won't ask for blind obedience.

> "The LORD bless you, my daughter!" Boaz exclaimed.
> "You are showing even more family loyalty now than you did before, for you have not gone after a younger man, whether rich or poor."
> - The Bible, Ruth 3:10

And that other vow ... Chaste? They would often chase! Imagine the Vatican suddenly annulling the old tradition of celibacy, and telling the priests and nuns that they can now do what they want. They are free to enjoy sex, to find love, to form families. Some priests and nuns would go about their habits (☺) and not change anything, but most might be curious ... they'll date, experiment, taste. Ah, the Garden of Earthly delights! Some might feel that old repressed passion burst out like a flood, and let the good times roll. And so it is with our reincarnated ascetics and renunciates. Yes, away from the confines of the constraining convents, these reincarnated choir boys and girls are oftentimes curious, experimental and hungry. They may still look over their shoulders, however. Religion retains the hidden reins, and other precepts can be recited. They may never lose that guilty conscience, for the vows were made, and years – decades – of chastity, of fighting the urges of the body, are running in the background like a computer (virus) program. This often appears like phases of lust and pursuit, then urges to control the body, and then times of quiet reflection – sometimes guilt and remorse. Or the reincarnated monk is an up-standing citizen with a secret mistress, or a double life; they must hide it from the Abbot/ society, keep up appearances ... This is stressful too. Some strive to tame the body on their own terms. Not with flogging and chastity belts, but a real struggle. Some just let it go. There is oftentimes a struggle with fidelity, monogamy, and the rules of polite society (remember obedience, and dis-obedience, the first vow!).

"Better is a poor person who walks in his integrity

than one who is crooked in speech and is a fool."

- The Bible, Proverbs 19:1

"Better the poor whose walk is blameless

than the rich whose ways are perverse."

- The Bible, Proverbs 28:6

And let us not forget that other vow – Poverty. My past life religious clients are often ambivalent about money, possessions and wealth. That old adage of the morally corrupt rich is flitting through the unconscious. Be humble, modest and poor! Then comes temptation. ... Ah, but they dream of the good life, of travels, fine dining, elegant and costly surroundings! Imagine! "That's the life for me! If only! ... But I don't want to be a yuppie/too material. Ah, perhaps wealth is not for me. Maybe next life." Envy may appear, or a certain self-righteousness ... "He may be rich, but I am ethical." These good citizens may not be saying "money is the root of all evil," but they may have their suspicions. Certainly one can look around and see cut-throat capitalism, dirty games and bought politicians. "If you play in the mud, you're going to get dirty." Better an honest buck than a dishonest deal. Indeed, the art of the deal, and the dishonest dealers, are a real turn-off. Yes, oaths, adages, sayings and aphorisms keep one on the high road ... but the struggle with money and the material world continues.

I have developed some therapeutic techniques to help these long suffering souls. In my Trance-personal Journeys, which are hypnotic techniques aimed at release and healing, I communicate with the *past* personality, a pious monk or a devout sister, and ask them to please release the *present* self from the old vows. That was then, much was learned and integrated, and now is the time for a new covenant. Please free your future self/ my present client, from the religious (or fanatical) oaths made so long ago. Thank you for the lessons, and let us release the old constraints, integrating the wise lessons and good habits, into the Now. Most of the time the past life nun or priest is very ready to help. The vows were for then; now is a new life, a new time, with new lessons. Amen, and pass the wine.

Jasa had had some wild rides, and some bucking up and down — in life and in her sessions. She feels certain times in her life that are fine, and other times filled with anxieties. There was a duality in her that I noticed, like her astrological water sign. She was intuitive, mutable, and enjoyed colorful dreams. With her various life experiences, three years of therapy, vivid impressions with my Winter Revery [7] – I felt she was ready to go. She wants to truly rise above her worries, especially for her young daughter's sake. Jasa wants to be a good role model, a good mom. And she doesn't want to be like her parents. Jasa's mother suffered from chronic depression, and her alcoholic father died when she was twelve; they were not good role models. This dysfunctional family could explain her worries and fears, but in trance we get to find out some earlier origins:

"I think I'm inside. It is day. There are many people around me. Strangers. They don't talk to me; nor I to them. I'm dirty, but not ugly. I feel lonely. I feel I don't belong there. Medieval times – everybody is dirty. Emptiness. Pure emptiness, no sense to it, a desperate feeling. I don't like this life! I was so poor. People call me Mary, but mostly they ignore me.

Europe... North... Ireland? Not Norway... up there somewhere.

---

[7] I created Winter & Summer Reveries some years ago. Soothing music and my guidance, specifically created for healing and inspiration. Don't listen and drive! - www.transpersonal.us/reveries.html

I have nobody. No friends. Nobody! Fully alone. I cannot... speak. I cannot speak. Somebody cut it? Some time ago ... - grimace -

... Father... is beating me.

I'm a kid... four, six, five. (Little Mary, around the same age as present daughter! People unconsciously contact me at just the right time. Trigger time.)

He is big. He is evil. I'm crying. I'm alone. It is only me and him. I want him to die. I wish him dead. I hate him. - whispers - I hate him.

He = is my mother? No. Not my mother. I'm confused.

(this might be blocked)

... He dies. ... Good.

I decided, with clenched teeth I say, 'I will be forever alone. I will not let anybody near. I'll be alone!'

... I'm 38 now. In my own way, I was happy, but I was unhappy and alone, really. (Just like her mother. Sometimes other souls reflect our own past ... a mirror.) I cannot trust. If you do not trust, you aren't hurt. No trust, no pain.

Dad died when I was around 11 or 12."

SP: So it may have been twelve. No coincidence. Your father today died when you were 12. (He was a mean drunk.)

"In the last days of my life, I regretted this (vow). I was so hurt. Really... I wanted to be loved, touched – to have another person there for me, loving me. - emotional - there for me.

... and then I died. Too late. When I regretted, I died. (Soul broke through the armor near death, probably.)

I breathe. I'm free and light. I will not be lonely again. No." (Yea!)

She learned in the end, and Jasa today has a loving husband and a child. Thus, she, Mary, made a vow in her life not to love (and to face disappointment) again. At the end of her lonely life she made another vow, to be loved, to try again. Jasa was born with the "residue" of that miserable life and found herself in negative circumstances, like poor Mary. Thank goodness she learned her lesson and made a better, more trusting and positive vow. She is reaping that promise today. This of course should bring each of us to also reflect … what vows and promises have we made? What declarations are you making now? Be careful what you ask for/declare, for you just might get it. As we reflect upon life experiences and free will, we must each learn the lessons, and decide anew.

ʺ☾,☽ʺ

Dr Marion is a Hybrid, which means her soul has had an incarnation on another planet(s), and may prefer those experiences more than earthly ones. A hybrid is a transplant from another world. (I will discuss our alien visitors in chapter 7.) Some of these worlds are less advanced than here on Earth, and yet other civilizations are quite developed. What is also unique to her, and to our sessions, is that she forgot her original contract for her Earth life. There was an agreement not only to be born here upon the earth, but to tame and to develop certain personality traits – which her present self has little time for! Yes, Earth was assigned, and she agreed to it (and forgot)! Her present personality was not totally pleased with this. Life down here is over-rated, she told me. We each have our preferences. I think to myself, I know others who absolutely love it here. Off we go... she is tranced out. She, or her soul self, is now in Spirit with her soul partner Arnie, who might be her junior guide...

"We sit there, us two. It is a misty place, exalted and spacious. An orb appears. ... a white eye? A robe? A form of a triangle – up to the eye. I get these quick images. A touch, a contact. We both sit there – very powerful feelings. I don't know where we are... It is powerful. Many thoughts. A plan. A mission is in the air.

There are several islands, brown, in liquid metal, not water, not hot. We have otherworldly bodies that swim on the surface. (Ah, signs of a hybrid life!) I get a symbol too, something wise and patient. I am feminine. He is masculine, a bit smaller than me. It is now Arnie, my partner. - emotional -

Oh, this freedom, ... to create something. Full of love. ...

To create – in fantasy, play, humor. I can make fun, be silly, have fun here. - red-faced, tears -

... and he watches me – so I don't overdo it. I can get carried away. Ha. All is beautiful. ... The mission comes to mind. We make a lot, *create*. This is our mission. We know each other. We aren't alone – there are others. I see that now. This is Home!

Oh ... I want to go home! This is real. Enough of here (Earth)! It is too banal. It is not my mission, my place. - tears -

... Mira. My name. I have a lot to do here at home."

SP: At some point, you got the assignment for earth? Please go to that time and place.

"Again, these colors. ... I don't know where I am. ... It is as if... a red crystal is here. Perfect, complete... lots of peace. Purple, pretty, transparent. I'm in this room, like a half sphere. Very pretty, I feel the power. Tingling all over.... Someone is far away, not wanting to interfere, watching. Here, before me is... like a little child, just crawling. Not aware. A little form, a being.... it waits for me. Huh?

But this is not my mission. I don't want that! I don't want to go into that body! It is so limited, small, weak." (Nice, she is reviewing a future baby body in Spirit.)

SP: Free Will is involved, true? Did you decide on this?

"Hmm. It has something to do with my development. But I really don't want to. (I suggest to go to the decision point. I have to be a bit of a lawyer, or chess champ, to get her to this decision. Ha.)

... I'm laying in a crystal...? A border or containment here. I look around. Behind me is energy, and color... on my right side too. - and before me are... three Beings. Lilac colored ... no, Violet, very dark violet. Wow. I have respect, even awe. They communicate telepathically. They explain the assignment. - all is very logical. I have to ground myself, essentially. *I have to remain One, in a separate body*. I haven't found my foundation, I lack grounding. I understand. ... They hug me. (she is moved, face flushed)

I have to experience my limitations. Yeah – also humility.... of what one does, of one's actions. I agree to it.

(I ask the Wise Ones, the Elders, to give Marion a pep talk. She forgot, etc.)

It is so difficult... it is not so easy down here. I have to beam more, shine, exert more. - tears -

Many things happen – many things are happening. ...

Understanding is coming. Wow. (Eyes in REM = rapid eye movement; things are indeed happening. Seems like a digital download!)

... This is most important. *I can do it – so that others can do it better, and can Be better.*

OK. I can work within these limitations, the structure. And create positive outcomes." - tears -

SP: May I also suggest the humor, play and joy of Mira, her wise and playful soul, can shine through too.

"Good. Ahh... Yes. This especially feels good and right. That is good for today. ...

I am now here, with you Stephen."

In the next days she fought various aspects of our sessions, and this went into a two or three week process, feeling the longing to go home; at one point describing that she was depressed and confused. She did recognize in the session that *she chose* this present life with her Free Will, and then forgot it. After our session she rebelled – but that is her nature. Then she worked on the material, talked with others, had dreams and discussions, and came to a point of gratitude and acceptance. During this process, she sent me an unhappy email, followed by a contented one. She found her peace. This shows that one can have the bliss of connection, the knowing that comes from on high, and still struggle with our (monkey) mind afterwards. I also recall the metaphor of the soul astride an earth body – the jockey on the horse. The soul sits upon the strong, instinctual earth-body like a rider on a steed. Our bodies have their own personalities and inclinations. One can say that the horse has its mind too, and may wish to buck you off. Hold on.

That is where Free Will comes in. We are constantly being tested, not only here, but elsewhere in our grand journeys. This Earth is especially a testing ground; this is a relatively tough school and we have tasks, things to do. Free Will implies choices. And as for our choices – for example between good and evil – many times we are confronted between self and selflessness, between an aligned Self and a private selfishness. As we are striving to find that mid-point, that middle way, we are searching for balance. OK, we have to have food, clothing, shelter, etc. But we also must give, we must help each other – our brothers and sisters – and if we can do it in a cooperative sense, we simultaneously are aiding ourselves and our soul development. It can be a balancing act, but this is one of the great lessons that we should be learning here: *cooperating upon the earth*.

☉

There can be some interesting twists to this gift of Free Will. I recall an advanced soul who planned to dedicate her life to aiding the poor in inner cities. At the last minute, as it were, she had a special request ... while still in Spirit: she requested to be a blond. ;-) Perhaps another lesson she wanted to teach our modern society was to move past stereotypes and have more respect for blonds, but in the meantime, the planners of incarnations had to find some Scandinavian stock for her incarnation!

Ask, and ye shall receive.

~ 3 ~

The Phenomenon of Bleed-Throughs:
Past Lives Skin Deep

We as souls circulate back here to Earth to learn lessons and to strive for and to achieve personal and social goals. To accomplish our missions we are given tools, abilities, talents, laws and rules – like karma, or cause and effect: What you sow, so shall you reap... whether we remember or not. Via Free Will we may choose, and we can choose poor paths. Thus there may be missteps, false directions, and even mistakes. Some path-finders believe there are no mistakes. I have slowly concluded that there may be some surprises along the way. I am reminded of the Cayce Reading that described a baby that was brain damaged in delivery with forceps. "This was not supposed to happen!" exclaimed the sleeping prophet. "This must be paid for." This passage was an eye-opener for me. We cannot say that "there are no accidents." This Reading implies that there **are** accidents! Karma is being created now; this connotes neither good nor bad, by the way. Karma simply means "action or deed." Karma yoga is the path of disciplined works or deeds. When we have a fond or loving connection with someone, for instance, we have a positive karmic connection that will bring us blessings in the future. "Give and thou shalt receive!" Yes, but know the whole dynamic: give and thou shalt receive, but not necessarily from the same person! Yes, there are many reasons to follow the Golden Rule. Thank goodness there is also the law of Grace, which is divine mercy and forgiveness. There can be positive surprises. These are universal laws, mysterious at times but good to know, and to pray for. Akin to karma are imprints, or bleed-throughs; we leave our own trail, the akashic trail. These imprints, like karma, can be good or bad. If we studied music in a previous life, we may come into the present one ahead of the game, or opera, which probably explains someone like Mozart. We could also have spent a past incarnation in ugly battles and scheming ventures, and the bleed-through today may be tendencies of confrontation and conflict. People do not come to me with complaints about their gifts and talents; mostly they wonder about negative issues and life frustrations. That is when it is time to hunt down bleed-throughs, imprints and reactions from past issues.

I have had several old warrior clients who regaled glorious lives of exuberance and daring. Those swashbucklers of old were also prone to impulsiveness and aggressiveness. In their present incarnations they are more theoretical warriors with smaller, weaker bodies. They intuitively understand combat and strategies and enjoy adventure films and books – and military history. Dig a little deeper and one will find that combative nature, but they can't "back it up" with an athletic body, or a military career, to match. And that was the plan. With a slower, weaker body these men, and some women, were "forced" to find other alternatives to war and brute force. Oftentimes this re-directed energy or drive was expressed intellectually or socially. The goal-oriented inner warrior had to work smarter, think strategically and develop team-work. Conquering was out of the question – such blatant aggression was previously over-done. Discussion, debate, argument and motivation are to be developed to reach goals this time around. Yes, Spirit choices of body types and temperaments are strategically planned – whether you, the now personality, like it or not!

Other "inheritances" can be more on the surface, for all to see. An interesting phenomenon of note are the past life origins of birthmarks. Oftentimes unusual and strange body marks are "explained" in my line of work by knives, sabers and guns from long ago leaving their marks upon the present day skin. Many times I have heard from my tranced clients something like, "Oww, the arrow hit me right here.

Wait, I have a birthmark right there!" Several clients of mine get red rashes around their necks when emotional or stressed; I am not surprised when they find themselves hung by the neck in some public square, humiliated and defeated. These marks can indeed be reminders of other times and issues *skin deep*.

A woman today had only one of her breasts develop. She had a left breast augmentation to correct this. In our session she was a soldier on the Western Front in WWI. The young soldier stood up from a trench and was machine-gunned right across his left chest. Surprised and traumatized, he died within minutes ... with strong painful emotions focused upon his left breast. This was the place of pain, and that past life that was *not* in agreement about his early demise. He did not want to die so young, and he carried that resentment on his chest.

Let's go deeper. How about the knuckles and bones? Some serious health issues have their origins in past lives. The definition of emotional and psychological Bleed-Throughs is derived from common sources: 1) The seepage of ink from one side of a printed page to the other, 2) The discoloration of a wood veneer due to seepage of glue, and 3) A weak imprint of magnetic information transferred to adjacent layers of audiotape, resulting in an unwanted echo. (Wiktionary) These definitions are appropriate for this topic and this phenomenon, but I'll add an emphasis on the blood. In this work I have had to deal with past life emotional issues bleeding through into the present life, showing moles, scars, and even deformities. Imprints. Not all blemishes are seen, however. Unseen scars from past lives "appear" as instinctual tendencies and emotional reactions – old wounds. From birthmarks to physical disabilities to neuroses and anxieties, strong reactions have bled through into lives today.

Reincarnation is accepted in Tibetan Buddhism and what is more, they believe that we return to earth remembering (subconsciously) and automatically doing what we did, and were interested in, from our previous lives. They call this the result of imprints (Tibetan: bak-cha) – what we did in our previous lives created imprints that shape our interests in this life, and what we do in our current life will therefore create imprints for future lives. Imprints are bleed-throughs.

Tibetan Buddhists may ask, "Are we thirstier for spiritual learning or for secular success and acknowledgment? Do we surround ourselves with Buddha images, Dharma knowledge and practice, or are we easily distracted by the 'attractions' of the samsaric world? [8] Is Shakyamuni's (Buddha's) wisdom stronger in our minds, or are we better practitioners of the eight worldly concerns? All of that is the result of imprints, and whatever our answers to those questions are a reflection of what we liked in our past lives." Imprints from past lives. Influences, voices and urgings – how many millions, or billions, might be affected right now from some struggle from far away and long ago? As we survey the world, there certainly appears to be a lot of suffering, and billions of people are affected. Past life regressions can oftentimes get to the bottom of things. The medical doctor and author Brian Weiss wrote,...

"I have found that about 40 percent of my patients need to delve into other lifetimes to resolve their current life clinical problems. ... regression to previous lifetimes is key to a cure. The best therapist working within the classically accepted limits of the single lifetime will not be able to effect a complete cure for the patient whose symptoms were caused by a trauma that occurred in a previous lifetime, perhaps hundreds or even thousands of years ago." [9]

---

[8] Taken from www.tsemrinpoche.com/tsem-tulku-rinpoche/autobiography/kentrul-thubten-lamsang.html. Samsara is a Buddhist term that literally means "continuous movement" and is commonly translated as "cyclic existence" (Wikipedia)

[9] "Through Time into Healing" chapter 2, by Dr Brian Weiss

A tall, athletic businesswoman came to see me. Besides her regret about being childless, she had been suffering from endometriosis, and suffered terrible cramps and joint pains – the latter growing more painful, a type of arthritis, in her 40s. Her ex-husband, an older man, was on her list. She wanted to understand his role in her life. He was very strict. It was his way or the highway. "He was definitely a pain", she said. And then she wanted to know why she had many dreams of a blue eyed man since childhood, although all her relatives were brown-eyed. Layers to uncover! We had our sessions over several days. I must admit, on the list of her issues I put the blue-eyed man on the bottom, but it turned out to be the key to it all.

We regressed back to a French life in a noble family. The teenage girl was spirited and loved her freedom, but was betrothed to an ambitious clan across the sea. She sadly went, a dutiful girl. The young man she married was a nice fellow, young, and a pawn like herself. He too was just doing the bidding of his domineering father. She did her duty, she bore a son. As far as the "man of the house" was concerned, I mean the Lord, her father-in-law and the real power in her fate, her job was done. Be quiet or go away; mind your own business. The baby boy was taken from her and given to a wet nurse, a governess, then a tutor, etc. Her job was done, and her dutiful husband was gone on his father's business. I believe the lady did protest too much – and the overbearing father-in-law, the lord of the manor, had enough. He sent her off to a spare castle. The next thing she knew, her body was wracked with pain: her joints, belly, head. She was so pulled into this pain in our session that she ignored my commands (yes, commands – it was yang time and I felt I needed to be assertive to help her) and suffered, crying and twitching, writhing and twisting, holding her belly, on my therapist's couch. "I've been poisoned! Oh! Awwhh!" The poor young mother, guilty of speaking up, died a terrible death at 23.

After she died, we reconnoitered in Heaven. We did our Spirit healing, which took longer than usual. Once the poor noblewoman could clearly speak in sentences, we asked her to cut the painful earth strings, the bleed-through, of the deadly poison – felt today in the various maladies my client was suffering. This release, a spiritual healing, for this poor woman was also longer than usual, but we got to that peace. In Spirit we could begin to identify some of the key players. The Lord of the poison? None other than the partner she had had for eight years, an older controller, an authoritarian with a temper. He already had children from his first marriage, and my client was a step-mother at the age of … 23. Ah, a significant age. She knew the rules. If she pretty much did as he said, there was peace in the home. She was supposed to support him emotionally and be there when he wanted her. However, after some years she developed her own ideas and by the time she was 30 she wanted to do other things. He was furious, and threatened her when she decided to leave. His blue eyes were blazing. But she gathered her courage and walked away from that abusive relationship. He used his kids against her, ultimately poisoning their relationships. But she was free and moving on. She made her break and became independent – something the young French lady would be proud of today. This took some time. Today she is a successful manager of a hotel that specializes in families and children's programs. Good for her. The only blue in her life now is the lovely blue sea.

"☽,☾"

Betty was in a good trance, and then her head turns to the side, facing me, and she whispered:

"Inside, but it is not a house… I'm alone. Hiding.

(Her voice changes, relaxes.) A natural escape. This is … an entrance to a mine. I see dark rocks, coal. I'm younger. 13? I'm eating something. I'm hungry. Starving. I want to eat it fast, while I can."

Ah, I think, a bleed-through. She is now robust, owns a restaurant, and complains that she cannot lose weight. In the course of our session my aim is to release the desperate emotional ties to that starving boy, to help him along, and in so doing to aid her to become free today. We did just that, and helped the poor starving lad to let go, and in turn to let Betty go. He was glad to do that. It was like a revelation to her ... those food cravings were coming from a starving teen two hundred years ago.

A client of mine was dissatisfied in a so-so marriage. Her more experienced soul sees both sexes as desirable, but her present personality, raised in a conservative religion, is uncomfortable with that. In our work together she came to know that she experienced parental love and support issues through many lives. One could say that relationships were "over done." Her Soul is now learning to be alone, and independent. Still, she was wondering about her sexuality. She fantasized being with women. In our first session she got an insight into her preferences and tendencies: with her early impressions she got a clear image: In her last life the body was agile, appeared to walk easily upon rooftops or heights. Looking down upon those sturdy legs, she laughed – "Ha! I'm a man, and a lusty fellow to boot!" This recollection put things quickly into perspective – this explained her "masculine habits" and the attraction to women was natural to that past life, and a source of tension in her present life. This little remembrance gave her a sense of relief. "This explains a lot!" Great. Now, what to do with these urges?! "Well," said I, "let's let things settle into a new equilibrium. Time will tell." This bisexual woman felt the natural urges and attractions of the heterosexual man in her past. This was an enticing example of feelings and tendencies bubbling up from a past incarnation.

I am reminded of body issues, body images and feeling comfortable in one's own skin. I wonder how many transgender individuals are dealing with bleed-through attachments, issues and emotions *coming from another gender* in a past life. Many souls have gender preferences and other souls switch to and fro, aiming for a balance or "the best of both worlds". Some individuals need to be pried from their preferences, however. I have come across some souls who get overly-identified with one particular sex and thus *need* to experience the other side. So I believe that the sex these transgender individuals "are given" in their present lives are probably correct and do not need surgery to fix "mother nature's mistake". The issue or problem is compounded by our societies and beliefs which need to expand their concepts of limited genders, male and female. Things are a bit more expansive than that which is socially accepted. I imagine a few bell-curves describing the variety of gender and sexual types beyond the norm. - things are not just black or white, male or female. Life is a buffet. Very likely these dissatisfied people are uncomfortable in their own skins, but societies can make this worse. What emotional issues and instinctual cravings are bleeding through?

Sara has had a fear of death since early childhood. In our preliminary discussion I couldn't find any early childhood explanations for this fear. She had several reasons to come to me, she confided. She has had asthma, which comes and goes. She went through a severe depression when her mother died, two years prior to our session. This death sparked her, and brought questions and personal changes. Sara wanted to know more about life and death, and spirituality became more important. Although her family was not especially religious, she believes in a higher power. I found her circumspect and observant; sometimes I got the feeling that she was measuring my words for their veracity. I immediately noticed her nice features, and the way she slants her head when listening. Short, somewhat pear-shaped; she told me of her weight problems. She is a yoga teacher, and sings mantras. She feels herself to be an older soul, and is attracted to both sexes. In the last several months the depression lifted, and she can feel more. This is when she felt that she is not so in love with her husband Eddy. He wants her to stay. She likes her engineer husband, yes, but now in a brotherly way. She met him as a teen, they married at 25, and now she is bored. Sara has two children, a boy and a girl. Sara has a seasonal tax business and one could say that she is grounded and practical. In our session we came across several bleed-throughs. We shall soon meet her past life personality Ginger, who was sad and angry – lots of issues for an old soul I thought.... Well, green-blue on the spectrum is not that old! [10]

So let's get to it. In our session I encountered the "long life" of Ginger, age 20 in 1940, and Sara my client was born in 1968, ... Adding things up, I reckoned that dying before 50 is not a long life, so this did not match. (Yes, I have encountered souls incarnating presently in two bodies – twin souls, but this is rare.) However, I did note, but only later, that things were detailed before age 20, and vague afterwards. She lost her best friend then – but loss is a relative thing, and grief can show up in odd ways. She saw her friend after this loss, but couldn't touch her – they were in two times! Curious indeed. More than a fear as she first told me, Sara has been fascinated with the death process her whole life. Her past life, and Ginger's death, was either blocked or she did not want to go there. This got me even more curious. Our session:

"I see a little girl, with long braids... outside. There is a spring or a creek... water, stones. Maybe I am age 8... playing alone, by the creek, … a blue dress... a sweater... red shoes.

I'm Ginger. I want to play. There is a cabin out here. Hmm... it seems I lived there... My father is not home. No mother. That's all right. … Father is gone, but he'll come back. He's visiting someone? Or working? ... He's been gone a while.

I know my way around the woods. I'm happy, carefree.

---

[10] We as souls vibrate at different spectrums which correspond to our levels of maturity, interest and evolution. There are young white souls, moving up the vibrational spectrum from impulsive and brave red to teen yellow to young adult green to a maturing light blue to a more mature deep blue and then purple, which is a very high or evolved soul. Interestingly, the next vibrational step beyond violet is back to pure white.

He doesn't speak with me ... doesn't talk with me ... much.

(switches to third person) She is dawdling ... doing this and that... hmm ... her father left in the morning and then in the evening he returns. He works in a factory. He is somewhat strict, moody. Not easy to be with."

SP: And what do you do when he is gone?

"I like to be in the forest... I'm always alone... no one to play with. This is not a problem. I love the woods, to play, wander ... And father works (... or he is gone frequently).

Ginger is again in the house. Now bored – looking around, disordered, disheveled ... her clothes unkempt, somewhat dirty... 'should I wear something else?' It is late afternoon, but it will still be some time until my father comes. – Ginger is bored.

(and so it goes, back-and-forth – first and third person; identifying and not identifying)

I'm waiting for my father, but he is not coming... It's late afternoon.

When he comes he brings something, something wrapped up to eat... I hope. I light candles.... It's dark.

I'm a little older. We are homeless... we're homeless. My father had work... then we found this cabin in the woods. After that everything was a mess.

Mother is dead... has been for a while. She died at my birth.

I lay down and sleep it away... I lay in bed. I'm a little hungry. (Eating is an issue today, and hunger.) I snuffed out the candles.

It's dark. ... Some light comes from outside. I sit on the bed... I can't sleep. It's not a totally dark night, but twilight. Ahh, ... now he comes – very drunk. I don't say anything. This happens more and more. He lays in bed, fully clothed. He says something I can't understand. I know this situation. ...

He is still drinking; he has a bottle... he can't stand... he tips over... he blathers. Pays me no mind. – perhaps he lost his job again. I pretend I'm asleep.

Morning... he's in a bad mood. I asked questions... he argues with me, complains about his work. I'm sad. (grimace) I'm sorry. He's not doing well. I dress and go in the woods. I just leave and let him alone. I don't want to be there. ... I go into the woods – smiles – yeah, it is lovely. I go again to the creek. I like to play with the stones."

Then Sara pipes in, "I don't know. She just keeps going? She seems stuck." (Yes, I think, this is a treadmill. I also wonder, is Ginger stalling? As bad as things are, is there something she doesn't want to see in her future?)

Ginger continues: "I don't want to hear him... I go into the woods. I jump, hop... I look around, like usual ...

No, unusual – some people took him, came to get him... not much later. I look on. Two men? Blue outfits, seem modern ... in dark blue. Father is drunk again. He calls me. A woman and a man are here to take him. I'm also supposed to go. I go in the cabin and quickly pack some things... a big bag, or big for me. The two people are serious, officials. ... I go with them.

I think I have to be taken to – turned in to a home. I was there before. Before me are bunk beds, mattresses... children my age.

My father is not there. (worried look)

Many beds... white sheets. There are other kids... nice kids. Orphans, poor. ... The overseers are strict. Father doesn't visit.

... I'm there now. In the orphanage there's a courtyard. No green there, just some dirt. Some place in the city. I can't get away. ... 1930? 1940? It all looks old-fashioned... in France.

- smiles - I have a friend. It looks like Eddy (present husband) – small, same age as me. He irritates me, but he is also nice. We play catch. The other children laugh about us ... we are always playing together. So there is some teasing. It's embarrassing. We're just playing. ... I'm 10... I've grown used to this place. I like it there.

Father is away – never returned.

It's not so strict anymore (at the orphanage). We learn too. There's a school not far away. There it's strict. My young male friend Eddy is also there. We go to school together; the girls sit on the right and the boys sit on the left.

Then I meet a girl... - smiles - She has long brown hair, pulled back, thick hair, pretty eyes... my new friend. ... I feel her, we're close,... I love her... We have such a connection... I have a strong feeling... like... Love. (cries, right hand over face – tears)

This love feeling is almost overwhelming. (cries loudly – covers her face again)

She looks at me... I feel the love. (Recognizes her best friend Olivia today) It is good to see her. I feel better. The school day is over – I don't want to go. I want to stay with her and look at her. (a wistful look) ... I sit in class. She touched my hair, laughs, caresses... touches me. (Ginger is definitely infatuated, and ... is Sara coming out? Tomorrow in our second session we will meet a past life gay man, so this soul can go both ways!)

Now we're grinning at each other. Just like two girls! I feel safe, free. We go outside... holding hands... like little girls do. - laughs -

Hmm, all are strangely dressed in this school. We all wear the same outfit, – a Catholic school in France. I like to go to school. She is there, not in the orphanage. Our checkered outfits are clean and ironed. Pleated skirts. I'm now in the courtyard of the school, a playground ... we're playing with chalk. We make little boxes for jumping, skipping.

I'm now an 11-year-old. I play with the other girls, and with my best friend Olivia; there are some girls from the home too.

... We grew up, graduated, carried on, moved. Wait.

I can't see Ginger – (serious look). She doesn't seem to be at home. I only see Ginger's best friend, now alone. (Olivia now. This I find interesting, and unusual. She can "find" her best friend in this past life, but not herself, or past self Ginger. She continues ...)

She smiles. She is now 20 years old. A young lady ... nicely dressed. Lovely. ... she's at a distance... wearing a wool hat, long knee length dress. She sees me, smiles...

I cannot go to her... I cannot get to her. ...

I see another woman... yeah... could this be Ginger? (third person) Yeah, it is Ginger. The hair is shorter, same color. Same face... But I cannot go to my friend ... our contact is... well, *she is not in my world... we see each other but... I am summer, she is winter*; we are dressed differently. (This mystery will be explained in tomorrow's session, but it is beautifully poetic.)

But it is all right that we can't touch. I feel content. I'm a young woman, no children. I am here, but she is not. She had an accident... how? I see many people with her. I see... many around her. She's in a crowd. She stretches out her hand... she doesn't want this. Hustle bustle, a busy place... the crowd pushes. It is like a current. Then she disappears in the mass of people ... going ever more away. I stood there – I couldn't do anything. She was sort of taken by the sea of people. ... She's gone, but I still see her.

She died, as I saw her, around 20. I could not reach her. 1940, '41?

The streets are gray... and the houses too. Things are more somber.

She went to a gathering... a rally? I did not go. (I was told that her friend Olivia reads a lot about the Nazi times. Sara worries that this is some kind of obsession. She too lost something then?, wonders Sara. Yes, Olivia is working out her own bleed-through.)

I live on the first floor; just making a living, working... where? In an office... early 20s... 22. I work in an office. I enjoy it. I like going there. But ... I'm tired...

... I see an old woman... sitting in the chair. Me? Not alone, but... alone inside. I can't really walk... I can't go. Very weak. A woman helps me. I don't ... no family. I see the old woman, I cannot speak with her. (We assumed this old woman was Ginger. This was the long life, or was it?)

- dies -

A light, it's blue. It feels like a transition. ... *I feel the love again.* The circle expands. Nearby is light blue... a point... yeah... I left the body very quickly. Now everything is bright. (whispers)

I'm in an isolated room, ... where there is quiet.

(She is in the recovery place, the bardo. [11])

There's an inner excitement in me."

SP: Welcome to Spirit! Time to recover. Breathe it in, rest, enjoy.

"I want to stay in this peaceful place for a while. I'm in a ... one can say room, by these shimmery walls, which are white. It seems I have a body... I am alone, but... I'm not afraid. Whew, what a contrast with Ginger's life. I feel a plentiful, generous energy, for I am exhausted; it feels childlike, naïve. Young.

I look differently... strange humanoid shape... not really... human. It is very bright around me. White."

SP: Is this your soul body, or something else?

"My soul body, elongated."

SP: Enjoy this place. Would you like to meet your spirit guide?

"I'm not sure if it would meet me. ... I'm not happy. I don't have joy. No joy in life ... *it came from down there.* I don't know if he'll see me.... I'm afraid. - starts to cry, then her voice changes -

Ginger worked a lot. Wanted only to work, or retreated into work. She did not help her friend. She (Olivia) disappeared... did she leave me? Was she swept away? - tears -

Oh, here she is, in Spirit,... she's not angry... yes, my friend is somehow here and ... apart.

She is somewhere there... not by me, though she sends me love.

... I sit here in this room. I feel guilty, but I don't know why.

I am happy where I'm sitting... in the Light."

...

It seems either a stunted past life personality (PLP) – Ginger? – or some other being! She seems stuck somehow. I believe it is Ginger, and she does not want to see or know some details; I use an ideomotor technique (unconscious finger movements) on her left hand to ask questions of her sub-verbal self – yes and no answers, past the mind.

---

[11] I had a chapter on this in-between place, the bardo, in my first volume, "Inner Journeys, Cosmic Sojourns". Tibetan Buddhism discusses bardo (an intermediate state), and rebirth in texts such as the "Tibetan Book of the Dead."

We get: Ginger did not live to be an old woman. She felt like an old woman, in a tired sick body. There are some things that Sara does not need to know. Healing is important. Forgiveness is important – and release. We continue:

"... I'm alone, I don't feel alone though."

SP: Can we meet your mother in Spirit? (This was a pain, a sorrow, in Sara's life, and her mother's death began two years of depression.)

"... yes. - breathing differently -

Sara's mother... she sends me love. She's not by me. She is outside – not too far away... I'm in this... place. (She starts to cry – Sara is upset.) ... As my mother died, I was not there for her ... I am again at the station, in the hospital. (Mother had cancer. Notice how this was similar to Ginger not being there for her friend at that other station. A parallel of grief and loss. She has waves of guilty feelings.)

- emotional - ... I stood there, motionless, at the end of the ward. I wanted to be by her at the end, but I couldn't. It was too emotional.... Then, afterwards, I came to you, mother. You looked so peaceful – I could not touch you anymore. But your hand... - cries -

I loved her... and miss her still."

(*Her left hand caresses the right hand!* Sara communicates to her mother, now before her:) "I don't know if you heard me, but I spoke to you. I don't know if you saw me, but I saw you... I gazed at you. I did not want you to be alone at the end. I was so afraid... that you were alone the whole time."

SP: Now hear your mother's side... Irene ...

- smiles, quiet for a while - "Yes, my mother Irene left when I was away. I just went down the hall. She wanted it that way. No blame, she says. All is well. – This is such a relief. ... I feel somehow filled up, replenished... with sunny, warm beams of light. I feel cared for, secure."

Irene: "I wish you happiness. You have children, family, like me. Love them."

"We hug, enjoy this time together... then she leaves."

...

After this poignant and loving mother-daughter exchange, she was peaceful and content. A good time to bring the four hours to a close. ... The next day, when she is in trance, I ask about Ginger compared to Sara's life today. Are there patterns, lessons?

Soul of Sara: Ginger's mother died in childbirth. Ginger did not get older – she died as a young woman. She... had terrible coughing... died in a hospital clinic. She couldn't live." ... - cries -

Sara asks, "Was this severe asthma? Ginger was coughing, perhaps she had TB (tuberculosis)."

SP: And could there be some health bleed-through unresolved?

"Ginger did not want to die. She was a young woman. She wanted a life, a family... but it went differently... She was pretty, wanted a partner. Too bad."

SP: Did someone, or a group, take her girlfriend away? What happened?

"I could not discover what happened, because I became sick... it was a sad loss. She was my closest relationship – my most important one. We had such adventures. We met men together. Had fun. Flirted. She was my best friend.... From my sickbed I went to that station where my best friend was taken. It was like a dream. I could not get to her. (This could have been either a lucid dream, or an out-of-body trip.)

Ultimately there were many losses. At the end, on her deathbed, Ginger was sad, angry and disappointed – and felt left alone, again. This was a recurring experience. Her mother died, her father left her, she went to an orphanage. And then she got sick – 'That was it.' (tears) I see Ginger sitting in the white room. She does not want to leave there. Sullen. Tired... (Poor Ginger died in a white walled clinic, and the white walls were recreated in the bardo.)

(Her voice changes) *There was a larger lesson at work. Ginger should have learned about loneliness – and separation. It was important for her to learn about loss. This was the plan.*

Ginger wanted that family, and didn't get it, but Sara did it. Part of this mother urge came from Ginger."

(How interesting that Sara having children came from a past life personality. Sara does not have much of a mother urge. We set about cutting the cords – the negative cords – between Ginger and Sara... after a while she speaks in a different voice...)

"*I am no longer Ginger.* She made me uneasy, restless – and then I was always exhausted. I could hardly breathe at times. Ginger died early, and this death process took months, maybe years... Sara thought of death as a child. Worried about TB, or coughing would lead to death. Heavy. This came from Ginger. ...

Sara now has more options."

Excellent. Sara is freed from the past. This tale indeed describes bleed-through feelings, explaining the heavy sentiments, loneliness, and worries of dying alone. Sara today felt like a lonely girl with images of enclosed white walls, sterile surroundings and feeling old and tired. Actually young Sara was insightful, social and even robust, so these ailing images did not fit. The personality of Ginger came through, and even the desire to marry and have children. The sufferings of her past life self explained much.

I have to ask myself, in general, how many urges, tendencies and reactions are actually "inherited" from past personalities? It makes one ponder.

Body Images

The theme is still bleed-throughs, and now we take a different turn. Blemishes, aches, scars and birthmarks have appeared thus far, pointing towards old injuries from past lives.

What's Going On?

Edgar Cayce said that "we are continually meeting ourselves." This is karma animated. How many times have I interviewed someone in trance, who is describing an unsavory past life self. "What a jerk. This reminds me of my bully big brother." Then a revelation comes. "Oh my, I bullied *him* in that life! My brother is mirroring my bad tempered past personality!" Yes, Karma; one sees this in society... recollect the "superior" whites in North America – conquering the savages ... and Now? A conquered savage peers back in the mirror. Meanwhile the past life Native Americans have been born as their enemies, the whites, some of whom lead ceremonies and sweat lodges; these pale-skins understand the old ways, and may be modern shamans and medicine women, revering the native ways they knew in the misty past. This helps one understand other groups, prejudice and tension.

<><

Here is a case of a woman who had a skin and body issue: she was too beautiful, and this beauty had consequences. First, however, she explained (in trance) how her husband was stuck, literally and psychologically. He had difficulties going into deep trances, so it was good that she could journey for him. Geneva's sessions are full of poignant stories; we confront Karma, cause and effect, and soul family members. Plus something unusual – her spirit guide incarnated with her today! We started with the idea of a broken body bleed-through, for Geneva has a difficult body and has endured pain and surgeries. She is middle sized, with a hump from scoliosis, hernia operations, and in her late 40s overweight (especially since cancer 1.5 years before our first session). This didn't dampen her spirit, for she is a real trooper. Geneva is entertaining, friendly, personable, and youthful. She lives in California and teaches English for foreigners. She loves to cook, especially exotic and foreign dishes. She already knows the name of her soul, Alara. Geneva is a good story teller, naturally intuitive, and an excellent subject. As a Libra, I was not surprised to find that beauty, love and relationships were her main interests. We find ourselves in a life in Mongolia, with her second husband Willard. ...

"We were married. I had a child with him – Alicia (her daughter again today). He was really a fierce fighter. 13th century ... with the Khans. He commanded others – now he does not (as Willard). He had enough of that. It was too much, like a raw power. He seems to be drifting now, but this is a time-out phase, a break. He killed so many people then; he needed to do something to purify, something very different. He died violently. - emotional -

I was looking for him. I took our young daughter to the battlefield to find him – There was blood, yelling; the field was so huge, so spread out, it took some time to find his body. What a sight. Frightful. There he was, stuck, like a porcupine. Oh, my man. … He was so reckless and fierce, he couldn't help it. He was one of the generals.... There I am by his corpse, I'm quite young when he died. I have a strong body, a good body. I can ride well, as can my child. It is essential to ride well. … Women were not so important. His position helped me. They didn't really expect anything from me. We were to focus upon children, the household, etc. I enjoyed the privileges; I was a beauty, and desired, pampered. Nicer clothes … respect … then it was over.

He didn't listen to me. I told him in general that he was too wild, aggressive, reckless... He was respected as a rider and a warrior. I did like that – I was attracted. I felt however that this could not last forever. Of course – fighting and war. … Now here I am with my daughter, just a few years old. We can't stay like this; we have to be with relatives, and I must get married quickly. It is impossible to stay single. My looks attract attention; it is dangerous, I am exposed. … Now that he is dead, I see how he protected me.

They sent me to his family; to his brother – I don't like him much. Now I have to do what other people tell me to do. … I think he wants me. I'm still young. I felt him looking at me while my husband was alive. He wanted me then … He is = Not him again! Mo'od, Alicia's father! (Her first husband, and a difficult man.)

Yeah, he wants me as his wife. He is in the army, not as skilled – always jealous of his brother's position and skills. The leaders, they could have multiple wives – and this brother did.

… Oh it's different now, with this man! I'm the last wife – hardly any rights. There are two other wives commanding me and my daughter – we must do chores that they do not want to do. They are contemptuous. When I was married, I was in a better position than they. We were better off, now they gloat. Now they humiliate me and my daughter = one is a colleague at school – Alicia's Spanish teacher. I don't like her much. Oh! I'm not sure, but the other one is at my school – we never get along well. A feeling of humiliation comes from her, or when Geneva is around her.

My Mongolian name – Sura. … This new arrangement did not last long…

I'm just laying there, very weak. I'm feeling that I'm going to die and join my husband. I'm 28, and worn.

But my daughter … only 8 years old. I'm leaving. … I worry, if I leave her now, she will have no one to turn to. I've been in this new household for about three years now. I am glad to leave, but I worry about my girl. They don't mind me dying – they have seen me as a burden.

… Strange, the younger wife is coming. My daughter is crying. I ask her to take care of my girl. I'm surprised because she promises to look after her. I didn't expect it.

- dies – tears -

I'm reunited with my husband … He is there, with a magnificent horse. 'We can ride on the winds,' he says, 'our daughter will be fine.' – He is healthy, and whole. He wants to, in his next incarnations, to have lives where he doesn't have to kill. He has to go into isolation – somewhat like a monk or hermit – for several incarnations. An adjustment. Karma. Guilt too. This violent life caused pain, for others and for him. He is still feeling it. So now he chooses families, and jobs, where there is no status, no power. Nothing is expected …

Off we go. Now we are reconnected! We are riding – two balls of energies. Vibrating. It does feel good." - smiling -

SP: Is there some Karma with Mo'od from that Mongolian life?

"Well, Alicia doesn't need to be afraid of him, if she needs him later. (He is presently not in her life, although he lives in California. He is from North Africa, and Geneva helped him get in the country.) He, in Mongolia, didn't treat her so badly. I had problems with the wives. He was the step-father. It's OK. That's good to know. Now I see that he was a buffer with the younger of the two wives, he protected her, my daughter. (and today he is the father of Alicia) What a relief. What a relief.

... She did very well. Very beautiful. She can ride well; she is a bit like her father. If she were a boy, she would be a wonderful warrior like her father. Her step-father respected her abilities. Alicia loves horses today (and animals in general).

Sura should have been more cooperative at the brother's house. She was very proud. She felt she was better than the others."

SP: Let us ask for healing, and releasing the resentment – then to now.

- several breaths - "Good! A real relief. The understanding is there. Great. Things are going to work out."

SP: Any advice from Alara, your soul?

"Yes – do that Five Element nutrition program, connected with Asian philosophy. Take the Asian food course; with Alara's knowledge, she can help me. She will understand ... and meet people. She can reconnect to the Asian wisdom. ... She will integrate. All of these blessings will come; this will open up a new dimension. One more thing – Go out and see the sky! (Geneva enjoys astrology.)

... One day it would be great to go to Mongolia or to the Aboriginal lands. (She was an Aboriginal boy in Australia 30,000 years ago; she got images of cave painting, and the awe of stars.) This will bring a lot through this environment, and joy, for self and for others. Seek out their foods and spices. This will help fulfill her soul mission to 'feed others.' Remember to feed body, mind and soul."

SP: Excellent. Any more information concerning self healing?

"Continue as you began. Organic food, your own cooking. Include, perhaps, body work – and the energies will start flowing. This will also positively affect the family."

SP: Can we explore lives connected to Geneva's health and body today? We believe that there must have been some past karma.

"... Yeah. Hmmm. These images first came to me a month ago during a massage. That life ... It did not turn out well. I see bells around my feet. I don't see the point, or should I say people make a big fuss about it, but it is a great honor to dance in the temple. You have to move in a precise way,... rather boring and restrictive to me.

I was chosen for this. My family thought I had the right body – slim, long black hair, long legs, arms and fingers. The special movements require such features. I see my skin is a bit dark. I like dark skin today. I dance in the temple ... but these bells! Ha ha. I am 15 years old. The things they put on my body! Bells and cloth ... so heavy to coordinate. You have to be careful in moving so you don't fall over! My dance teacher, – she is trying hard to work with me. She says I have the perfect body for this.

The priest in the temple is here too – they both watch me. They are strict. They keep telling us that our movements invoke energies that help them in their work in the temple. (I assume that a bad performance would bring negative energies to the temple.)

I feel I'm totally the wrong person – I hear my name, Lalumay.

This is a lonely chore and discipline.

I recognize the female teacher, a colleague, now retired. Supportive then and now. She is trying hard to teach me, but I'm so stubborn,... I didn't choose this, but I'm bound to this. My family would expel me. I'd be a disgrace. Such pressure! And an exam is coming. Oh dear, I'm not good enough. Not good enough. – I'm called in. ... I have to talk to the high priest after my performance. I don't know what to say to him. These priests are so powerful. You cannot contradict them. He is severe. He eyes me, looks at my body... I can't recognize his face; he is wearing a mask. A middle aged man.

He tells me, 'I'm disappointed, this would be an honor. If this doesn't get better, you will have to die.'

I am shocked. This would be my punishment, for something I didn't even want! I go back in, this is my last chance. ... I realize, they tell me I have the perfect body, I should be able. It must be my mind. I think I just don't want to do this. I feel trapped. Maybe death is the only way to escape. ...

I feel tense. Tension. I expected something holy with this religious role. There is not that floating now, or the expansion feeling, like the Aboriginal boy. Such pressure.

I know I'm going to die. But I'm so stubborn. I don't want this. There seems to be no solution.

… Suddenly comes a scene on the top of the hill, over the ledges, tumbling into the sea.

That was it, a perfect body broken. The plummeting fall onto the rocks … such terror, at the end.

… It is a relief! To die.

Geneva's body carries the memory. It was that nice body that got Sura into another mess, going back to Mongolia, and again here in India!

The priest – always the same person! Mo'od again! (Lighting strikes outside, literally.)

He humiliated me. Sodomy. And then threw me to the sea.

Lalumay – Her perfect body for the dance became her trap – and she died. … This was the 17th century. Not so long ago. Centuries after Mongolia."

SP: What was learned?

"Learned... Even if you are born with a perfect body, there is so much more. Society, intention, using it. It was a prison. … In this present incarnation Geneva was able to separate herself from that man, Mo'od. He could not kill her in this life today. Aggression and violence lay simmering in this relationship. Geneva wanted to kill him, but she chose to break her ties instead, – divorce. Furthermore, Geneva with her imperfect body was able to cope with him."

SP: We integrate all of this with your soul, Alara … let us now focus upon healing, releasing the pain of Lalumay's last minutes.

"Yes, this is needed. – Geneva feels the result, a flowing energy."

SP: Good. Letting go of the karmic tension between Mo'od and yourself. This healing shall continue for the next days and weeks. Rejuvenation, peace and recovery are yours. Alara, can you please give a sign that you are near Geneva in the future?

"Yes, a blue aura will be an image of protection for her. My Soul help is always here. I feel at peace, and there is a hug from my soul. This is a blessing. Great!"

She made her peace and found resolution. Some people are not so resourceful, nor lucky. Some individuals are stuck, some are trapped. They too have their stories.

~ 4 ~

Personalities Stuck in Dilemmas
– Before and after Death

We often discover what will do,
by finding out what will not do;
and probably he who never made a mistake
never made a discovery.
- Samuel Smiles (23 Dec 1812 – 1904) Scottish author [12]

Carol, a Gemini by birth and a soul that is drawn to dualities, to contrasts, recalled a life as Lizzy, an American housewife living on a farm in the 1800s. In the same session we come across another life as a young man, born right after Lizzy. Her descriptions are rich and nuanced. Her voice and tone change when he shows up...

"... He is young and scrappy. In a city. Philadelphia. I see him swaggering.

He's poor and he's doing something about it. He just signed up. It is 1917. Then shipped.

… He just died fast. He hardly got started. Sad.

SP: Yes, that was quick. What is his name?

Hmm, his name? I can't decide. Tom or Clark? … Clark Thompson.

And he smiles ... even in the midst of poverty. Regardless, he and they – those around him – are positive!

… We have a big family. I have many siblings. People asked me, Why sign up?

---

[12] Samuel Smiles was a Scottish author and government reformer, but he later concluded that more progress would come from new attitudes than from new laws.

Ha. I give them that smile and tell 'em, 'You have to do what you have to do' and that is what I did. ...

My brother Phil already joined. He is older than me by two years. He went first. That is not why I went. It's what had to be done." (Ah, social conditioning from another era!)

SP: I know that "he just died fast." So, please go to when he, when Clark, died, and right after.

(jerks) *"Hey. This is not a slow fade! It is a quick yank.*

It is not beautiful. It is dark. Jarring, somewhat like the military ... By your bootstraps! Sucked in and out!

Here I am. But where? ... I don't sit by anyone. This is so different than the first death when I was that farmer's wife. This happened so quick. Rata tat tat – right across my chest! Boom boom! Bullets. Across my chest. Bullets everywhere! The battlefield ... I get somewhere in France.

You don't really expect this. I don't think, 'I'm going to stand up now and be dead.'

Now this is strange. A voice from the future talks to me."

Carol asks: "Aren't you sad to leave your family?"

"I say, No, they are fine - a big clan. *The weird thing is, I'm surprised that Carol is talking to me, and she doesn't know the answer. Aren't we related?* (Ha. Two lives with a shared soul are orienting. I love it.)

She talks to me. I tell her my name is Clark, but they call me Boxer.

... Anyway, it was all too much, this war. ... They tell you that you are 'doing the right thing' and give you a gun! Do IT with a gun. So I feel I was doing the *wrong* thing; Shooting someone. Then I get, 'If you don't do that, you'll be in a lot of trouble. Follow orders!' ... But I was taught, thou shalt not kill. But that's what you do! It's not so easy to pull that trigger. I hesitated more times than I'd like to admit. It's not easy! You have to kill someone, and against your upbringing. It's not easy."

SP: Boxer, what happened after this?

"Don't call me Boxer! It's odd coming from you.

(Ha, a past life personality who died in 1917 not wanting me, a guy from the 21st Century, getting personal.)

No, this is not like Lizzy and her death. This place, after death, is a darker place. Not scary though. Calm. ... A stillness, but energized. Lizzy was in an alive place.

I don't see too many people. I see two... One feels like a teacher – a person of wisdom. One feels like a friend, who winks at me. Huh? It's Kendra, my best friend. Am I making this up?

She laughs at me now. ... She has a message, but I don't like it. She is laughing and tells me, 'Pull yourself together, you are totally on track!' Huh? How can that be? Shooting, being shot?!

She goes on: 'Just accept. Accept that it's all right!'"

Carol: But it feels like shit! (Ha. We've got a three way talk or debate happening, in trance.)

"Yeah, I hear, but it's all right; accept the shit. You 'know' that it is the universal plan, just manage."

Carol: "I tell Kendra, 'I'm going to kick your ass when I see you next!' We both laugh. ...

Boxer is leaving. He did what he needed to ...

I just got shot and died! Stood up when it was time to stand up – and got shot."

SP: He questioned society in his last days. Carol does too.

"Yes. His doubts had consequences. Question everything!"

One derives many insights and lessons with such stories. He questioned war and killing. That past life soldier got some tough lessons, and my present life client learned from her past self. Contrast is good, and teaches lessons. These opportunities to walk in other's shoes also offer empathy and perspective. When we add past lives and their unique outlooks, we expand the story; and insights enlighten. My aim with every session is to discover past tendencies, talents and lessons; if healing and integration is needed, then attend to that. Then it is time to channel the wisdom and ask ... how can we make our present lives better in the knowing and integrating of these past personalities and gifts? There is much to learn.

"To get everything you want is not a good thing.
Disease makes health seem sweet.
Hunger leads to the appreciation of being full-fed.
Tiredness creates the enjoyment of resting."
— Heraclitus, ancient Greek philosopher

∞

Donald quickly goes into trance, and then the fireworks begin. I am not surprised, for he does everything else quickly! His sessions are edifying, for he has keen observations. Today we will be exploring his political inclinations, their origins, and his sado-masochist fantasies. ...

"... Millions of lights, not static, not a wave. It's really alive! I am light. Darkness doesn't exist. Ha ha."

SP: Welcome, soul.

"Thanks, soul says." (Ha! He's translating for me.)

SP: (He is so quick, I intuitively treat him like a test pilot.) Where would you like to go, in nature or in the Spirit realm?

"I enjoy this floating feeling. We will land in a meadow later. Right now, I'll float. ... I feel my hands getting larger, bigger; a lot of energy in my hands. (A natural healing gift, we discover.)

I occupy my body. I feel the body. I feel my feet and hands more. I cannot move the hands. They are like ... big hands. This is a good feeling. Everything is vibrating. Warm, and light. Yes, a good feeling. - deep breath -

I can switch to the Great Room. Well, it should be big or great...

It would be nice to bring everybody there. A reunion place, to unite. (He is community minded. Here and there.)

I'm now in... a cathedral. It's a strange mix... people with gray-black capes. I don't see their faces. Are they called the Dark Ones? I would call them that. There are other people too ... a blend of different people, and energies. Such a mix. A feeling of... Ha... like when you cook, you have these different spices, ingredients. Some don't blend together – until the third element is included. This is needed to cook a good meal. And so it is in society.

But some would say, 'Oh, not him, don't put him in the mix!' However, a blend, a balance, is reached when prepared right. This includes, in the simmering pot some... poisons. Not bad in essence. When some other ingredient comes into contact with the poison, it could bring out the beauty. Something can be cooked or brewed this way – very special. Oneness is made of this. Everyone is important ... even something or someone deadly. It adds a special flavor. (This is a mixture of his dark past, plus his present past of brewing ayahuasca in Peru adds a particular tang to this narrative. At the same time, this points to a cosmic truth that some could say "explains" evil in the world.)

In these days it is important to know this. I see... *they* want to come. The dangerous ones. We may not allow such things, usually."

SP: Is this *We* you and your soul group, or you and your guide?

"It is more a greater or universal We. ..."

SP: (Referring to his inclinations...) Did you play a dangerous role? Where did the Sado-Masochist fantasies originate?

"Yes. Something special. People enjoy playing. ... Some people are really cruel. But is this an illusion? A play, nevertheless?"

SP: Is there an origin to this, some connection to a past life?

"... I go back to the cathedral,... I'm in black... There I am, with a beard. A Calvinist style or era? Catholic? Hmm, ... sometimes it looks like my father. Is this him or me? ... This is me, then. I'm inside. ...

It switches. I find myself in a room, under the cathedral. Then I'm a woman, naked, tied... then the man whips me; – then I am the man. I can feel the pleasure of a man doing that. I can feel the pain, and pleasure. This is it. – I know I am going to die. Ecstatic, hurting. ... A great sense of power by the man. Control and power. ... At the same time, the woman, tortured and burned. Pain, yes. Then transcendence. ... strength and power. Ecstatic. It becomes sexual, orgasmic, especially for the so-called victim. That sounds incredible, I know. ... It is like dying in the ancient Roman Colosseum. When the lion bites and attacks and eats you. You become one with the lion, feel its strength. There is ... so much love for the lion... teeth, doing that – an ecstatic moment. All the while, knowing who you are ... a certain detachment. ... There is also a spiritual experience, going beyond all that. – Power. The games. We play all these games – and many more. ... The tension rises. And then afterwards, a sense of peace. Like sex. ... la petite mort.

... then death.

In Spirit, the man and woman forgave each other. They experienced... the joining and dissolving, then it's over, - a certain balance. After she was burnt... And I... I still feel both. I know both. ... He goes back to the church. Prays.... maybe he says, 'the world has been freed of the devil. We are cleansing the land of dark spirits. The Church has decreed.' He kisses the cross.

An important man, yes. A high position. ... He didn't have to do that, but he went to the inquisitions, participated in the torture.

It was a pleasure to be there. He liked it. And ... all the while cleansing the community, the world, at the same time. Very satisfying.

There he is. He's between 40 or 50 years old. Doing something good, he says. 1282 came to mind.

This has always happened. It is still happening.

Paul Greguar is my name.

... Oh, I don't know if I want to be here. ... Spain, or South France. Cathars. Persecuting them ... the pattern is the same. ... I know I have been a part of the dark brotherhood. So I know how to control, to keep people ignorant, to lead people astray, to veer them from their purpose, how to delude and confuse them. I have been a part of all that. I'm interested in that today, as Donald. - How to control people. I view, and observe, this time. Now I'm on the other side. The counterpoint, contrary. Now I'm observing how they – the dark ones – play. I know the game. ... These are crucial times."

(Another voice states,) "I want to bring peace, joy, gratitude, forgiveness, to this world ... so that we can all forgive each other."

The soul of Donald continues: "When it is all said and done, we can say, Hey, remember when we played those roles?! Oh my! – What times! Those were such interesting times."

SP: Interesting perspectives and viewpoints. Please go to the end of that life as Paul.

"In the end ... I just wanted to be alone. ...

His fantasy dream would have been to get on a boat and leave; start a new life, where nobody knew him. Later came guilt. So much guilt... and a conflict 'doing what he had to do'... but, what did he do?! ... He realized he had been lied to. It was a huge conspiracy, lie. He had been manipulated. The manipulator had been lied to. Curious, he read books, later, from the heretics ... – the evidence. And the lies of the Church. Where was the devil?!

He would *not* do that again! Never again! *I want Nothing to do with religion again!!*

(So he was born to an atheist father and a history of freethinking. A free spirit who did not wish to have responsibilities, nor power, over others!)

I see the big picture now. – American Indians, the natives, met determined Christians in the New World. Fanatics became fans. That thing called Conversion, just lying, killing. It happened there too. An old story.

... Paul, is at the end of life, now quiet, worried ... what had he done?

- death -

It's a good feeling. ... I look at the body – *I will never again be this body. These 'clothes' have been used.*

60 years old at death. I look deeper... at the body. So much joy, pain, suffering. Everything. He was important, for his time. ... His sexual

pleasure was mental, sort of stuck in his head. He did not know what love was. He fantasized, as I do.

Then died.... I left the body."

SP: It is time to release anything that may be lingering, and with this wretched and complex person, Paul, there may be some baggage, and some sado-masochist fantasies. Let us now cut or dissolve the cords – for him and for Donald.

"Yes, freeing. I feel lighter. New energy coming into this place that was occupied – the never, Never, fear, guilt, etc. ... gone, ... now the quiet. (integration, reinforcement)

... It's like I had this in the room with the woman downstairs, in the basement. The dam broke, it flowed out. Damned. Now the dam breaks again, and the power flows in. – I was afraid of it. Would it judge me? I judged.

It is strong. However... more power means more love, compassion; letting go, too."

SP: You, Donald, sailed away on the boat that Paul dreamed about. You traveled to South America, a Catholic land, and you helped the people there to wake up. You started again, fresh.

- hands over heart – smiles -

SP: And what of the tortured victim? That woman below the cathedral? She touched Paul's conscience, yes?

"Yes, she was the one. Here we are ... in Spirit... like two birds coming together. I am a wing. She is a wing. Now... she is Jackie. We met two times, twenty four years apart. We were drawn together, and pushed apart. I left her twice. I was drawn and repelled to her. She doesn't want to have contact now. I can't blame her."

SP: May I suggest sending an energy love ball to her, to gift and bless her.

"Yes, this feels good. May our past tensions be finished, or this is my intent. (sends the energy ball) I have done all I can do. I will let go and let Spirit. Thank you."

Pale death, with impartial step,

knocks at the hut of the poor and the towers of kings.

- Horace or Quintus Horatius Flaccus (8 Dec 65 BC – 8 BC)

Roman lyric poet

₪

Stanislav is an out-doorsy guy, a recovering Catholic, and recently divorced. Waves of guilt have accompanied him since he was an altar boy. Secrets were part of his family, and his community. He is metaphysical, intuitive and has vivid dreams, sometimes violent. In general he is healthy, but he has upper back problems, sometimes stabbing pains. We are at that place in the inter-life where he is floating and able to move about in the Spirit World. I ask if we can communicate with his guide. Yes. ...

"... He is a demanding character, but kind. I don't exactly trust him, but I know I can call on him. He is my soul guide after all."

SP: Why are you so distrustful and hesitant about him?

"I am uncertain. I was wild and reckless, full of energy, said my mother, who was worried about me. I then also wondered and worried. I was strong, impetuous, lusty. Was that bad? Was I wrong? (He was athletic, into sports, and shy about girls, but with longings.) So I put the handbrakes on, and things got hot under that brake. The brakes are still on. ... I am afraid of letting off the brakes. What will happen? The brakes ... It might be on my mother's side. She was more cautious. But my ego ...

There was a past life. ... I don't trust myself.

... I sense my last life as a woman. I was willful. I died in childbirth.

I wanted my husband to return from the war, but would the military bend to my wishes?

I was dark haired, I see a large belly from a pregnancy. Good looking and yet a bit masculine. Strict and willful. Iza. Nickname? Living in East Prussia. It is 1942.

We visited, my husband and I, and then he left, again. I didn't want him to go. I already have two children. Now the third is coming, and I will be alone! 'No. Stay here!' I yell at him.

He is the softer of us two. I see that he has reincarnated as a wealthy female friend today. We dated, but I felt that I would have no worries, or challenges, with her.

Iza... my heart is beating heavily. I wanted to change things, but things did not go that way, my way. I had several people dancing to my flute. I was so willful. Only later did I know I could not maintain this.

I died in pregnancy. I slowly bled to death.

I stayed by my body afterwards – then things slowly dawned on me. I watched on the sidelines after a while. I stayed ten days after death.

... I looked at the child who was born. Alive. I separated from it. I left. ... a yellow light came to meet me. It drew my attention away. I had to go... I couldn't change things. Sad. I wanted, but I did not want, to change, move.

Stanislav is afraid of this willfulness. I am skeptical now, hesitant. I put the handbrakes on – but I sought a fire sign birth-date! So ... the willfulness is still here."

SP: Would Iza please withdraw some of her strong energies from Stanislav?

- quiet - "The yellow energy is like my father, but ... I am not sure.... she expands or floats. Iza is then escorted up and away, after death. It is lighter. ... I hear music." ...

Good for her. I offer positive assurances. Stanislav is quickly into another past life ...

"I see myself as a young man, wearing sandals, 20 or younger. An 18 – 20 year old. Outside, sandy ... a village, a street or alleyway. Others are in and around somewhere, but I'm alone. I have a stick or staff in my hand, like something to guide animals with, but I'm in the village and not herding sheep ... I'm relatively small, dark haired, black actually. Not really muscular, but strong. I am Machmood, ... I'm going to see someone, in a house. I'm outside, ... hesitant. It is afternoon – I'm going to my mother, who is wearing black. She is in the house. There is another woman, my sister, who is also in black. A normal color for the women.

Mother is stronger and thicker. Distant. ... it feels like a reverential or respectful relationship. But I feel a warm feeling to my sister; we share a warm glance. I bring news?

I thought I was quiet, but perhaps I have ridden here, or run here, with a message, on a mission. Confused now. I get two images – news of an attack? I see myself running. Like another scene. A hesitant approach ... vs ... running to tell. Odd. Yes. Two scenes, 2 different times, coming to this same home, the same women. ...

The first time, quieter, I give news of things going well. Checking in. – I didn't want to go home, I wanted time for me. Time for them vs time for me. Like ... I *should* visit them.

One of these women is now my younger sister. A good connection. It is around 600 AD, ... in Saudi Arabia.

The second scene: caring for animals. A group of riders, warriors, attack the village! I'm on the outskirts of the village, away from our home. There are fighters, and fighting. My father is in danger?! Terrible, frightening! My father and brother are fighting, defending ... I watch. I'm younger ... 13, 14? No, younger ... I'm 12. Shocked. Horrified. I run to the house and tell my mother; my sister is in another room.

Father dies, and one of our brothers. Such fear and grief! I had such fear, but I thought I should protect. I felt helpless. I did not fight. I was afraid. A feeling of shame.

The village is now being ruled by a new clan, a regime, with new rules. The language is similar but different. Many villages succumbed to the conquerors. This was the end of the carefree days for me.

Some time passes.

... Inside, with someone, together, yeah ... violence, and I'm involved.

I'm now mid to the end of my 20s. I am angry, enraged, with a woman. I sense she belongs to another...

I feel she belongs to the other side. I wooed her to get revenge for my father and brother. I feel hate and retribution. I recognize she had nothing to do with it, but still ...

I will kill her.

She doesn't get it yet. She is here because I lured her here.

I choke her with my hands. She is under me. She looks at me in disbelief. I yell with hate and rage and pain. It was over quickly. She didn't expect a thing. - tears -

Oh, she is Selene, my new girlfriend! (They had just started dating six months prior, perhaps triggering this old memory, and this session.)

When she stopped moving, her eyes were open, and she was dead. I closed her eyes and took her in my arms. I then felt love for her. I spoke to her, caressed her. After the hate comes the love. I did it, I am satisfied, but feel unhappy. I flee the room, the house.

I feel that others knew that I had visited her, perhaps saw me. She belonged to the family of the leader.

My father was also a leader.

But then I felt my love. I was surprised. And so the triumph was hollow.

… I go to my family.

I am accused. Fingers point at me. It is known, or suspected. A blood feud. … this was one of several reprisals.

I am torn. I expressed my hate and rage and indignity to my family. Yes. But I did not expect the love. I am torn apart with remorse.

The other side, the ruling tribe, knows, or suspects, who committed the crime. There is no proof.

I am broken, shattered. I could not move forward. Life was lost. It was no longer worth it. Others thought my revenge was good and right, but I couldn't live with it.

… Then, a few years later, … I was hit in the back of the head. It was like a decree.

No. I was knifed in the back – exactly where Stanislav felt the block. (upper back pains today)

I fell forward into the dust, and died quickly.

I felt him coming. I knew it would come. The killer = is now my friend today. He was the brother of the young woman. The blood feud continues. Now without me.

I floated over the body. It was right. I expected it. I am satisfied.

Then I notice lights. Bright lights, white. … at least two. White, and then the violet.

… Now I get a white light rain, like a shower. Soothing.

Lessons …

I need to look at my heart, and not the hearts or needs of others.

I felt the duty to others and not to myself. I did something for others and damaged myself. (both hands over heart)

I feel a healing to my back ... I can feel the quiet energy ... now warmer. I meet the white soul. Deep and close. Ah, the young woman. She was innocent. (breathing heavy) She is not angry at me. No. I am surprised.... We feel a close connection. I do feel hurt, remorse. Regret. My plan to choke her, kill her. I can heal this part, for I feel close to her. - tears -

I feel her as my new partner. I get another chance. She gestures that all is well. This is how we wanted it.

I must stay closer to my heart. It opened with her. She opened herself to me, to my advances, but it was planned. She sacrificed herself for the wrongs done by her family. She gave her life. I see that she is a noble soul, an old soul, and she loves me."

Machmood: If we could try again, and try living together ... may it not end so soon. May I be worthy.

Stanislav's soul guide speaks up: "There is karma, and now they have a new chance. It is a good possibility for each other. Follow the love."

♥

Marilyn is an Aquarian stuck in a rut, in her job, and in life. Still hurting from a failed relationship – it has been a long recovery time. The romance lasted 1 ½ years and that was 7 years ago. Perhaps she's playing it safe, waiting, but this is rather long. She has worry lines on her forehead. She has worked for the city of Richmond for the last twenty years in real estate or property administration, but she is tired of it. Her past life will help to explain this need for security, property and home, as we will see. Marilyn is tomboyish – androgynous. Curly black hair, round face. Slender legs, stocky torso and busty; a sporty type. She is overly cautious, sensitive – even superficial. I sense she has put a lot of emphasis on looks in her life – with partners and herself. Time is passing, however. She has lower back pains, suggesting relationship issues (in my experience); and migraines connected to hormones, as they are cyclical. We shall see if a past life can shed light on this. Part of my therapy was a pep talk – get out of your rut, get a new job and location – stretch, risk, get moving!

I look at her list of people. It is nice to know that she has many spiritual people in her life, so she has support, and needs it. Marilyn's mother is loving, humorous, spiritual, and generous. That is a blessing. Meanwhile her father is loving, honest, and security minded, but too serious, material. He had a very strong influence, she tells me. I discovered that there is a certain triangular relationship between her and her mother and father; this could keep her single and uncommitted.

She had interesting dreams just days prior to our session: a sports car with no engine, so needing to push it; and in this dream car with her was an unknown passive companion – no energy there. Interesting. If I were to interpret this, she is the vehicle, pushing herself to go to work; and she has no companion. Another dream found her stuck in a factory, doing drudge work, - and she dislikes her job today. These were definitely appropriate dreams for her worries and issues! So it was time for the journey ...

"... Red, orange colors – rich colors. The light, ... blue now – bluer;
the red is receding. I feel I'm in a place somewhere and the clouds
come to me... it is foggy. A feeling, a breeze, like a scarf over me....
Floating. (I suggest healing for the back pain.) Now I feel my
shoulders relaxed – something shifting in my lower back.... a blue
light comes. Now a hand, seemingly pulling me. Bluish and bright.
Very light, moving forward, slowly... It's a feminine feeling. ... in the
light, bright, air.

(This was the abbreviated version; I tried to get her back – but it
took time – she likes the in-between space, and the light feelings and
pretty colors.)

Floating. ... I see from above, slowly flying over landscapes ... a
dark stone, strange – large rocks, glacier, ice, crevices. I move further
south ...

It is day... I feel I'm alone, and yet others float around me. (I find
this interesting. Her floating soul, aware of other souls, took a long
route to meet her past self. She was in the north where there are
glaciers, and then went south to find her past life personality. No rush
it seems, or was there a deliberate delay? Eventually she lands.)

I am a woman, 20... long dark hair, white dress, or whitish, tan. I'm
by a spring or well ... fetching water.

I see this from the outside – I think this is me; I don't know this
being or personality right now.

Simple clothes ... brown shoes, a simple tough leather. A village
with tents. I see it all from outside – apart. (Safe? Soul distance? And
it took a while to get here. These are often indicators that something
unpleasant may come.)

In America – North America. I see inside the tent; not much.
Simple. The people there... simple and hardy. It's a cool day. I am
called Nerion.

My father has a brown robe, some colored patterns; a sparse beard.
I see a brother with dark hair. I feel good here.

There are many tents but hardly anyone here. Did they die out? It
feels like they did.... should we travel on? Look for others? ... No.

Some people in uniforms came. White people. Blue jackets, soldiers. … we were destroyed – wiped out. My family, some of us made it – we hid till they left. All this is so painful. Now we are really alone.

My aunt died too. She was special. She was the sister of my mother. She had children my age.

We were decimated. Afterwards, my mother is in the tent, crying – wondering what we should do. Is she wounded? I am surrounded by maimed and dying friends and family. It was all shocking. The fear then, of the attack, the killing and loss – and now to be alone.

But my family is here. We're together. I'm happy I have them.

1845?

… I go through the forest alone... many mountains. So many hills and mountains. I get lost.

Age 22. I'm searching for a village, or town, houses, homes – which direction? Difficult. We got separated.

Daytime... confusing, somehow sad. What to do? I don't know which direction to go. Windy, clouds in places. Warm, but windy. I'm barefoot? – I come across a river, or creek.

No one. No person. (A long trek, barefoot? Where did her surviving family go?)

It's been five days. Where am I getting food? I drink from the creek. I feel lost. I wander.

… I come to a village. I don't know. There are many white people there. They look at me strangely. I do not feel good here. I don't fit in here, but I'm starving. Then I meet an old man, a smithy... working with horses. I ask if there is something to eat. I gesture. I don't trust myself here. He gives me some soup, vegetables – more a broth... it is something.

Should I stay?

English language. I have another language - mine. I understand some, but cannot speak it. We understand each other, however. He has a place for me to stay. He's 50 or 60... white hair, strong. A nice face. I trust him. I can work in the house – and then eat and sleep. His smith-work keeps him busy. He talks to me, but I don't understand everything. He jokes, sometimes.

… I see myself older. How old? 60, or older. I live alone, in the same place. They've accepted me. I knit, sew, make clothes. I'm busy. Time passes.

The smithy had an accident at work. Iron, fire. He died quickly. (So Everyone died in her life!)

We were like father – daughter. We helped each other. We watched out for each other. They, the others, accepted me more and more. I do not really trust, and so had no man. This was for me okay.

I lost a lot, but *I am the person who looks always forward.* (An Aquarian thing to do, but this tendency helps explain some blank past – she would rather look forward.) *One can't change certain things.* I had a good life, eventually.

… Not too many contacts. I was mostly alone; I preferred that. I was careful, kept to myself. Cautious. (It seems Nerion dissociated, unconsciously separated herself from all of the loss and death. Marilyn inherited this and more, and is alone today, so we have some personality bleed-through.)

I invited an older wise woman for dinner now and again. She needed food sometimes. We did not discuss things. Well, she talked, I listened, mostly. No real friends. No.

Then came the end... It simply happened. There was a stool … I sat down, I was so tired. I closed my eyes. I fell off it. Without pain, I died quickly.

I was 65 years old. A good life." (Right!)

This is yet another example of a person who dissociated from her unpleasant life, going about the motions, but keeping a distance. Nerion was numb and traumatized; a shadowed past. Today we would call it post-traumatic stress disorder (PTSD). She is definitely a personality stuck in a dilemma. We will find out just how much in our next chapter!

"The soul has neither beginning nor end. Souls come into this world strengthened by the victories or weakened by the defeats of their previous lives."
- Origen (185 - 254 AD) *de Principiis* – early Christian writer

In transpersonal psychology one hears of the Shadow, and shadow work, etc. One can give credit to Carl Jung and other psychological pioneers to aid us in integrating the unhappy and unsavory parts of our selves – which is called the shadow. "Everyone carries a shadow," Jung wrote, "and the less it is embodied in the individual's conscious life, the blacker and denser it is." Jung stated the shadow to be the unknown dark side of the personality. He also said that it could be negative or positive, dangerous or creative, but it is almost always unconscious. Working on one's shadow is very useful and certainly not the focus of this book, but I have come to the conclusion that sometimes what could be applied to a shadow may be a past personality who is sometimes in turmoil, and can also be positive and creative. Strong emotions can bleed-through to our present personalities, clouding our thinking and throwing us off track. You have read of some examples of such cases here - and there are more to come.

Ghosts – Stuck in Emotions

There are those who, after death and as souls, got lost on the way home. We have met many so far. Essentially they lost their way. Did they err? Did they go astray? Interestingly enough, the original Judeo-Christian concept of "sin" can be linguistically followed back to "missing the mark" such as an arrow, and thus falling short of the goal, or perfection. In essence, if we stick to this earlier meaning, this sin is not so bad after all. This type of sin is a delay, and maybe a detour. Obviously sin developed later into the "terrible" thing we know today. Some of my clients discuss this missing the mark, being thrown off, and getting bogged down in some issue or other. Other souls, some of my clients, get completely thrown off and lost for a while. Edgar Cayce described a "borderland" where souls transition after life and sometimes get disoriented. I have had many of my clients tell me of past times when they stayed earth-bound after physical death; they were brooding, still working on something. One could say that they were haunted by some event or reaction. Some were confused and disoriented; others were just taking a time out.

> "...many an individual has remained in that called death for
> what ye call years without realizing it was dead! The feelings,
> the desires for what ye call appetites are changed, or not aware
> at all. The ability to communicate is that which usually
> disturbs or worries others. Then, as to say how long — that
> depends upon the entity."
> - Edgar Cayce reading 1472-2

Marilyn, who we met in the last chapter, is in a strange place. She just left the Native American life as Nerion, who lived with white settlers after her tribe was wiped out by the US Cavalry. After she wandered into this town, she kept to herself, had little trust for others, and one day keeled over and died. The sojourn continues…

"I feel I'm 'laying' somewhere gray. No body of course. It feels good. … it's dark around me…. some lights come – from the dark. A dark light from afar.

Still some darkness. I am – like buried... under the earth. A sad situation in some respects. Where am I?"

SP: Nerion said she was happy at the end of her life, but she only survived. She lost everything and everyone close to her, and only had a place to live. (I let it sink in …)

"Yes, a sadness... but then a sort of peaceful quiet, a resignation. *I lost a part of myself.* There is a sadness. So I stayed there, afterwards. *13 years buried. I accompanied her to the grave.*

… I saw where Nerion was buried. A dusty place. Sand. I saw this from above. There, not far away was a little cemetery. It was a peaceful quiet place, much better than where she was buried."

(The white settlers buried this Indian outside of their cemetery, so she ventured to this official burial place as a ghost, and *buried* herself proper.)

SP: And what happened after 13 years?

"I see light around me. Bright, around me. ... then came blinking lights. ... Lighter... bright.

I float now, feel free. ... a hand – or a blinking energy reached out to me. Sometimes bright, then dark, blinking; all bright and light. It appears... like a blinking traffic light. It seems like energy. Nice.

... I stay in this energy world, recovering. There are various vibrations, around me. And a point near me, around me. It is all pleasant, resting here. I need that."

SP: Great. You have found your peace and recovery. Please bring some light and peace to Marilyn today.

A fascinating case. Not only was she a ghost, burying herself in her own grave in a Mid-Western hillside, but the pattern remained. Today Marilyn has been unconsciously looking for a place to rest. Her profession is working for the city in plots of land, working on official real estate agreements. I find this interesting, and appropriate. She is tired of this administrative work, however. May she move on, as her ghost self eventually did.

Hungry Ghosts

In the Taoist tradition it is believed that hungry ghosts can arise from people whose deaths have been violent or unhappy. These wandering souls are hungry for connection, for touch, food, revenge or a thousand things that humans want and have; the thing is, they can't get these things so easily without a body, without the third dimensional contact. They have left their bodies and are in search of ... something. Chinese Buddhists have old traditions of appeasing these lost souls through prayers, incense, offerings and special days. Many Asian families also pay tribute to other unknown wandering ghosts so that these homeless souls do not intrude on their lives and bring misfortune. The concept of ghosts, wandering spirits and even fairies and invisible beings can be found in many cultures. Modern thinkers might believe these hungry ghosts and lost souls is the stuff of superstition, but I don't. I have met some.

Entities are souls. Cayce often referred to our souls as entities when detached from our bodies. I use this term here in describing specific souls who are earth bound, sometimes attached to a person for company. Sometimes these entities are lost, lonely or stuck in some emotion, and very often a friendly child is good company, and comforting. Perhaps the child is afraid, and so is the ghost. There is a resonance, an attraction. Yes, sometimes invisible friends to children might be lost souls, entities that might want to attach themselves to a sympathetic human. And so another being, this ghost, "settles in" and shares its thoughts and feelings with the earthling. Do some people hear contrary voices in their heads? Psychiatrists do believe they know the answer to that question. Parapsychologists may have alternative views. Perhaps these voices belong indeed to separate individuals or personalities, and they are too close. Usually these ghosts or entities are hanging on too long; when I come across them I request that they leave, often asking an angel to help us. "Go to the Light, the Source. Go home. Find your peace and family."

It is time for some more ghost stories.

Nancy came to me to re-connect to her departed father, who had died about five years before. He visited her briefly after he died, and she wanted to renew that contact, to check in on him and ask how things were "over there." She got a bit of a surprise in our session.

"I am in… like a place in a city, with many people. Hectic,… a market square… gray. All gray. I am bright though. …

I'm there, as if frozen. It is daytime. Still there… on my left, some green, more color. … On the right is this place, with the people. I want to go left."

SP: You are in the middle. Searching? Frozen. Have you lost something? Did you just die?

"I feel a transition… I go up, float…I'm high, relatively high. I don't want to look down. – No fear up here. I'm not on the earth. I am gone … somewhere. Here by me it is light, around me … it is darker.

– I feel a bit lonely. *I want to make contact, but I am in this capsule, I cannot make connections.*

Upon the earth, a Medieval feeling, gray. Like the place before – the hectic market. Twilight now. I see myself, still, bright somehow. Others are darker. I roam around, but where to? No beginning or ending? I'm a girl. That life passed too quickly.

Now I see myself in a carriage. I'm a woman. 33 years old. There is an accident, a river, I drown. I don't get where I want...

Nancy has been a wandering ghost for a long time."

Yes, after that drowning so long ago, she was lost for a period of time. I prayed for her and asked for an angel to come to her aid. Please bring her Home. After her spiritual allies came to her, she was released and could move on. She was known to be absent-minded; I dare say she was more than that. I have come across many like her. And so we have to call some folks home. With the help of divine beings, I ask for a return, an integration and a resolution. Blessings and positive outcomes please.

"... pray oft for those who have passed on... it is well... Those who have passed through God's other door are oft listening, listening for the voice of those they have loved in the earth – this is the nearest and dearest thing they have known in earthly consciousness. Then, thy prayers direct them closer to that throne of love and mercy, that pool of light, yea that river of God."

- Edgar Cayce, reading 3954-1

A couple came to me for a dual session, a *simulcast*. This session was inspired by the wife, who had read several books on the subject and arranged for our journey. Ting, which means graceful in Chinese, was fascinated with reincarnation and was quite curious and motivated. When it came time for the session, however, she was somewhat blocked ... but her husband, who was "just coming along for the ride," turned out to be the central figure (fancy that). He recalled an emotional past life – and things were not finished. It was quite a ride. ...

Jeff (J) lies down and Ting (T) is next to him – close but not touching, as we begin our pair regression. After an induction, I (SP) start off with who I thought would be the slower of the two to perceive images, in this case the husband who is here because of his wife:

SP: Take a deep breath ... going back beyond the body to a specific time and place of importance. Describe whatever comes into your awareness.

J: Just gray, and a light in the distance.

SP: Very well. As you bring your awareness from the gray, bring your inner perception down toward your feet. We can begin the exploration there. Please describe what you're aware of in that particular time and that particular place; perhaps you may note what you have on your feet... or maybe you're barefoot; and then describe from there up.

J: My feet are heavy.

SP: (Looking at his face, which seems anxious) You're also feeling emotions, is that right?

J: I'm scared. I'm very scared.

SP: Are you by yourself or are you with someone else?

J: I'm alone. – I'm a young man.

SP: Why are you scared?

J: I don't know.

SP: Ting, are you picking up on this? (She is next to him, her eyes closed but twitching.)

T: I don't see anything but I don't want him to be afraid. ...

SP: Please describe further, young man...

J: Thick heavy clothes. Pants and a jacket. My feet hurt. I feel like I'm upside down. I'm nervous. I'm upside down. I'm stuck. My legs are stuck. Someone's pulling on my arm. There are rocks.

T: I knew it was rocks. I feel like it's dangerous. I don't want him to get hurt. ...

J: I'm fine. I'm flying in a plane and ... something's not right, something's not right.

SP: In the plane?

J: Yes. We're in the wrong place. There's not enough gas. Oh God! (suddenly hysterical) That wasn't right! Somebody blew it!

SP: Calm down, relax now. It's like an old story. See if from afar.

J: Yeah but something wasn't right! Somebody screwed up. Somebody screwed up big time! It's not fair. It's not fair! (hysterical, louder voice) Oh God, why?! Why?! (anguish) We trained so hard. Oh God.

SP: Are you in the military?

J: Yes! Why?! (voice getting louder) We're not going to make it! No way! (hysterical) God! What a waste! At least let us do something ... before ...! No, ... It's all over.

SP: What happened?

J: We crashed. It's all over. I can't go anymore. Up-side down, then the rocks.

SP: What time was that? What year?

J: 1943. I'm floating, suspended. ... I'm angry. (crying) There were five of us. Why?! (The hysterics begin again) God why?! I'm on the ground, but we're stuck here!

SP: Are you stuck in the body?

J: In the body. ... O.K. but the others are dead. (crying) Why?! It's not my fault.

SP: No, it's not your fault.

J: No! (hysterical) Stuck here... and they're dead. (crying) And we can't leave. Why?! Oh God why?! We were so ready. What a waste! What a waste! (voice raised) Why wasn't I hurt? (He was, but shocked.)

SP: What happened to you?

J: Why wasn't I hurt? The others are dead! (hysterical, almost yelling; Ting is no longer in trance, eyes open, staring!)

J: They're going to come for us here, but we can't go.

SP: Did you live much longer?

J: NO! NO!

SP: How long?

J: An hour! (still hysterical, panicking)

SP: And then you left the body? (I try to get him some distance, to separate the personality and soul, move a bit away from this.)

J: Oh God! I didn't want to. Where are the others? We were together. ... No. Get back! Get back! No! (hysterical) I'll shoot you! I'll shoot you bastards! Where are we gonna go? ... They see the smoke. They see the fire. Where can I go?

SP: Where was this?

J: 1945. On the ground. Where can I go? I'm not going to lose my wits. No! They're coming. I don't know where to go. They closed in ... and it ended right there.

SP: Is this the Pacific or Europe? (Jeff interrupts)

J: Yes. On the ground. And they're coming. I can hear them; I hear rustling, and they're getting closer and ... I don't know where to go.

(louder) Oh God! (panics) I'm gonna shoot those fuckers... Come and get it! ... No! God!

By this time Jeff's wife is wide eyed and crying. He is not himself; the past self is front and center. The last minutes of life, so intense and emotional, are being re-lived. Not much can be done for the poor pilot at this level, so I strive to bring him to a higher place, ask for help. I snap my fingers, a hypnotic trigger, and make multiple suggestions, even military commands.

SP: (snap) Attune to your soul, attune to your higher self! You've left the body, left the body, leaving the body, leaving the body now! (Jeff groaning in pain) (snap) Leaving the body now. It's now the present.

J: No it's not.

SP: Yes it is, right now.

J: Oh God! Not it's not! Ohhh! No it's not! I'm not leaving him there. No, God damn you! (definitely hysterical) Oh God that hurts! Oh God! (in pain, yelling at someone) Oh come on, don't just stand there and look at me, get it over with! Oh God No! (groaning, holding belly, breathing hard)

SP: And it's over.

J: I didn't give in and I didn't talk and ... I didn't give in. They took me but fuck, – if they can have it, (hysterical) Go ahead Jap Nazis! The others are dead!

SP: Open your eyes. Look Here.

J: Forget it. I'm beyond that. (Yelling at the Jap-Nazis) You're idiots! Shoot again. Shoot some more! Pretty tough huh?!

SP: Coming back now.

J: Oh God! It's like I'm back. Somebody better get him! Somebody better get him. Those butchers!

SP: We will work on it later, but...

J: But I don't want to go.

SP: Be here right now. Listen. Will we work on it?

J: Yes.

SP: O.K. I'll make a deal with you, we'll work on it, but be here right now.

J: No deals!

SP: With me.

J: Straight up. No "deals"! You and me.

SP: Yes. What's your name, soldier?

J: Douglas. I gotta get out of here. Oh God! At least we hit them first! We hit them. God! O.K. (calmer, talking to someone) Stay here. You stay here. I'm going to look around. ... Oh Boy. We're in deep shit! This is busted up. Nothing works. The crash was too rough. (crying) ... good plane though. She's tough. So tough. They're gonna hate us, we wrecked their plane. Sorry Chief. (laughing) Can't help now. ... Maybe I'll get to the beach. I don't know.

SP: How old were you? (Obviously he is not "coming back" so I continue the questions.)

J: 17, 18? I lied. I'm 17, then took the training. God! Maybe 21 (at age at death)?

SP: Where were you born?

J: ... Indiana. On a farm. I remember home. ... Big silo. The biggest one.

SP: What did you like to do as a boy?

J: Run, explore. Be outside. I drove a tractor.

SP: Describe your Dad.

J: Short hair. Spiky short hair. Tough. Dad is tough. He never smiles. But I know he loves me and I know he knows I'm tough. And I'm gonna help and I'm gonna fly and we've all got to do our part. And I'm sorry, but I have to go. (To war, never to return.)

SP: Can you describe your Mom?

J: She has curly hair. And she wears a dress and ... she's scared. She's so sad. (crying) I'm sorry Mom, but be proud. I'm... They're gonna know about me and they're gonna be afraid of me (the enemy). I'll come back. I'll come back. You'll see.

SP: Do you believe in the soul, Douglas?

J: Yes. (laughs) He [Jeff] is still here. *And I'm not ready to come back in.*

SP: Because Douglas is not finished, is that right?

J: No. No! No! There's a score to settle. You killed us. You killed us!

SP: Who's "you?"

J: The "Boss." ... Yeah. He's the boss, the Brass. Idiots! Charges and charges. I'll tell you what we do ... but we don't do that.

SP: What was his rank?

J: Colonel. Or... I don't know. We call him the kernel. (laughs) That colonel couldn't wipe his own butt. If that guy's still in charge we're in trouble. ... This is a bad idea, but they'll never say "go." This doesn't hold water. It's not going to work (this mission).

SP: Can you take a deep breath and attune to your soul again, because I have a very important concept to bring you?!

J: There's a lot to resolve.

SP: Yes indeed and that's fine. We can have time to do that. Are you ready to concentrate right now? In your mind's eye, on the left hand side is the life as Douglas. You got that? On the right hand side is the life as Jeff. You got that? Tell me when you got it.

J: I got it.

SP: I want you to realize both sides, Douglas and Jeff, and have them look at each other, O.K.

J: Oh, it hurts.

SP: Are they looking at each other now?

J: Yeah.

SP: What are they doing? How are they communicating?

J: They know. They look, knowingly. They know. They know.

SP: Tell me what they know.

J: They know it was wrong. Why? Why? What a waste!

SP: And yet you see that there's a difference between them?

J: Is there?

SP: Yeah, Douglas...

J: Name, rank, place... (classic soldier answers, the bare facts)

SP: Look, perceive.

J: Hah, Jeff's bigger.

SP: What else?

J: He's smarter but he's not as... gutsy ... yet. He can be. He's learning. He'll learn. He'll be fine. But … what's in the middle? I'm stuck. (Yes indeed.) They took me. … the middle. It's empty. *There's something holding me. It's screwed in the middle. Tied up.* Scrunched up.

SP: Do you also notice something, like invisible strings or cords, between Douglas and Jeff?

J: Yeah, and they lead to the tie-down.

SP: You know what that is?

J: No.

SP: They're the emotional connections, cords.

J: We know, but we gotta carry on. (crying) Why?!

SP: Who's saying that?

J: Me. Jeff. He was a good man. He was so good, that Douglas. And they're Evil. I swear. We hit them first! It wasn't supposed to be one phase (?) ... They knew it though. God! A real person would have told us. We would have done it. We would have volunteered for it. But they could have told us! (crying) I got two more (killed two more)! They were animals! I wish I had more to work with! I need more ammo. I need more ammo! More guns. I'm out. What do I do now?!

SP: Douglas?

J: What?!

SP: The war's over.

J: For who?! (hysterical) For who?! I don't know what happened! I hit them hard.

SP: Would you like it to be over for you?

J: Yeah, but why, why? I want to know why first!

SP: You know where you can find that out? One way.

J: It hurts. It doesn't matter. They can hurt. I can't feel my body. I'm leaving. You jerks. Bullies! Evil bullies. You're weak. If I was there.

... I'm cold. You're lucky I'm dying! Huh! I'll show you – you'll have paid. Uhh. ... yeah, bleed.

SP: And then the body dies and the soul leaves.

J: ... I tried to go. My body's heavy and it's cold, and I'm so tired... They can't do it. THEY can't do it! (laughing in scorn) Ha. You have to try harder than that! No character! No guts. You're gutless! You're gutless! But you are gutless. ... You're gonna lose. We got you. We're gonna steam over you!

SP: And they did lose.

J: (laughing) What do I care? I'm just one. A number. Oh, do it again. Do it again! Why don't you cut some more?! Ohh (pain) If you haven't noticed, I don't care. You cheap son of a bitch. I don't know why it won't end, but I don't care. You're not gonna take this! Understand, you're not gonna take it. *Only I can let go.* You try so hard, but you're weak. You don't have a soul. - That's heavy.

SP: You *can* let go, is that right?

J: I don't want to, because I don't know why it's happening. Why is it happening? ... *He's in a box.* He checked out. He doesn't want to feel so bad. It's too sad. It's so sad.

SP: Would you let go for Ting?

J: Yes.

SP: Then let go now, for Ting.

J: Can't let go, but you can look. I can never let go! I can't let them go, the others (his team mates in the plane). There were others too. (crying) For them, I will carry on. We hit them. We socked it to them. I don't know why I lived. Oh it hurts. (sigh) But... Oh (pain) I don't care that they make it hurt, but I care why it's happening. Because it shouldn't have been. I could have done this 100 more times and I could have saved 100 more lives 'cause you wouldn't had to deal with them ... because they would be blown up - because I know how to do this and I'm damn good at it (bomber pilot). And... that's why I lead. [Evidently to the Colonel, the Boss] You know you made me look bad, they trusted me, and I do what you said ... and where'd you take us? Gas for one way, one way! And they would have volunteered.

They would have volunteered. You didn't have the guts to ask. I'll get you. I'll get you.

SP: The boss, the Colonel?

J: He's getting fat on the ship. He's eating dessert right now. (laughing, crying) I'm sick of him. He ... is now smoking. Piece of shit. I busted my butt to do my job. How many more are you going to kill?

SP: Hey, listen. We're going to come back. Focus upon Ting. Can you focus upon Ting for me? O.K. focus. Take a deep breath.

J: (sigh) I don't want to let go. It was sunny when we took off.

Ting: You have to let go.

SP: It's all right. We're going to work on it later.

J: Oh, oh God! (in pain)

SP: Hey, focus upon Ting now.

Ting: Jeff?

J: Don't pull. I'm here.

SP: It's all right, he's there. Focus. Are you ready to focus on what I'm about to say?

J: Don't be angry. I tried. I tried.

T: Please let it go for now.

J: You know of all people I would try and stick to it. Believe it.

T: I do.

SP: Douglas, can we talk to you later?

J: bwvoooo (clenched fists, groaning)! What? What? Why are they standing over me? They're just waiting.

SP: Jeff, listen, listen, listen...

J: Promise me we'll work on it.

SP: Yes we will. I promise. I promise.

J: Who are you to promise?

SP: You don't know me, but I promise.

J: (big sigh) Well, I trusted him (the Colonel) before, and look at me now. (crying)

SP: Look at me.

Ting: Jeff, please. (crying)

J: All right. That makes sense. I'm not going to trust you, but I understand.

T: Jeff, you're not going to lose me, I'm here.

SP: (Counting down to get him back.) 5, good, 4, coming back to your wife, 3, 2, 1.

J: O.K. Come on back. - I'm here. Oh God. (sighs) This is so real.

SP: It was real.

J: *He's been stuck there since it happened.* (crying) Oh! All this killing. - But he doesn't ... he plans for these emotions and he works around them.

T: Who?

J: Jeff. He's not going to forget. They were good men.

SP: Jeff, have you had other memories of this particular thing?

J: No, no way. It looks familiar though; pictures.

SP: I imagine it does. The imprint was so strong.

J: Ocean. I love the ocean. I love to be above it. It's so big, but (voice changes again) what we're doing, I'm in charge and there's no denying it, because you can't argue with this, because it's coming for you ... and it's gonna getchya. (sigh)

SP: Jeff, can you come back here? Look at Ting.

J: Hi...

SP: There we go. Need some tissue? It's right there.

J: No, I'm dry. I dried up in the sun.

SP: Yeah, I bet. Let me continue.

J: Who are you? (laughs, reverts to Jeff) I don't mean that in a bad way.

SP: I understand.

J: You weren't there.

SP: I wasn't.

J: They closed in ... and it ended right there.

SP: So many emotions! It's unresolved. You know about karma? You know about such feelings and unconscious reactions?

J: A little bit. [To Ting] You were there. (cries) I tried to save you. ... Oh how I hate those people. I know I shouldn't hate.

T: I was there? Do you know who those people were, besides me?

J: They listened to me and they would do anything I said. (crying)... But still, it was down here in a box (the plane?) and we picked it up and brought it up here. And it's open and it's big. We were a good team, and they worked hard ... and you worked hard and ...

T: I was a man?

J: You were the best and that's why you were in my plane. Because you could shoot.

T: I could shoot?

J: You sat in the back.

T: No wonder he wants to take me to the shooting range all the time. Now I get it. No wonder I want to go!

J: You could hit anything. ... You were the last one alive, but you were banged up bad. Blood. The others were dead. I crawled to you, watched you die. I told you, "I'm going to get you out of this." Your eyes then sparkled and you said something strange. You told me that You were going to get Me out of this. Ha. How could you, ... dying?! I looked you in the eyes, and you died. (Tears) I felt you go. Then I got my pistol and waited. They came ... with bayonets. Damn them! ... (To Ting) You had a reputation. Yeah, aircraft carrier and ... it was funny...

SP: And you were fighting which group?

J: Japanese.

SP: That's right. You were fighting the Japanese. And do you know why you married an oriental woman? (Striving to discuss the reincarnational healing choices.)

J: She's Chinese. She's Chinese American!

SP: Yeah, Asian though.

J: Way different. I know because I've seen them. And they killed me. (laughs strangely)

SP: It's a karmic connection.

J: I know they didn't get my ---- (uncle?) though. He was already dead.

Ting: I recall Jeff's father. He always said, "I never thought my daughter would be part Asian." (laughing)

J: But she's Chinese and that's good. And they helped, and we helped them.

T: That's why you married me.

J: I can see you. I can see you! (crying, seeing his teammate)

T: It's O.K. Jeff because I'm here now.

SP: That was then. That was then. Yeah, the emotions are there, the emotions are strong. (Jeff leaves the room.) Ting, I wouldn't be surprised if your awareness was attuned more towards him and maybe, on a soul level, you knew how this was going to affect him... You set up this regression session and had the interest, and brought Jeff, and Douglas, to work this out. (Jeff returns ...)

J: When I was in the sixth grade I built model airplanes all the time and I built the same plane over and over, and I kept breaking it and burning it. And one time I made something big; I took a big piece of plywood and made it, like hit the ground hard ... I crashed it hard on that wooden island. I was such a little modeler, that was my thing. I had contests with my friends ... model airplanes.

T: He still does them.

J: From the 6th grade and ... (voice changes) you were laying over the side.

T: What?

J: (Douglas) I had to pull you out and the plane was fried. I couldn't get the others.

SP: That sixth grader...

J: He knew. (himself as a boy) ... Even now! 3 days ago I was asking, I want a 1:48 scale Dauntless; that plane, over and over, everywhere we looked and ... that one company that makes mediocre models stopped making them, and at the hobby store they told me whenever you're at Longs Drugs, because they have lots of models, and they don't move them at all and there's probably an old one on the shelves somewhere. And I always go there to get pacifiers for the baby and I go look at the models. [13]

SP: Looking for your plane because Douglas wants to work this through. Because Douglas wasn't finished.

T: (Taking in the fact that I am talking with her husband about karma and past lives. Pointing to Jeff.) This guy is a totally conservative, Mr. Upstanding, who has just recently learned to express his feelings kind of guy, so...

J: We were so tough, we were so tough.

Ting: But we are now! Our whole relationship was ... no one believed in us; everyone thought, He's never going to stay with you Ting; and his family thought ...

J: I will stay with you forever! (We all laugh, then Jeff changes mood) ... Somebody dying. Someone being killed. Killing for no good reason.

SP: That's the theme, right?

J: I died for no good reason, because they blew it. Sent on a dead man's mission. I wear my uniform ...

SP: Are you in the military now?

J: Not now. I was remembering.

T: He wishes he was. That's all he thinks about. That's all he watches on TV.

J: That movie Battan, this 1943 propaganda movie with the evil Jap-Nazis ... that just gets under my skin, I swear, because they make a point of making the Japanese out to be evil ... When they horrifyingly kill the Americans one by one ... I can't stand it, but I have to watch it. Yeah, it hurts, and I keep watching.

Breathe.

That was the first of several sessions. He made me work, but it was fascinating to witness. We scheduled another session within the

---

[13] I later researched the Dauntless aircraft. It was definitely used in the Pacific in WWII, but Douglas must have been also a pilot of a larger bomber with five crew members and a gunner in the back.

week, as promised, and went back to retrieve poor Douglas. More of the story came to light. Douglas soon died, there on a rocky island in the Pacific, but stuck to his post, and stayed with his men ... for years. Shot down in the Pacific. A soldier ghost protecting his men. After he was bayoneted his soul hid under some rocks. He fought until the end. At first hysterical, determined, fighting and protecting, things got slower and gray. Time passed, in the rocks. Then one day a gentle soul, a warm light with a friendly smile, came for him. *It was time to go.* It was time. A warm white hand, bigger than normal, see-through, urged the lost pilot on, and upwards. The memory of Douglas was by then diminished, suffused and less determined to keep watch. He felt the warmth, got lighter and felt a pull upwards. He met his bombardier in Spirit. They knew each other well. That soul, now Ting, chose to be born into a Chinese American body to get one step closer to the old Asian reactions, and planned on meeting Jeff. The next thing he knew, he was a baby boy born in California, next to the Pacific. He was very interested in planes, models, the military and flying. Something kept Jeff from the military, but he got into security work – appropriate. One intriguing part of this is that, although the same soul came back as Jeff in California, a part of his soul remained on that Pacific island, keeping watch. Thus, we did a soul retrieval, instigating the release of poor Douglas. This couple, through their love, made a spiritual contract to retrieve the young pilot Douglas. We would get a chance to heal, to retire the earnest soldier, and through Ting's interest in spirituality and reincarnation, she brought him to me to finish the mission. Bless him for his service. Time to retire. "At ease, soldier."

Jean is round. Overweight. She was skinny as a child, she tells me. She talked of recognizing her protective armor to keep her step-father "uninterested." So came the layers of protection, at puberty. Jean has a nice pleasant face, with brown eyes "from my real father!" Strait blond hair, to shoulders; she started to get premature gray as a teen. Hers was a very dysfunctional family beginning with the tyrant and mean spirited Grandfather (with cold hazel eyes), who abused and damaged her mom, who then became an alcoholic, liar, controller and manipulator. Her traumatized mother divorced, then came the lecherous step–father; the result includes three broken unhappy siblings. A sad story, too often found in the world. I worked with her a few times, orchestrating some healing TPJs (transpersonal journeys) in Spirit to aid her to break out of the spider-webs of unhappiness. Jean is a talker, imaginative, with one foot in the fairy/ soul/ angelic world; I later learned that she was somewhat absent to the unpleasant surroundings – she was asleep as it were, which was a bit of a blessing. This was protective, perhaps an unconscious strategy of coping. Her school time helped her to be in books and with friends – and away from the family; these things saved her, I thought, … but I would soon find out that it was more complex than that.

Jean is a motherly–type who did not have children. George, her husband, manages a chiropractic practice; he was married before and brought his three daughters to the marriage. Jean became a good, nurturing step-mother to them. He's wary of this stuff that I do, but he trusts her, and paid for her sessions. He is tall, looks masculine but "rather emotional" she says, soft and sensitive. When he heard of the details of our first session he got teary–eyed. Our session:

"I've had this picture before… a past life. On my arm, there is a child = Michael. (older brother now)

We have to flee. Refugees. … Rocks, dirt, rough going. My feet hurt; I'm holding my child. My girl Tina (now sister) is here too. A war came… and its aftermath. We are wearing heavy linen, which is dirty, heavy, and coarse clothing. I'm the mother. 29? I'm nervous, overwhelmed. I don't know what will happen?!

Their father is in the background – a dark face, sharp sneaky eyes. Ah, I recognize him. He is a colleague in the office. Andrew. We understand each other, but he can get aggressive. I'm not afraid of him though. I tell him if he doesn't like me, I can go. George protects me too. Andrew is difficult. He sometimes loves me, then he hates me. He is so changeable! But I show him my strength. He can't intimidate me.

... We are refugees in Austria. Turn of the century? 1800?

I'm Deborah, I feel my belly, rub it. .... I see my son on my arm, Michael (His name today as her brother, but sometimes in these sessions the past personality keeps the name of today. Okay by me.). He is stubborn, stoic. Doesn't say a word. He just observes. I look around. Panic in the streets. Various people run, from the village. We separated. Now only us three – Tina, Michael and I. My husband was separated from us. Good. ...

We found refuge. Tina is anxious. She goes into her fantasy world. Yeah. Okay. ... We adjust. The outfits, clothing ... a farming community. We started anew. This new start came with hard work, but this was fine. I had my children and we are away from the danger, – this was good. It is autumn. We're alive.

... There is a new man in Deborah's life. Nice.

I'm 33, 34. He's like George (husband today, and probably the same soul) but taller, slender. Joyful, and jolly.

He takes my hand and we go. He shows me things. 'See how pretty the flowers are!' How different this is!

I don't sense Tina... Michael is still stubborn. It was another opportunity to reach him, to get him out of his pain, trauma. My baby was lost in the calamity. I was pregnant, and lost her. Lost my husband. – That father was no gift. Just as well. My child, Tina, is in her own world. Still.

Now I, we, have a new life. No, it is not important to have another child. (And in Jean's present life she became the good stepmother to another person's children.)

Now a farm, with my new partner; a cabin, straw… Fields, corn, grain. We grew what we needed. More than surviving - thriving. Things flow easier.

...

Our time was not long. He died earlier then he should've. Too soon. I'm sad, despondent.

He was face down in a creek. Heart problem? Young Michael found him. That was hard for him. Another loss. It was hard for me, for us all. I couldn't maintain the lightness after this loss. *I lost my will to live, and lost my love for my kids.*

Why?! It was finally set up nicely…but… then shattered. I can't take it. I feel alone. We only had three years together. I am devastated.

Tina dances around, in her world.

...

I can't get any more oxygen. I'm older … just a shell. 68?

My daughter looks like a witch. Poor clothing, disheveled, wild hair. I cannot care for her anymore.

Michael moved away. He quietly went his own way.

- dies -

I'm received by many hands…. They take me, bring me in.

This feels good. Like a 'complete' feeling, whole. Kind. Such good feelings.

As Deborah I could not grow or develop, inside, after …"

SP: Let us invite Deborah to the spirit circle for healing.

"Yes … there is a hammock. I'm in it. This form … comforts, a rocking. A gentle wind, a flowing. I feel it. A rocking. Tingling. I feel like a baby… I get bigger."

SP: Excellent. What was learned?

"What can I say? This feeling of pointlessness. I did not want to feel anymore. I was numb. Now … I do not want this anymore. … I couldn't even believe that such a man as my 2nd one could exist. And as I began to accept it, it was over. After that I shut down. I did not feel a lot. I called it the 'death time.' ...

I woke up at 27. (In Jean's life! This is an interesting twist, and something for the (para)psychology books – past life Deborah shut down and dissociated with grief. Thus, she was a "ghost" before her death. She was doing time, what she called the death time. Then she died [in 1930 or so?], left the body and continued to grieve; numb and detached. She, her soul, was then born as Jean, and the heaviness and unhappiness was reflected in her dysfunctional family, which she dimly noticed. 27 years into Jean's present life she woke up, and started living again. My guess is that this half-aware living, in Jean's dysfunctional family, may have also saved her from further turmoil. This suffering family, on one level reflecting her own past grief and resignation, damaged her siblings, but Jean came through it relatively unharmed, as she wasn't paying much attention. Thus a protective bonus of being detached, or asleep! She continues describing herself at 27...)

Then the clock started. I realized that I was responsible for my life. I needed patience, but now I have the rewards. *Time slips, when I am not paying attention.*

Now I feel waves of warm healing … The part of Deborah has departed. She was finally lighter, relieved, ...then she ascended."

SP: Great. We bless her and wish her well. Was Margaret (Jean's difficult mom) in Deborah's life?

"Probably. Yes. Mother then. Another reason to leave. ... It is nice to see that she was softer then. However, she 'married me off.' She chose that husband. She ignored my wishes, my heart. She didn't want to harm me, but it was a poor decision. Even today, right now, when I hear her name, Margaret, I say Oh no! - But good to see her as a softer person. She hurt me though, then and now. One didn't argue with one's parents back then. I just accepted it. I married him, and suffered.

… Mom's soul is not here right now. Other souls are all around, above, near. Caring. I was taken to a cave. I was there for the healing. They wait, observe. Then, after some time, they say 'Stand up and free yourself. *Feel your greatness!*' I am moved, touched, and more.

Hmm, funny, … from my back, I have wings. I can fly! I fly quickly, turn, play. Yeah! I fly up." - smiling -

SP: Simultaneously a release for Jean, an uplifting, freeing.

- breath - "I can't really throw it all off."

SP: Shall we ask for help from your spirit guide? Please help us here.

"Kara is here, wagging her tail. Ha. She seems big and soft. (Could her beloved pet dog be a spirit guide? Ha. She certainly trusts it.) Sweet, and so warm. Loving."

SP, looking at her list of questions.: Let us address the abortion. Was this Kara? (Her question! I don't believe it!)

"No. Just a wish. The connection is older, and different. There was a dog when I was born. She protected me, - my buddy and companion. She saved my life a few times. Then she was run over. I have no picture, but it is the same dog soul. So Kara returned to me. It was strange. I did have a cat. Momo. It felt like a brother. Momo reached 17 years old. A character, that one. But Kara is special. Kara doesn't want another animal or pet around. Protective? 'Be content with what you have' is the message.

Today I make a stand for animals. *I am sensitive to cruelty to animals. They are born like human babies – they cannot defend themselves.*

Oh nice. An expansive field of energy, all over. Wow. – This cannot be compared!, hard to describe."

SP: Lovely, the healing shall continue. Blessed beings near you. Any advice from here?

"Yes, … 'I'm on the right path. Keep on going!' and 'See for myself.' I'm curious about what's coming next. Then I get, *If I know too much about my future, this could slow me down.* When I need more, I'll get it, at the right time. My life partner is at my side, which is a gift. George - he's the right one, and accompanying me. He is here. He smiles, contentedly. It is all there."

…

Super. We slowly return, reinforce the healing, insights and lessons. More will come, she intuits. She's thoughtful, grateful. I offer her a gem stone for a reminder and keepsake. She chose a pink quartz. She intuits that this will aid her in her on-going healing, and a reminder that her soul is here and on her side. Pleased, she thanks me. Perhaps her George will come one day. He has a story too. In the meantime, she has carried out this duty long enough. It is time to enjoy and be here now.

~ 6 ~

Angry Souls: Fallen Angels

"Before thee are set good and evil. Choose thou."
The Bible, Deuteronomy 30:15

One person in trance was angry at his spirit guide, and also angry at God, but that perspective came later. He started with "My spirit guide is pissed off at me." Hmm ... unusual, I think to myself. Actually it was the other way around. "Why didn't you intervene when I got lynched?" Ah, the story. After some exploration we discovered that this soul had condemned another to die four hundred years earlier. His earth personality forgot. That same victim then came back and organized a lynching. Perpetrator, victim, perpetrator ... Get off that wheel!

We have stumbled upon some lost souls, some ghosts and soldiers keeping to their posts – beyond death. Some entities have attached themselves to welcoming children, and to drifting, unhappy loners. Evidently hospitals where medications are administered and bars where drinks are poured are also hang-outs for entities. There are hungry ghosts, searching for something they cannot quite grasp. Some entities are just waiting for things to settle down, and then they can return home. Some individuals, however, get really lost, hurting themselves and others. There are dark forces in the world. Hold on.

We are not finished with Jasa yet. She had her adventures and lessons, as described in the second chapter on Oaths. Things will get more complicated. Her troubled and addictive father was born near the Romanian border, and hated "those people" across that border. She married a Romanian (to spite him, or part of some plan?) – and had a past life there in Romania too. When her father died, she was left with her cold, unloving mother who was "absent, screaming, hurting" – no wonder Jasa was an emotional roller-coaster. Her sister was born when Jasa was five – and jealous Jasa picked on that little sister, who in spite of this mean treatment grew up to be intelligent, caring, and sensitive. She admitted to me that "I wanted her to be worse than me, lower." Jasa apologized to her poor sister a few years ago. We will see that a mean-spirited entity entered at this young age of five. What came first, the jealousy of her younger sister, or a negative entity that wanted to pick on another person? Shadows and negativity. Now Jasa's daughter is five – is this triggering the cycle anew? She books this session, and the negative entity is sent out. Yeah. Full cycle, the end of a mean phase. But this was just the beginning, I was to learn. In Jasa's past life she was a sadistic killer, and more. This perversion went to the soul level, and this is what I mean by a fallen soul, a fallen angel. Yes there is a difference between an evolving soul and a mighty angel, but the spirit of divinity animates both. We read of fallen angels but seldom of fallen souls; I am creating a link here. Perhaps souls who are caught up in the "deadly sins" have succumbed or fallen. Her description of the review and transformation in Spirit after this ugly life matches Edgar Cayce's information about being "cast unto Saturn" and being reprogrammed! Evidently Saturn is where one goes for deprogramming and rebooting the system. Interestingly enough, our souls learn lessons in the special vibrations represented by certain planets and stars. More information on planetary influences are found in an addendum. Cosmic information, and worth distilling.

We started with a past life personality as little Mary, beaten by her father. He thankfully died when she was 12 years old. (I note the parallel age in Jasa's life, who also lost her father at 12.) Young Mary was so destroyed that she vowed not to talk to nor trust anyone again. She died lonely, and remorseful. This hurt and distrust turned to rage, and festered. Jasa then tells me a secret. *There is another part of me –* accepting, yes, but another part struggling, contrary... a scornful voice says "Everybody's bad."

SP: Follow that negative voice back...

"Grey buildings… outside. (voice changed) There are also other people. I see them.

I hate them.

I'm a man. This may sound weird, but I'm Romanian. (We joked before about how she, as a Pole living in Germany, has so many Romanians around her.)

I'm very small. A small body. From an illness? No, but not growing up. A runt.

I'm evil. Very evil. I can kill, and enjoy it. I look very ugly. A dwarf? Or perhaps I feel this way? (grimaces. She doesn't like this past life personality! There is a tension in the air; I'm uncomfortable too. I pray for protection.)

I'm very evil.

I'm 40? … I have a loving mother... but I was born very evil. My whole life – alone? Or... sometimes a partner?

I kill people. Eat meat. Oh?! (realizes the worst)

I'm very aggressive. I'm strong, weird, mean and dangerous. I scare others. I enjoy when people cry.

I've a typical Romanian name... Maraiescu?

1800s? A city. It's very dirty, everywhere. I'm living in these dirty places.

I'm dressed normal. Pants for small people. Children. I can play the innocent.

I roam and live in a big city... many people I can hunt. I can hide, remain unseen. Stalk.

There are some people who come close – but I don't let them close. I can reject them, or kill them, eat them. ... I like to reject them. I get relief, satisfaction, from rejecting them, putting them off.

... I think I just killed somebody.

I'm inside. Afternoon... there is a dead woman in my bed. She was lured in... she believed...

We had sex. I put a knife in her belly.

I look at her. Her eyes were so pretty. They are closed now. Why did she like me? Trust me?

...

Green, foliage, trees ... a path. I'm walking in the forest. I'm 60? I'm happy I think. ... but I have nothing, materially. I am more quiet. I'm not so evil anymore. I don't want to be evil anymore. I had many phases. I accepted what I had done. I feel relief now. I have my walk. I live in the same place? Maybe not. I'm away from the city. No aggression now inside of me. I'm different. I don't want to hurt people anymore. ... I learned that it is painful to hurt others.

I think I feel happy because I feel pain for what I did. Conscience? I feel a certain relief.

...

I'm in bed... a bit scared, panicky. I start to feel very guilty. What have I done? What have I done?! – a huge tension is building up inside. What have I done? I'm old. I'm sick. Oh my God. - A tension ... which is very familiar to Jasa. 'No exit, no way. I can't avoid it.'... this is what I'm feeling – the inevitable. (And possible/ probable judgment and punishment in this Orthodox Christian background?)

- dies -

I see the body... down there. I'm not so relieved. I feel calm, but heavy. ... like something didn't happen like it was supposed to happen.

I was not supposed to do what I did. I was supposed to manage my aggression. My mother tried to teach me, be an example. I thought her weak.

It was a wrong life, or bad deeds. I wasn't supposed to kill that lady. I'm not okay with this. I want to make things different. ... It was about this lady. I did it against my will; I felt I had to. Instinct. It is what I did. (Evidently little remorse for the other victims. This one got to him. My guess is that this soul made a contract – to meet him and possibly to be harmed by him to awaken his conscience, but he crossed the line with her. In that case she sacrificed herself so that he would awaken. How often do we see this in history, in the news?)

I'm afraid to meet her now. (In Spirit) - but I want to...

- smiles - Ah. My ex-boss, Blanca. I bow my head in remorse. 'I'm so sorry. So so sorry!'

(Recalling present life memories of her...) There were conflicts. I was very afraid of her. It was like she knew things about me. Could she read my thoughts? I'm very afraid of many people."

SP: Is this a similar fear that your victims felt? Contemplate karma and the emotional mirror. We are confronted by our past.

"... Blanca is a nice person. Warm. Not easy, but nice."

SP: Does she have a message?

"I'm afraid of a message from her." ...

Blanca: "Follow your path. Be more attentive to people you meet."

Jasa: "Do you forgive me?

... She is hugging me. (relieved, emotional, and speaking to me in Polish. Ha.)

Mareiscu was attracted to her. He opened up a bit - he was touched. And regretted killing her. He realized too late. - Life could have been different.

(Yes. But he had many victims. I set it up so that he is confronted by people he killed ... in Spirit.)

... they are small souls. Poor and downtrodden. I made them small, or they were small in my mind.

I'm so so sorry.

... I don't quite believe this ... they look to me with understanding... they have a wisdom. Compassion. But I also feel pain, and ... understanding. We are crying... there are no words.

... then the word 'silence' (whispering) ... John, my spirit guide is here. (smiles)

He is very patient. (she is quiet, taking it all in)

I am in some space. I don't know where. I'm stuck there. ... in energy. No shape. It's not so good energy. It is heavy. I cannot understand it.

... something to be understood, accepted here. I cannot let it ... go. Or it will not let me go. I cannot get inside this vibration. It's strong, contradicting, stopping some impulses. - On one side and ... I want to do it, go, but something is stopping me. It's like I have no legs. Of course in Spirit, I have none, but I cannot go, walk, leave. I cannot move.

I'm afraid of that Light. (I get images of a fallen angel, a damaged soul, afraid of the Light.)

I don't see it, I sense it. If I stay in this space, it is just what I need. ... but it is so narrow, and thin. I cannot get inside."

(This reminds me of a re-programming place and specifically of Saturn, one-dimensional, as described by Edgar Cayce – souls were cast back to reform, or re-molded there.)

SP: How long were you in that space?

"I was... 100 years there."

SP: Good, much was released and relearned there. And after 100 years...?

"I'm flying... quickly. - smiles -

I think I'm lighter. The vibration – like a hand came, 'Come,' it said. I go ... and I'm more high, in a place of songs. Wow. Everything is here. Sad too. Gray. Golden light.... a bit of gray. There is a heavy gray.... what is this? My guide comes.

John, her spirit guide, explains: Jasa needs to understand. And she can. She knows this place.

"Yes... Gray... it is this fear. I would rather concentrate on the golden good light. Ha. I'm passing through the gray, however. I must, ... but it is part of the gold. Gray is a challenge – to search for strengths. Gray is painful. Doubt and uncertainty. *The heaviness of our own deeds.*

She is feeling it now. It is a pain for all generations. It's hurting now.

Oh God, it is hurting... it is painful. (Was she sent to Neptune? [14] Weltschmerz = the pain of the world. – a Pisces redemption place? The empath feeling the pain of others, of her/his victims?)

I'm trembling. (breathing hard)

Here is … the gift of healing. Empathy. It is good. But painful. It is almost too intense. (She is suffering. I suggest she employ a volume switch. The effect will still occur.)

'Okay - down to minimum.' … Now I feel my hand again. I had so much pain that I couldn't feel it. From my heart to my left arm. … Empathy is something good for Jasa."

(I ask questions – there is yet another change of voice; she goes in to a very deep trance:)

"Jasa's mother now was in both past lives. Unimportant, however.

And her Father too; - s/he was the woman who was lured to her fate. (Could this explain her alcoholic father? She was meeting Self again, that evil past life.) He started drinking after I was born. - quiet -

I don't want to speak. This is all so exhausting. I have a feeling of going home to sleep. Tired. And relieved."

Okay. We call it a day. 3 ½ hours. There was a lot to take in, to integrate. I give suggestions, review, renew, …take a winter sleep to a new spring. "Recharge, re-new... there will be a sunrise."

She later said, "I feel strange. Not like my old self. It is quieter, there is an inner peace." Excellent, I think, but what a difficult, and disturbing, story. I ponder … as we go along our ways in our modern, complex world, who else is laying in wait? We read about similar predators in the news, but here was an example of a savage personality who did foul deeds, and came to regret them in his older years. This soul, tainted by that perverted personality, was sent to a

---

[14] In an addendum I list the planetary influences as described by Edgar Cayce.

re-programming place and then felt the sufferings of his victims, opening up remorse and empathy. Furthermore, this soul got another chance, in another body at another time to "try again, and do things right."

> "There is no coming to consciousness without pain.
> People will do anything, no matter how absurd, in order to avoid facing their own soul.
> One does not become enlightened by imagining figures of light, but by making the darkness conscious."
> ~ Carl G. Jung

Angry people, and souls. The previous example of a hunter and cannibal is unnerving. A look at history, and the news, shows us many scary and ugly humans hurting other people (and mistreating animals). Sad but true. From my experience I believe there are predators among us. Perhaps they still feel the primordial imprint of instinct from the early days of the "fall" to earth; perhaps they identified with a predatory animal, such as the soul who remembered being killed by a lion in a Roman arena and felt some strange fascination and identification with the hungry beast. Other people and souls are stuck in heavy, bitter and enraged emotions, and they want to lash out – blindly. They cause harm, and innocent people need to be protected from them. M Scott Peck (22 May 1936 – 2005), an American psychiatrist and best-selling author of the book "The Road Less Traveled," also wrote "People of the Lie: The Hope for Healing Human Evil" in 1983. Dr Peck explored the shadowy world of evil in this study. Although thoughtful, educated and scientific, he came across several patients in his practice who maintained an essential evil, a notion that other psychotherapists would dare not admit. Peck described these people as maintaining a "militant ignorance," which goes beyond an inability to have empathy for others. These people have personality disorders distinct from sociopaths, he asserted, and they instinctively avoid self-examination and project faults and evil itself upon others. They often want to bring other people down to their level, and below. In my next case, a victim becomes a perpetrator and a bleed-through reaction erupts with the birth of her child. This was a trigger, and it was about time.

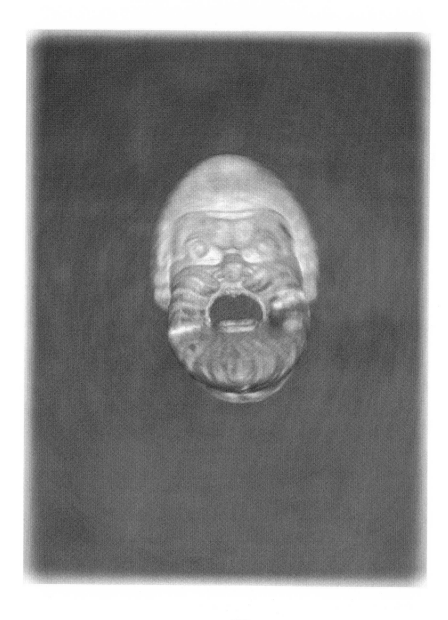

Sandra contacted me in desperation. She had suicidal thoughts since her C-section seven months prior. Her baby son totally triggered her and pushed her into a crisis. One thinks of postpartum depression (PPD), also called postnatal depression, in such cases. I have wondered if mothers, and sometimes fathers, affected with this were meeting a past life conflicting personality in this newborn child. Her complaint wasn't very satisfying: He's either crying, or happy. This seems pretty normal to my understanding, but there was a strong and mysterious story to discover. For some months, postpartum, she was severely depressed. As she closed down, her understanding husband took charge of the baby's care. This young Gemini mother, I discovered, was a ghost two times, and one of them was a mean-spirited specter, the type that Hollywood would love. She became a ghost that wanted to scare people. I can only recollect two other times in my thirty plus years of conducting regressions of something similar. S/he was so evil in Ireland, happily torturing, that, after death, he was "taken away" for rehabilitation, as was the Romanian killer in the last story. This experience in the inter-life was beyond purgatory. We discovered that s/he was a victim in one life, became enraged and became the perpetrator in the next life. The birth of her son triggered despair, and the unconscious pattern from an anguish 400 years ago.

The plot thickens: Sandra's mother is disturbed. Did she use Black Magic?, Sandra ponders. This mother is a complicated, manipulative nagger. She can manifest destruction, even break things, like a poltergeist, Sandra told me. And then her alcoholic father was sometimes "an asshole and then nice. Like me." He said mean and destructive things. He complained that his buttons were pushed by his nagging wife. Besides this, Sandra's family was poor. So … basically not a happy childhood. She was the only girl; her brothers picked on her. There was some karma to this, as we shall see. Sandra's husband is probably an older soul on an assignment to help guide, and evolve, Sandra. He is patient, and understanding, an educated man from a well-to-do family. I found Sandra to be intuitive, dreamy, and a good subject, even though she got dizzy, spinning, in the suggestibility test! We are ready to go ...

"Blue, violet and white, ... and stars. I feel expansive." - laughs, pleased -

SP: Welcome to Spirit.

"Oh, I like it, and want to suppress it though. (?!) - tears -

On the right is a waterfall. I come here often. A peaceful lake, with quiet water, grass, the waterfall is on one side. The sky is expansive, and a light–blue color ... the sunshine, very vibrant! Maybe one other person is there.... The waterfall is before me, with cold gray rocks. There is a sadness there. I look away, to the sky. ... I'm spinning again, a bit dizzy.

I sense that I am not alone. There is a male, near me. He's quiet, serious, perhaps too serious. He has a lot of knowledge. Like twenty times more than me!"

SP: Your spirit guide is here, probably. Great. Does he have a message?

- cries – red nose, tears -

"I don't know what this means... I spin forward... Then I come to a stop. Confusing! I'm spinning.

He says, 'Then don't.' - Ha! He appears now as a ball, before me. I can spin, but out of control? Can I let go? (This self trust is a theme.)

– breath – ... He is white, and a bit of gray. Is this his name? Gigi! Sounds funny, ok! So he is not so earnest. Ha. He's tricky, this one! This name = means Peace.

Gigi says, 'Sandra has anxieties and fears.'"

SP: Yes indeed, and your guide brings Peace, Sandra. Breathe it in.

"... So I have this war, this conflict, inside. Ah, to find the peace!"
- cries -

SP: Feel his peace, like a shower... take it in.

"Ahh, ... within me, - the same peace as my youngest brother! I really admire him. ... I'm ashamed... that I can't be laid-back, or take it all in, as he can. – I resist."

SP: Why would you resist the good traits, and feelings?! Is there a message here?

"I have 20 heads, all busy. Ha."

SP: (This is way beyond Gemini. ... So I ask...) Do you sense some entities, lost souls too near? How many?

"Uh ... 4 or 5? No, 3."

SP: So it is time to send them home. What do you say?

"I think I'm afraid of being alone."

(An unusual response. This makes things complicated. We continue, orchestrating the release.)

SP: Angel, please help the lost ones to go Home, to the Light.

"Is it possible that I am clinging to them? she asks. - Yes, comes the answer. - breathing heavily -

My head says, 'Then Gigi has to leave. I want to be alone.' (Hmmm. Spiteful!)

Then two dangerous eyes stare at me. An eagle or devil."

SP: Who could this be, a past life personality?! What happens next? What do you perceive?

"What will come? A place, gray and dark. Oh no! Fear! (agitated)

(I must reinforce protection. It is safe to explore, etc. – She calms down.)

It was dangerous, now it is fine. I'm okay. ... things have changed. In the dark night, the sky opened up, then, ...

I'm in a dungeon. I have fallen.

Torture, tools, crying, screams! Wheels, instruments, crying people, terrible! Such feelings, emotions, pain!

I'm a man, 40 or 50 years old. ... Two images, faces. I left this place – this torture scene. Oh...um... It is like I'm both - the torturer and tortured."

SP: Could you be sensing two lives?

"Could be."

SP: Then let us go to the first life...

"... Inside, dark and musty. Torture. I'm an old man, quiet, knowing. Being one with nature – at least, before this imprisonment. Nature is my solace… Then I was brought into this dark cellar. (emotional, tears)

I found peace and oneness in nature, and then I got tortured! …

I was so angry that I tortured in the next life! - cries -

I knew it was wrong. Now I understand - when I have two options, good and bad, I go for the wrong one. (Contrary, spiteful, and very angry – over many lives!)

I now go to the 1st life – death and thereafter ... I see everything from above. - deep breath -

At first I was observing the body… then I left, and was looking around in nature. I was seven to nine years… in nature. (OK, a nature spirit, as it were. From such beings come legends and myths.) It was very peaceful after death. I wanted to reconnect to nature - like before the torture."

SP: Shall we meet the perpetrators? Do you know them today?

"Oh I know this mean one: my friend's step-mother. S/he was the torturer; she is bossy and imperious now. S/he was being 'too clever' back then, leading this 'work' in a thorough way.

My best friend comes to mind too; she was in that life - a little girl, quietly trying to help. We were related then. She brings light, smiles, when she can. He he. She's so funny, like now; a little witch. Ha. She was the daughter of a servant there.

- cries - Oh, oh! … My son was here! He was tortured too!

(And it was his birth that triggered her depression and suicidal thoughts, eventually leading her to this session.)

We were together. I tried to show him the peace I found. I couldn't! He suffered!

(wails, cries, tears – nervous, emotional, I hand her more tissues.)

My teeth, chattering, I feel my hands bound, knees aching. The ants crawl all over, bite. And ... this person next to me, - cries - my son now! He is not doing well. I had a peace in me. I wanted to comfort him! Hold him. *I wanted to die first, to help him on the other side. So now I want to die again, for him!* I thought then, perhaps as a soul, a specter, I could help him … on the other side. I would be released from my own shackles, and then aid the poor boy. Oh oh! I see. I understand my suicidal thoughts after his birth. I would die for him!

- cries -

(breakthrough revelation) Thank you Stephen.

- tears, heavy breathing -

Oh. Ha ha. So sweet. My boy. My sweet boy. He cannot be still. He wants to catch up, get on with things, to be grown.

… *But I didn't help* after I died. I was curious. Detached. Happy with the peace, relieved to be out of there. I drifted away, went back to nature. I left. – I enjoyed nature."

SP: Do you see this as a recurring pattern? (Hmm, leaving him to find her peace, to pursue her hobbies and interests. Her present mother instincts are not so pronounced; now her husband is caring for their boy.) Invite both men to the circle, here in Spirit ...

"On the left, Gigi my guide, and then my son, who is dark green. Then me, the old man. - The light came. All of us… Oh! Big and strong. Independent from one another. May we live in freedom with and for each other! But not enmeshed. I fall into the feelings. I take things to heart. Then I feel bad. I have things to do … and my son has things to do. – Gigi has things to do! All independent. It would be ideal if … I can concentrate on my own things. It's okay. Important. (This is essentially good but it could be taken too far. She could pass on the chores now, and be irresponsible. The old man with the good intentions went about his own way immediately after death, leaving the now son to fend for himself. Patterns.)

… I hear the conversation – how can I achieve this in my everyday life? Breathing has helped. More than yoga, meditation. Take a big breath! In my suicidal times, I was told to breathe. Charles my husband tells me that too.

Thank you Stephen. Now more joy can come!" ...

SP: You're welcome. Good, now for the second part, recalling the next life, the perpetrator…

"… I'm inside. A man. Uhh…ohh… I reacted, joined the dark …

I am like Dracula. Great. (Ironic, dismayed) While the people are tortured, I laugh in their faces. Cruel. It was so bad - I'm so intense. I'm so big too. Such a rage, an energy, and such anger. I'm agitated, enraged.

I feel the people from the inside too. Such nice, innocent people, many are good souls.

I torture them with zeal. How can I treat them like this? How long did I do this? Where?

I was in Ireland. (She dislikes it today. Bad memories, and guilt.)

It is the Dark Ages. I'm wearing an old costume, with a white face, big teeth, like a theater piece. Ridiculous. Chilling. Grotesque. 'Dracula'" - tears -

I had an apprentice, a young boy. I taught him my tricks; it was like theater, and ugly fun. Ah, this little sorcerer = became my mother today. She likes to show off her magic, but it is warped."

SP: We are seeing the cause and effects now. How did this start in that life? Let us go earlier in his life…

"I see myself younger, a boy. A simple life. Oh my! My now husband = then was my mother! (And he has motherly qualities today.)

I was playful, but one half of me was already mean, angry. She did not know how to deal with it. She did not stop it. She avoided it. She retreated from it.

I could express it. So I was playing alone, being cruel. I hurt little creatures. She did not know how to deal with it. This is an important developmental lesson, for my husband now – for our son. There needs to be limits and rules. I need limits."

SP: Yes, limits are needed. And so you became the torturer. Let us now go to the end of that life.

"I'm sick, alone. No one cares. I'm frustrated. I didn't get rid of my frustrations. – Oh, I am old, 80 or 90 - I die alone in bed. …

Detached from the body, I'm not detached from the earth. I'm a gray fog. ... Nothing much happens. The house is quiet…I go in a forest. Thickets and underbrush.

I'm disoriented, frustrated. I seek out people.

I try to frighten people as a ghost. I'm laughing. I know how to go home, but I want to stay and be mean. I kick trash cans on the street. Break branches off of trees.

… I lost my motivation, after some time. Then… Nothing. An emptiness. Then came … little feelings. I was 70 years a ghost, a wraith.

….then, once I was empty, Gigi arrived. This was the only thing I could feel – I tell Gigi, 'I lost myself. … I have to 'step back,' get back to my core. I lost something.' I had to regain it ... *Like after a person has a stroke, they have to relearn walking, talking.* I lost my humanity, my spirit. So we go to a bright place. Gigi and I. …

I'm sitting, waiting... feeling my head. An energy, light everywhere. Gigi is waiting, pacing. Yellow comes. It seeps in. Light to my head, my thoughts. I was 30 – 50 years there.

(Soul renewed, rehabilitation! Re-winded, re-booted? Retrieved that lost goodness. I think of infamous characters in history going through this restoration. Fascinating.)

These horrible things – I see where this came from. I get it."

SP: Good. And the people you have met today, on the list? - any who met Dracula?

"Oh! I understand now! My three brothers! The 'torture' or teasing that I endured in this life today is nothing compared to what I did to them then. I can be thankful! Also … a teacher, Martina. She was a substitute teacher. I had to torture her too. Repercussions today. She was intimidating, punishing."

SP: And how about Lawrence, your son?

"Was he a little brother? To Dracula. … Yes. He was the mother's boy. I was the big brother. A big age difference. I didn't see much of him." (Thank Goodness!)

SP: And your father Arnold. Was he there? (A difficult character)

- cries - "He was my father then too. He left or died early. So much love came from him." - tears - (In that life, not this one. Still, this love did not check the "mean side" of Dracula.)

A light comes. ... Gigi makes a suggestion: "It is how it was. It is okay. Leave it at that. It is done."

Soul: It would have been easier for me to learn this, when *I* was tortured.

Gigi: "Don't ignore that. Now is a Time out. Sit it out."

Sandra: Ha Ha (relieved) But then I think, if I sit it out, I may get too passive, then my son will not have the limits, like Dracula's mother didn't set?!

Gigi: Lawrence will be okay. Don't worry.

Sandra: I can be a good mother. I am really feeling the bond with baby Lawrence. Now I remember how I had lost my patience; I regret that. I want to re-write the impatient scene with him. There we are. He is crying. This time I send him peace and patience. 'It's going to be fine,' I tell him. I feel Love. Simply love. - smiling -

Oh, I'm allowed to love him so much! I love him, I do!"

SP: Excellent. Nurture that love, follow the wisdom and stay close to your soul guide Gigi.

...

And so we wrapped it up that day. Ugly stories, and lives, with relevance today. Towards the end it seemed to me like a group meeting with several viewpoints; interesting. Notice also how her soul guide, Gigi, urges her to Let it Be for now? This could refer to a break or a time out. It has been promised that there is always a way out. There are vacation lives, for instance. Yes, sometimes souls get to have a recreation lifetime; this is a relaxation lifetime for souls who need a break from a series of difficult lives and are spiraling downward. Blessed be! This soul guide advice to Let it Be may have a darker hue however; it could point towards a certain distance exhibited by some souls in regard to pain and suffering upon the earth. Add that part with her first life as the man of nature who was tortured also fits this "hands off" detachment. Although he wanted to help the poor lad next to him in the cell, once he died he just drifted off. We will discuss this further in the chapter *Hands Off and Far*

Away. In the meantime, one can get inside the heads of serial killers, torturers and sadists in this spiritual work. Unsettling. Not only have people been killers, cons and hungry ghosts in the past, but much more. ...

Spiritual journeys – it is not always pretty. It is however always fascinating, and multi-faceted. There is more to explore, and often a lot to heal.

> "It is absolutely necessary that the soul should be healed and purified, and that if it does not take place during its life on Earth, it must be accomplished in future lives."
>
> - St. Gregory (257 - 337 AD) early Christian writer

~ 7 ~

Aliens Among Us

I recall a client who is a scientist and more comfortable with the consistencies of physical laws, engineering and mathematics. We went back to a past life in some primordial jungle – it was her first incarnation on earth. She was fascinated and proud of her strong body. Wow, could she run and jump! She was a strong vibrant physical specimen that found herself one day pregnant, with no clue as to what that meant or how it happened. Totally lacking in maternal instincts and not aware of cause and effect relationships, she simply found her belly growing, which slowed down her hunting and running. When she gave birth, out in the jungle that was her home, she viewed the wet thing on the ground as foreign and not so interesting. She did notice that her belly was smaller and that she could now move easier. That's better. Her friends were near and wanting to go. Leaving the thing on the jungle ground, she bounded out, able again to move more quickly. 1500 years later the results of this abandonment would surface. The present self could not have children, much to her sorrow. When we left that jungle life, she floated up, found herself in some spacesuit, and boarded her spaceship. She debriefed her comrades about the strange and fascinating earth flora and fauna. It was an interesting study, she reported. Humans need more studying.

There are aliens among us. When incarnated they are called *hybrids* by some people in this work. This means that they had previous lives on other planets, some having advanced civilizations, and then they were *planted* or transplanted onto this Earth and thus are hybrids. Is there a thin layer of earth civilization? A thin veneer of humanoid is more like it; they may not catch on to the unspoken rules down here. Are some of them autistic, trying to tone down the noise? Many find it harsh. Some want to leave. Many are innovators, mathematicians, scientists, teachers, and too many of them are socially different, odd and may not have that many close friends. Misunderstood often; with spirit memory, friends are "thoughts near," or energies to sense, or mergings of auras … which others don't understand. If only the space brothers would come!

No, it is not so easy for these other-worldly beings; things are somewhat primitive here on earth and it is not always an easy fit. There are many types, temperaments, and tales; hybrids are mixing with the "natives" or with those who had a head start here on Earth. Although some hybrids are loners or not too socially adept, they have unique gifts to offer. Some are leading the way and have the right stuff.

We return to Aqua, from *vol. 1*, for this ride into outer space. [15] She had the worry of a large belly and an old fear of pregnancy. A big belly, a pregnancy, gave her away in a past life in Medieval Europe and the results for this unmarried woman were terrible. This free thinking herbalist had an other-worldly perspective on love, sex and the body that her social contemporaries found licentious. We resolved those shaming and confusing emotions in Spirit, thank goodness. She relaxed and could allow more ease and acceptance in her life. I saw her a year later, after another trip to her beloved islands of Hawaii. There is always more to explore! She quickly drifted into trance, and Aqua was again swimming, and quickly:

"So fast… I'm flying, with the dolphin – then it turns into, … like a dance, in the air, spirals, playful! Then we Dive… Now deep in the water. Darker, the depths… Oh, the presence of a whale. Immense. –

---

[15] "Inner Journeys, Cosmic Sojourns" volume 1, by Stephen Poplin; pp 148 - 155.

I feel something, deep in my pelvis, (right-hand over womb) ... my right side... quickly, up and down. On the right is – like a light. Beautiful... a presence, masculine. ... A yellow, a bit of orange, in my belly. It lifts me up. - quiet -

I get an image... a young man... with a spear? A long staff? There, on my side. I see him from far away. ... He's in his 30s or 40s. An oar or punt in his hand. He is a servant, now in service of ... rowing the boat, a ferry man. I'm in the boat. (At this point she could be in a past life, or symbolically transiting across the waters of consciousness. I'll wait and see.)

I see flowers – blue, green... I am landing on an island in the Pacific. A wave of emotions. I feel sad. Nostalgic. ... I see a native woman. It feels so much like home. - deeper breathing -

There are others. I see her on the edge of a village. I perceive her ... long thick dark hair. Her skin is brown. This ... sort of dress, a simple skirt. ... She is One with the Earth, Gaia, there, peeking out from the bushes. There is something on her body, but you don't notice it at first. A necklace? Emblem?... She reminds me of a woman that I know. The ex-partner of Martin, my friend. (By this point, dear reader, you may know that sometimes our friends and loved ones take on a shape or size, or a personality, that is a reflection of our own past.)

... I arrive on the island with this boat; the woman in the underbrush, waiting there. I think I'm more ... a man. Around 30. I'm white...

I'm not from here.

I feel a sadness... on the left side ... (rapid eye movement – REM, something is going on)

There is a romantic connection with this woman. I come and go I believe. She won't leave this island. This is her home – it is her self, almost. I can't really reach her. She is like, embedded in the bushes, plants, flowers. (This could be an archetype, symbolic, an earth goddess? or a true native, "at one" with her island?)

There is a hesitation, and a big longing. ... I'm still in the boat, very close to shore. She looks up. She looks at me – interested. I feel my pelvis energized. (Hand still there. The attraction is palpable.)

... I don't know if I am the man coming ashore, or the woman... or both? I'm still a bit more the man.

(now both hands over pelvis) ... She waited for him. They are running hand-in-hand through the forest. She is leading. The energy feels very young, fresh and playful.... In the middle of the island is a village – a round yurt type thing, but more modern. Sci-fi. I have an internet image from yesterday. Geometric, radiating. - gestures -

It feels like a secret place... where beings live. No one knows. It is an assignment, an outpost or station. ... I don't see the beings. From far away I see this structure, this complex. Geometric-lines directed towards the middle.

This woman is a nature being, natural, a native of the island, of Earth. I feel there is a parallel existence here. – This outpost is not native. I feel it is from another planet. ... now I feel that a Being is greeting me with a lot of love... a purple blue energy.

- emotional, tears -

... I feel ... this love in my head. An energy transfer from this being. My body wired, moved – and even contractions."

SP: Is this "wiring" okay with you? It must be okay, or get your approval. How does it feel?

(Aqua gets straighter, different breathing)

"A ripple – around my chest. My body is like a ripple. My skin is like a tube. ... I don't know if I like that. ... My body – new colors. I get very uplifted – I'm flying,... I'm leaving Earth, in a UFO. There are others here, on this craft. Strange, some ... very slow travel, or seems to be. - smiles - Oh, there are colors in space! Ha ha. I can fly very quickly. It is fun being up here with them. (stretches, arms overhead, then back down)

We are now approaching their home planet. A greenish light in view. (smiles, then tears, moved)

We all go out. Still very spacey, but this substance here, other than gravity. It feels so familiar... There's a busyness, but in a nice way. Others go in & out of the UFO. My body, and head, are swollen, long. A change. I see ... They don't have a clear body form... rather floating, pulsating. Ha. A bit like a salamander. But not flat, on the ground. Upright. - quiet - They are a bit taller than humans. I don't see this clearly. And ... I feel this endless love. - quiet -

Ah, this love and energy. Now a sharing, an energy transfer. We 'look' at the complex on the island... They are there on earth, and want to understand, to comprehend: their mission... to imprint patterns, the geometric forms. Is this part of their communication? - tears -

Love touched me.

This familiar feeling... The geometric form receives information. It reminds me of a temple complex of ancient Egypt, but ultra-modern. There are outposts on other planets, and on Earth. The one that I was at ... It is on this very green island. It is big, and round. I have not been in it. I see it as a whole. Perhaps it is the UFO itself. If so, I was in it. They create a close contact between the Earth and their planet - again. An interplanetary friendship – like it was. An old connection. This is really needed, - emotional - so that the earth can survive... and reach its goal. The Earth, it is like a child that is reconnected to its mother again. The origin. Spawning.... I sense, in my body – a release in my head and neck... a field of unity. It feels good. (hands to upper chest)

Something like a helmet is put on me – it has all of the information; Colors, vibrations. I get more information, a transfer.

(right-hand to side of the mouth, just under her nose, beside mouth, then to neck. Gets quiet – She told me later that the helmet was removed.)

... I'm more... on earth again. Now comes a sort of ... a memory. Images of the Incas... and their temples. And a deep peace inside. My head says, Maybe it is the Sun, or via the Sun. ... A new friendship with the Earth. When I say that, I feel a concept of the Sun. I think, 'It is hot. One can't get too close to it.' There is an interplay between the earth and the sun. The beams of this planet – green, loving, matches the energy of the Sun. I can be there, on Earth, and in between. I can't get burned... Ah Sol divine! It is the true energy – what we really are. We're made of Love. This is also crystalline – beautiful.

It's not like one would get burnt by the Sun. I feel this fear, mine and humanities', – about getting close to the source. Our source is the Sun. (hands out, from the blanket, over chest)

I feel the Source, beaming … It is very green, light green. Strong. … There are other energies, beings, here, in Spirit. I intuit ... is it a memory? *An agreement that we will go down to earth. We are family.*

I feel like one of them."

SP: Excellent. Let's see more. See yourself. Find before you a magical mirror, what do you look like?

"Hmm... more like an energy. Green – yellow. Then the feeling... I could be a form of a person, but the substance I'm made of is different; it's light and fresh. I feel a pull down – to the Earth space. That is okay."

SP: Fascinating. Let us look at Aqua, incarnated here. What about her next phase, her mission – any advice?

(her legs open, yoga like.) "I need to look closer at the island.... On the island, I come out. There is a cape on my shoulders. We walk very slowly, dignified. Ha. Like a... picture of a delegation; the others have capes too. My family, the same family. Hmm... it is working in my belly. Very strong. Pulling me down. Gravity. I see the capes; white beige dresses or outfits. Janie is here. Also Heidi. (Soul sisters, and evidently foreign emissaries too!) I feel their energy... also Donald, my partner. Plus two other friends. We're all incarnated together, for a purpose. (head and forehead touched, like a salute – leg now straight)

We come – with good news! Ha. – corny, but *We come in peace!*

My mission: connecting different parts of the Earth ... I almost 'hear' a form like... - gestures - a triangle, with the planet at the top. Four points. A Pyramid shape? Technical, mathematical. Digital too. We are here to help connect these places on the earth: Hawaii … the

Green Island. Then I feel the Inca energy. Plus … the mountains of Austria and Switzerland, and then Tahiti. Earth and Water. …

I think of the woman I met in the beginning. Strange that my belly got such energy. She is the one who knows Earth. It feels like it is my mission to be this connection between that planet and Earth, so then … I really need her. She is so pure. Grounded. Earthy. I need her as an anchor."

SP: Is she a person that you know, or she might be like Pele´ (Hawaiian volcano goddess) or a nature goddess?

"It is important that she stay pure. It is nice to invite the white man, but she should not go away with him. Ha – I got this vision of Columbus coming to an island. Don't trust him, or keep a healthy distance! (both hands over pelvis – breathing deeply)

My belly hurts a bit. It is round, like it is full of air all of a sudden. … an image of the boat returns. The pain grows ... It moved away from the neck, and now down to the pelvis. …"

SP: A birth? The next phase? The boat could be masculine. It comes to the island, which is feminine?

(legs up, contractions, deep breathing) "I get images of Pele´ the Hawaiian volcano goddess. A stream coming out of my vagina. A voice – the Goddess. New energies, something concrete wants to flow over the earth. A Change is coming. (contractions, movements)

A serpent is coming. I see us doing things. There is my friend Heidi.

- rhythmic gestures -

Sweeping of the earth... white cords... touch the people, touched the Earth. Touch. Songs are needed, and Hawaiian dance moves.

- arms move, rhythmic, like a dance -

I am in a sarong, dancing. Touching the earth. I have been doing that recently. Sounding the feminine energy. … I felt this from the planet, far away – they imprint the earth. A rhythm and sound. Me, in my limited body ... all I can do is give this to the people right now.

- arms still moving, to an inner music! -

And so the Earth connection, places on the earth, can and should vibrate, move. With Heidi, and Sarah, my dance friends. In Hawaii –

I'll bring the sound healer there. It feels like an alibi, an excuse, to go there again. Ha. I now dare to be the sound, and loud, to be myself, singing the sounds of love! On the island is the feminine power, the dance. I can work with that man I met there. He uses a stereo for the music, but we can have something more natural. Live music. … I will return to Hawaii to sing and dance."

...

And so we return, integrate. She is very pleased. Happy and even astounded. And then we debrief: No, I do not think it is weird that she mentions UFOs, other planets, etc. I have met with many people over the years who tell of other planets and dimensions. We are not alone. Aqua then added, "Funny. It was years ago that my partner Donald was connecting to UFOs, etc. I thought it was all wild, just his imagination – now I get this!"

Yes indeed. From out of our own super-conscious minds can come surprises. How many actually know who they are? What extraordinary things might we discover? What lurks within, and beyond?!

~ 8 ~

Soul-mates and Soul Companions

"And think not that you can direct the course of love,
for love, if it finds you worthy, directs your course."
- Kahlil Gibran (6 Jan 1883 – 1931) *The Prophet*

It is the stuff of poetry, songs and legends. A love sublime. We long for a partner, a mate. We seek love, romance and happiness. There are millions of stories of how people came together, fell in love and married. They manifested a home, had children, enjoyed their families. Then came old age, infirmities and eventual death. For many people, that is the end of the story. Not here! After the release there are reunions, celebrations, and plans for the next round – with an important amount of circumspection. Who will we share the journey with next time? How can we burn off some of this karma? How shall we pair off, connect? Which roles shall we play – and in which countries? And how will we meet for the next cycle?

♥

There are many ways to connect. In some cultures marriages are arranged by families and religions. In other places individuals strike out on their own. Where to get advice? Who you gonna call? I remember talking to an ex-Catholic priest who also perceived a higher order and could no longer be contained within the old vows. He left the church and married; he found another way. He talked about one of his priestly duties, namely advising couples on marriage. He had a sense of humor and could laugh about it later. "Can you imagine?" he said, smiling incredulously, "What did I know? I was a celibate and knew nothing – and I was supposed to counsel married people about sex and intimacy!" He laughed. How incredible.

Yes. The things that humans do!

I then get serious again. Yes. The things that humans, and institutions, do. There are rules of etiquette, strategies of approach, traditions to follow, and then, in the end, God has other plans! Since love/ romance is the number one question of my clients (money/ career is number two), I have paid more attention to this theme of love over the decades. My slant, of course, is striving to know what the *grand plan* might be. Thanks to the insights derived from thousands of sessions, I have been able to outline some basic themes and tendencies on this subject. In my first volume I went into some detail about the various types of relationships us humans might be inclined to find ... based on the spiritual dynamics and lessons wished. In short, there are, besides hybrids going their own ways, the following main categories...

o   soul-mates
o   soul companions
o   twin souls
o   guides, teachers and coaches
o   assignments for the lost ones
o   karmic relationships
o   communal or tribal companions

"They say a person needs just three things to be truly happy in this world: someone to love, something to do, and something to hope for."
– Tom Bodett (born 23 Feb 1955) American author, voice actor, and radio host

♥

soulmates

Romances are made in heaven. Yes. For the most part there are agreements and contracts arranged in Spirit before we are born. I also believe there are contingency plans and 2nd, 3rd and 4th options for partners. We have free will, and so we can choose differently than planned. However, if we stay tuned, listen to our gut, or to our hunches/ intuition, we will probably be better off in the long run. I present some of the highlights from these various ways to connect...

I begin with the most compelling, and the type of relationship that most of my clients wish to meet, to experience – *soulmates*. These souls are close partners in Spirit, in the same soul group or family. In astronomy, imagine two stars revolving around each other. Some people expect such a dyad, a duet – two souls who repeatedly incarnate with each other, and there are indeed millions of these pairs here. These romantic soulmates plan to meet upon the earth while still souls. Imagine also a tight group, a soul family, and there are pairs planning there. I know of a foursome vibrating in a song dimension, two pairs. One couple has chosen to incarnate multiple times upon the earth together, and their dual companions in Spirit, part of the choir, choose not to incarnate here. The Earth adventurers report back to their vibrational pair, and all grow in understanding. Whilst in Spirit, preparing for the next life, most all souls, future pairs, go to a preparation place where they choose and practice "giving signals" when they shall meet each other. These outward signs can take many forms such as meeting during a holiday or event, with colors, music or other specific signs and locations. When these partners see or hear these triggers in the flesh, it is almost immediately recognized. Ah! There you are!

"Love is that condition in which the happiness of another person is essential to your own."
- Robert Heinlein (7 July 1907 – 1988) science fiction writer

Some people are surprised to learn that there may be two or three soulmates for them in Spirit, and thus for them here on Earth. Some of my clients are relieved to know that there isn't just one special partner or soulmate. This is true especially if a person lost a great love and is now widowed. After this loss the worry was that that was it. Just one. Love life over. For some this could be true, but for many there may be several soulmates out there. Oftentimes an intimate relationship is an excellent way to learn, for one opens up on deeper levels; Spirit is all for that. Some bereaved souls have come to see me. I have helped many, in trance, meet their beloved who had passed away. These loving partners often encourage the one left behind to move on, love again and find happiness with someone new. There were a few partners who told us in a session that they were sending *the next one*, and soon! How generous and loving.

There are other times that do not seem so generous. One can indeed be born with one's soulmate, but the relationship is not as anticipated – well, more accurately, not as desired as our present earth selves/personalities. My client Sara, from the Bleed-Through chapter (3), is having another session with me. This mother of two was no longer in love with her husband, but she had no clear path forward. She had wondered if she was bisexual. I repeat the recollection upon meeting her soulmate in the 1930s in France ...

"There is a girl... - smiles - She has long brown hair, pulled back, thick hair; and pretty eyes... she is my friend. I feel her, love her... there is a special connection... I have a strong feeling... like... Love.

- cries, right hand over face, tears -

This love feeling is almost overwhelming. - cries loudly, covers her face again -

She looks at me... I feel the love. It is good to see her. I feel better. ... I don't want to go. I want to stay with her and look at her. (a wistful look) I sit in class. She touched my hair, laughs, caresses... touches me. Now we're grinning at each other. Just like two girls! Nice. I feel safe, free."

...

The sparks were flying! Sara met her best friend Olivia from today in that life back then. You can read the love and affection between them. They are soulmates, which is one reason why Sara contemplates bisexuality – she is in love with Olivia. They are friends now, as back then, and they are choosing not to be mates, again. This is known, and smooth and easy on the soul plane. Their souls wants to learn other things, and they have been loving mates in other past lives. As an earth personality, however, Sara has felt lonely, and a repressed inner longing. She would love to be with Olivia today, but they are both married, with children. Olivia is definitely heterosexual this life, so a romantic relationship is not in the cards. Best friends is what they are, and this is how it was planned. In Spirit they are very close – soulmates.

Perhaps next time …

♥

"Let there be spaces in your togetherness, And let the winds of the heavens dance between you. Love one another but make not a bond of love: Let it rather be a moving sea between the shores of your souls. Fill each other's cup but drink not from one cup. Give one another of your bread but eat not from the same loaf. Sing and dance together and be joyous, but let each one of you be alone, Even as the strings of a lute are alone though they quiver with the same music. Give your hearts, but not into each other's keeping. For only the hand of Life can contain your hearts. And stand together, yet not too near together: For the pillars of the temple stand apart, And the oak tree and the cypress grow not in each other's shadow."
— Kahlil Gibran "The Prophet" 1923

soul companions

I ask my impending clients to bring me a list of significant people in their lives, like parents, siblings, partners, etc. The usual suspects. Family members stick around for a lifetime; blood is thicker than water, they say. Some people remain with us for decades, for lifetimes. We all recognize that other acquaintances and friends come and go. Soul companions are often best friends, colleagues and long term connections, even family members. One can even marry a soul companion. They have much in common, enjoy each other's company, and may share similar hobbies or pursuits. They are often on the same or similar wavelength. Now and then a client is surprised to find that someone not on their radar, their list, was in fact an important person for their development. In one session my client realized that there were workers in her company who were actually soul companions, and she was a role model or teacher for them. Here on the earth plane she was told that she should be nicer to them. She intuitively knew this and was very helpful and kind. They came to her for advice. I bring this up here for it is interesting to recognize that sometimes those on the periphery of our lives might be more significant than we imagine. Be on the lookout for these companions when joining groups, clubs and associations, or at the office. Most of our close connections, our compadres, are soul companions. They will make good sounding boards, and they need your input and friendship too. They may challenge you; we need perspective and contrast.

♥

"The cosmos works by harmony of tensions,
like the lyre and bow.
From the strain of binding opposites
comes harmony."
— Heraclitus (6th Century BC) Greek philosopher

twin souls

When one soul chooses to incarnate into two bodies/personalities during the same time, this is a twin soul experience. As we have free will, and curiosity, our souls are free to do this. We "send" from above portions of our energy for incarnations; for instance, 30 or 40% to animate this earth vessel. Do the math. Thus, one soul could indeed incarnate in two people around the same time. I've had several tranced clients tell me of some part of their soul incarnated somewhere else, right now. This is rare in my experience. Sometimes the soul wants to work off some karma and this seemed to be an efficient way to do it. Their motto: double the work, get "it" done twice as fast!

"Whatever our souls are made of, his and mine are the same."

– Emily Brontë (30 July 1818 – 1848) English novelist and poet

I recall a client who incarnated as twins. He went back to Switzerland in the 1700s, where he, or rather It was born as fraternal twins – a boy and a girl. His soul described this as an experiment. As children, the kids were best buddies, friends and siblings. Things got off balance after puberty, however. The female twin was courted by a nice partner, got married, had a family and was content. The male part missed his sister and sort of drifted. He did not meet and marry someone special. He was off track, traveled around, seeming to search for something, or someone, and was rather lonely. He died in his thirties. His twin soul joined him again in Spirit some thirty years later. In Spirit this soul admitted that this was an experiment, and he/It would not do it again.

A rather advanced soul told me that his twin soul was twenty years younger than himself and living in another country. He thought it would be great to meet her, but felt that she needed a little time to mature before their lives could cross. I imagine that it would be a fabulous meeting.

guides, teachers and coaches

Thank goodness for teachers and guides. We all need them, and within these pages I have described quite a few. Most often they are more evolved souls, and they may play roles for shorter or longer periods of time in our lives. Each person has a soul guide, a highly evolved spirit who most often is not incarnated. However, I have a few instances of these guides who indeed accompany the "pupil" to earth. I remember a young woman who was only on her second earth incarnation. She got way off track on that first life, and made some serious mistakes, like getting duped, led astray, and getting into drugs and alcohol. So her spirit guide decided she needed closer attention and incarnated as her grandmother. This older role model was so popular with her fellow schoolmates that most of the kids in her elementary classes would come over to hang out with grandma too. She was definitely the most popular person in the village!

I recall a fifth grade teacher who made an impact on me; he sparked the curiosity in learning. In one trance session he was there in the background, in Spirit – not so close to my soul group, but there in my life at an important time. He wasn't a soul guide but played the role of a teacher for one school year ... he guided hundreds of other kids through his career. Bless his heart, and his mission.

One of the interesting things about this category of assignments is that each of us can play this role. We may meet someone in need, or a friendly or lonely child, or someone at an event; our inner urge (conscience is the soul's prodding), if we follow it, is to talk to this person, to offer advice or simply to be kind. When I am aware of this at the time, I thank Spirit for using me. Yes, I want to be of service down here. Every now and then I meet some advanced souls who are, in the Spirit World, the equivalent of nannies and scout leaders, or nursery or elementary school teachers. On the Earth they are drawn to similar careers and positions, and they contribute positively to many lives. They are following their callings.

"The heart has its reasons which reason knows not."
– Blaise Pascal (19 June 1623 – 1662) French mathematician,
physicist, inventor, and writer

Ξ

The good teacher has to first get the attention of her pupils. In love, how does one get that attention? Friendly dialog, flirtation, good times, eroticism and sexuality join people together intimately. Once together, Love forms deeper bonds. From there one can work out other issues, reactions, aggressions, grievances, sadness and dozens of other emotions karmically "planted" from our past interactions. The glue of love and relationships aid people, and souls, to work things out that lie in the shadows of the unconscious. Ah yes, the glue. Passion and lust merge with the heart, and Spirit motivates much of it for specific purposes. Once the lessons are learned, the teacher may move on; couples part. A parent dies. People and partners disappear. There are many contracts, and many lessons.

assignments for the lost ones

There are times, and assignments, when guides, teachers and coaches are not enough. There are stuck or lost souls who cannot (or will not) get back on track. They have forgotten their spiritual natures and their divine origins. A coach may be ignored or rejected. These entities need help, and this brings the assignments for the lost ones. According to the Bible, the daughters of Men [16] were mated with light-workers, more advanced souls – assignments from on high – the "second wave" of souls who came to the earth to aid the lost ones. I went into some detail in my first volume about the "fall of man" as described by Edgar Cayce; it explains a lot. There are millions of lost souls down here who forgot their divinity. They got caught up in instinctual reactions and baser emotions, or they fell into selfishness and the addictions of the flesh. How to break this cycle? Erring personalities, hungry ghosts and negative personalities are cosmically teamed up with caring souls. There is a good chance that you have met such a pair – a kind and patient person partnered with a loud and obnoxious cad. Many ask, Why are they together? Poor woman! Too often these lost or contrary souls choose to be born as men, for they willfully gravitate to aggressiveness and positions of power. They want to be the bosses, sometimes callous and brutal, even predatory. Of course I have seen the genders reversed in this pairing and tutoring. In my experience, however, usually it is the fairer sex that warms the hard-hearted macho dudes, bringing lessons of patience, humility and kindness. Thus there is a path for these wayward souls, who forgot the big picture, to join, to connect and mate – and through love, they are coaxed and coached to a more humane level. Personal evolution is seen here akin to interventions, and thank goodness there are assignments – caring souls – for these lost ones. This takes time, lots of time. Many lives. A mission of this type of love one could call saving souls. Perhaps you have met such odd pairs, wondering how

---

[16] "And it came to pass, … that the sons of God saw the daughters of men, that they were fair; and they took them as wives." (The Bible, Genesis 6:2)

this patient, nice woman could be in a relationship with this hard and harsh man. Now you know. Bless them.

"Marriage is a great institution,
but I'm not ready for an institution."
- Mae West (17 August 1893 – 1980)
American actress, singer, playwright, comedian

karmic relationships

There are millions of karmic relationships playing out in earth. A bully in a past life will be a domestic victim today; and the perpetrator? – the past life victim. When strong emotions between two people are expressed, there is probably karma and a contract. In relationships there are attractions and repulsions. Tensions pull and twist, storms blow. I do declare, if more people understood the spiritual agreements made in heaven there would be much less animosity in separations and divorces. Many karmic relationships are set for specific times or length of connection, which can be concluded earlier or later depending on the progress and lessons learned. I have come across many pairs who planned only a set number of years together. Penance and patience. There are forgotten agreements, debts to pay, and lessons to be learned. Sometimes the romantic contract ends as soon as the woman is pregnant. Sometimes it ends when a child is three or four. Sometimes the passion fades on the seventh anniversary. – Debt paid, now on to new assignments. Here in our temporal physical perspectives there may be some gnashing of teeth. Many err, thinking that things did not go according to plan. Ahem, who's plan? More karma accrues by how we handle these disappointments and challenges. Buddha warned us not to get attached to certain outcomes. Many of the tales within these pages are karmic connections.

Remember that there is positive and negative karma. We of course hope for positive feelings and close connections, but negative karma is like a magnet. We will meet that person again. The scandal sheets happily describe the theatrical outcomes of these karmic attractions and dramatic marriages and separations. Sometimes bitter enemies in one life are born today into the same family. Hopefully the lessons of patience, understanding and respect will be front and center, but the animosity could be confrontative. A person who killed another in a previous life is now the parent to that same individual. A life was taken, and now given back. It's all in the family, they say. This could be good, but it may be bad. According to statistics, most assaults and homicides are committed by family members. What goes around comes around. Karmic.

"Ah me! Love cannot be cured by herbs."

– Ovid (20 March 43 BC – 18 AD) Roman poet

communal or tribal companions

There are so many relationship options! These communal or tribal companions are interesting, and explain certain romantic attachments, and multiple marriages, here on Earth. As above, so below, so imagine a star cluster such as the Pleiades in the heavens; some aggregate souls come to earth together – a group incarnation. They live in Spirit as a tight group, sometimes like a multi-celled organism. Could this explain some teams, sects or tight groups? They are never alone there in Spirit and often find it rather lonely and separate or isolated here as individuals, even if they are married. They are definitely group oriented. Some of these multi-oriented types get pulled into societal or religious restrictions of monogamy, and indeed follow this tradition ... about four, five or six times! Serial monogamy is the result for these "butterflies". Otherwise these and similar souls are attracted to loose, tribal connections on earth and could be attracted to several people at the same time, such as in polyamory relationships or extended, intimate partnerships or open relationships. Many societies are not so comfortable with such lifestyles and these individuals, if not discreet, are labeled, judged and even harassed. There will be a time in the future that they, like homosexuals in more liberal lands, will be recognized as yet another sexual orientation group that should be accepted and given equal rights.

> Just as a cautious businessman avoids
> investing all his capital in one concern,
> so wisdom would probably admonish us
> also not to anticipate all our happiness
> from one quarter alone.
> - Sigmund Freud (6 May 1856 – 1939) Jewish Austrian neurologist, researcher, theorist, writer, and psychoanalyst

In a variation of this grouping of communal or tribal companions we also have more advanced souls who left their soul groups or families and joined a special interest study group, somewhat like graduate students or members in cooperatives or educational or philanthropic societies. These individuals may or may not be in passionate relationships, and may also be attracted to serial monogamy or, like their tribal siblings, may have several marriages. Some are also into polyamory or open relationships or extended, intimate partnerships. Friendships and altruistic connections are often prized. These souls may not be protesting for free love, but they may be quietly demonstrating the wide spectrum of love and loving in their relationships, families and communities. They intuitively understand Platonic love and empathically care for all living forms on this precious planet. This is sometimes termed Aquarian idealism, and the world could use more of it. Even Jesus Christ's advice to "love one another" is closer to a non-specific love and taking care of one's brother or sister in the community. There is a bonus in such actions: by giving, by loving unselfishly, by being thoughtful and kind, we can actually create new, positive, karma. There is a relaxed, even Buddhist, ideal working here. For those hoping for romantic love and intimacy, this may not sound so filling, or fulfilling. The teacher within, that still small voice, is looking for something else.

In the end there is Life and Love, Spirit and Matter, and we are heading towards the One. Love is the bond.

"I am not an angel,' I asserted; 'and I will not be one till I die:
I will be myself. Mr. Rochester, you must neither expect nor exact anything celestial of me - for you will not get it, any more than I shall get it of you: which I do not at all anticipate."

— Charlotte Brontë (21 April 1816 – 1855), "Jane Eyre"

Of course we all live in complex social relationships and thus we simultaneously interact with many people. I recall a school teacher who had married someone she had some karma with, and this husband was not her soulmate. He was a communal or tribal companion, and yes, there was karma from a difficult past life. In Spirit they are acquaintances and they have volunteered to play roles for each other from time to time. Their tribe is large, with smaller, closer family groups here and there. Her husband's contract was to sire her children – and then they should part, but her training, and money worries, kept her holding on to him. She was actually in love with the principal of her school. In Spirit she got lectured, and how! – let it go, move on. All is well. The children will be fine. Her children are part of her soul family, as is the principal who she longs for. Her grandmother, always with her, is a coach or teacher. She had quite a troupe working with her.

"Nobody has ever measured, not even poets,
how much the heart can hold."

– Zelda Fitzgerald (24 July 1900 – 1948)
American socialite, novelist, and painter

The following story describes a complex dynamic involving mainly four souls who keep choosing to incarnate together. They are part of a larger cast, a theatrical troupe as it were, who play other roles, but it is these four souls who intertwine in complex stories. I introduced some of these characters in the third chapter on Bleed-Throughs, Body Images. There are other tales. Today Geneva is married to Willard, her second husband. He is a good guy, but her first husband Mo'od has played difficult characters in the past, adding karmic twists. Geneva had a daughter, Alicia, with her first husband,

and now Willard is a caring step-father. Alicia has often been a little sister or daughter to Geneva's characters in many past lives. These souls do their dances, have their theatrical personas, and lessons are learned. Let's follow them for a while ...

"I find myself among pine trees, a clearing or meadow in a forest. Wonderful! The sky so blue ... The smell of the rain recently on wood, that fresh cut wood smell. ... I am barefoot, my feet look smaller than my real feet. I'm wearing a strange ethereal greenish dress, layers, shades of green, like a ballet or fairy outfit, light. I am female, I can't see my hair color – I'm looking down at my feet and dress ... hmmm. More clarity, I sense blond–reddish hair, fair. (Geneva is brunette) Nice, it feels good here. I am a teen, slender. It's as if my feet are not touching the ground – like floating! Yes, I can float if I want! (She is connected to her soul. Nice.)

I am carrying a basket – with wine? Elixir comes to mind.

... Quiet, peaceful, centered, purposeful – especially carrying this basket – it is important to protect it. I see a woman at the other edge of the meadow – a mother figure, with gray clothes, in her 30s. Immediately it is clear to me: "The color gray does not fit this scene!" She's waving, she wants the basket?! There is something sinister here; she's wearing a cap or hood? She is impatient, she wants the basket, the bottle! No way. ... I float up – and she can't fly. She waves her arms, but too late. I'm glad she doesn't get it."

SP: This is an interesting beginning. Mysterious. Is your spirit guide near?

"Yes ... seems to be a man ... then he fades into the background. ... I am back on the ground, away from the woman, who is smaller now. Much smaller. Ha. I'm almost enjoying this, she has no power over me. I have gotten big and strong, I can feel the presence of my spirit guide ... in the background, supportive."

SP: Yes, you feel strong, soul, and your guide is not far. You are empowered. The gray woman: who is she?

"She is not from Geneva's life. She might be a nun. – Oh My! She's from my own past, my past life! (feeling very emotional)

153

… I am now somewhere else, … outside. On a beach, looking at the sea.

There I am, wearing the gray dress, waiting for someone, … someone coming from the sea … my love.

But I'm a nun! I can't be waiting for a man!

In my 30s, by the shore, the water is almost touching my feet. I feel wooden beads, a necklace with a cross. I wait but … the person isn't coming … I feel a tremendous loss. It is a man … he seems to be dead. I still feel the love, and loss – inside me, even though I'm now a nun.

… I'm not a nun voluntarily. My father sent me to this convent. I believe this is Wales. 1271. Where did that year come from?!

My name is Gwendolyn.

There was a conflict about that man; Father didn't approve of my choice."

SP: Let us go back to an earlier time as Gwendolyn …

"… In my room, by a window – looking down into the compound or courtyard. Father has received visitors. They arrive by horseback. I'm curious. One is really handsome. He can't see me. A feeling comes… This could be important.

I am 18 years old. Protected? Father is important in this region.

It is time for dinner. Time to meet the guests. … Food and wine. I've a beautiful dress; purples, and pink. I like it. … I can't help it, I feel an instant love with this man. He too, it seems. He is eating and drinking, looking at me from time to time. The air is charged. He's tall, brown curly hair, brown eyes. Oh my goodness, I recognize him from today = he is Bob, my 1st love, an Austrian.

But there is Father, gray hair, somewhat stout, and strict. I respect him … He is distant, hard to get close.

We are an important family – Brithewaite, Baythewaite? Father has other plans with me. He wants to marry me to someone else – in a higher position. But, I don't like this other man. I've met him. He is loud and uncouth. Wait, Father has another face. Oh, he is now Dieter

– (Her first husband, older, controlling but more stable and secure than Bob.).

My younger sister is here too, pretty; she is comforting me about this dilemma. ...

I have just arrived at the monastery, because I refused to marry the man father chose. Now I am 21, it has been three years, and I'm somewhat resigned. – It might be a better option than marrying that Luddite man. So I am putting on my new clothes. I will wear gray, and black. Mourning. I must cut my hair. – My lovely hair, lying on the floor. ... My younger sister cries. = she is now Alicia, my daughter. (They have had shared haircuts with each other that were significant – when Geneva had cancer and chemo in the summer before our first session.)

I try to comfort her now, even though I need the comforting. Perhaps I will find peace here – although I have lost my love. He wrote me letters, I believe. He was a foreigner.

The man who my father wanted – loud, uncouth, with dark hair; a family bonding through marriage. This is about money. He is rough and unpleasant; 10 – 15 years older. = I see that this man who I rejected is now Mo'od, my African ex-husband. (He sucked the life out of her, used her. Rough and loud today.)

Alas, I hear that my beloved sailed to Southern Europe, on a mission or for work. Father was glad, I was told. Sad. A question comes to me, 'But what happened in those three years since I first met him?' A blur in many ways – why didn't he try to contact me?

... I felt I was waiting for him too long. Meanwhile there was the pressure to marry. Oh God, I'm supposed to marry this other man. ... I feel trapped, and so, I consider going into a convent, to wait. I can try to hold out. ...

Time passes. Some months. It is so drab here. Monotonous. ... I decide to marry him – my beloved did not come back.

Wait, this groom was killed the night before the wedding! He comes to my room the night before. He was menacing, perhaps drunk. I am so scared. His lecherous smile ... 'We're getting married anyway! You are mine.' He wants to rape me. We struggle. I smash his head with a pewter dish. He falls and hits his head. He dies. I cannot believe it! Oh my, it happened so fast. My father and sister rush into my room, horrified. – I try to explain to father what happened. He laments, 'my daughter is a murderer. What shame! A disgrace.' I'm shaking. Father declares, 'We have to send you to a convent. There is no choice. Jail or convent. You can't get married after this shame.'

My head down, I must agree. It seems the only way out. I have many thoughts … I hated that guy. He deserved it; but I have to go away. I had no choice. And then the ultimate reason… my old love disappeared. Maybe I loved him more than he loved me. I feel that my life is over – at 21.

Can I find peace in the convent? …

I can say that I did, after many years … Time passes, my younger sister visits me from time to time., I look forward to that. – Now I'm around 36. I was fifteen years here. It's not what I wanted; Father did. Ultimately I lost the will to live. … Time passed.

Yes, I made some friends in the convent. My Mother Superior was quite supportive. I took my dowry to the convent. It helped them.

My father hardly visited. I was glad. He knew about my secret and never forgave me. His plans were turned upside down. I vowed never to allow a father power over my fate, or marriage. I'm responsible for my own happiness. (Her strong convictions, vows, were also felt in present life. She will marry whomever she wants.) This came back to bite me. In this life, Geneva's father disapproved of her marrying an African. The same soul she didn't want to marry then! Now I know why Mo'od hated me! I didn't want him and then killed him – and this explains why I went out of my way to help him adjust, to thrive in the USA, in California. But he was loud and uncouth as ever.

... And that was it.

Gwendolyn dies of fever.

… I am pulled upwards. I see myself lying there, the other sisters are crying. – I'm not ready to go. Something is pulling me up, but I resist. I want to know where my love went. … There are souls coming to me, now closer to me. My father, mother ... my father soul feels he went too far ... he is now feeling regret. ... I'm ready to forgive him. Maybe he couldn't help it. I understand his viewpoint now. ... My parents' souls want me to come up with them. No, I need to know. Where did he go? –

'He's still alive!' (As Gwendolyn died, and thus he was alive during her whole time in the convent.) This revelation just comes to me. I thought he was dead. I intuitively know about his life ... after me. He is a merchant. He lives a care-free life. He is well to do; he married ...

He was too afraid of my father, who helped him professionally. Helped him? Was he paid to leave me? No. He was lied to. We were both lied to. Father told him that she, Gwendolyn, had changed her mind and that she had fallen in love with another man. That ended it. Deceit.... so sad.

After this revelation, the wind just left me. I chose to go up.

... I seem to go through clouds and bright lights; I see the earth below. Going up, traveling fast – feeling others. It gets lighter. I feel lighter. (smiles, laughs)

Oh, my spirit guide! A male, understanding, soon we are embracing. This makes me feel very good. We melt/float into each other. Ahh, I can get some energy back, as if he is feeding me with energy and life. I feel rejuvenated. ... There is a sort of review. I am asked, what did you learn?

I learned – *Listen to your heart. Be true to that.* ... Don't give in to parents' wishes if they are contrary to your heart."

SP: Very important. What was the meaning of the first scene – when the nun wanted the elixir in the basket?

"Gwendolyn wanted nurturing. Something was denied her. She wanted to drink of life. My Soul didn't want Gwendolyn to have the bottle. *It was planned* that Gwendolyn would not have intimacy. ... My Soul had many sensuous lives. Somewhat frivolous, wasteful and indulgent? *'Get more mature about love'* is what I hear. Patience too. – Gwendolyn had to live a life without it, without love and romance. That was denied, so no elixir. There was a pattern ... indulgent love.

157

It was overdone. The hunger for intimacy has over-flowed into Geneva's life too. Love and partnership have been the main desire of Geneva today."

SP: Love of course is not wrong. It seems it is the balance. All-encompassing in previous lives, it is time for healing now. Let us help poor Gwendolyn, and find the balance.

"Yes, this is good. The scene changes … I am back in the meadow.

I now feel compassion. My soul gives her the bottle of love. She is grateful, takes a drink. She transforms back into the beautiful 18 year old, with long hair, the pink dress. She smiles, full of joy and life. She suffered so much. – Gwendolyn can now aid, heal Geneva. A healing wave to and fro, between us two. - touched, emotional -

Now we are looking at each other. – There is a glow, a healing energy. Geneva is also in the meadow, standing opposite of Gwendolyn, who is stretching out her arms, sending love and healing to Geneva."

SP: Beautiful. Does Gwendolyn have any advice for Geneva?

Yes. "Be more open and accepting of the love of others. Show your own love. Feed them the wine like you did me." (Geneva wants to feed others, loves to prepare food and have people over. She shows her love through nourishing others.)

SP: Wonderful. Bless Gwendolyn, and let her go.

"Yes, this is good. She waves, turns around, and goes to the other side of the forest; she is her old self. She doesn't wear the habit, the old gray clothes any more. Her purple pink dress now fits the beauty of this place."

Very beautiful and satisfying, a happy end as it were, – but not in Gwendolyn's life. That is the thing here … one can change the perspective on the dynamics and even heal the old hurts and memories. The past is the past – it's a done deal, but the release can be achieved here and now, and *now* the present self can be relieved. We are ready to explore some more with Geneva, a Libra fascinated with Love...

"I am outside, near some woods, a lake. It is late fall, barren trees, hilly, gray sky, chilly. This is a meeting place of sorts. This ground, this place is by the lake. Here is a settlement, with log houses. There is a woman, – me? She is young, 17 years old, ... I know she is a Christian.

I'm wearing a long black dress, a white apron and white cap. I am outside, getting water, carrying a bucket, I am strong in body. I am Murielle – I like to be called Marie.

English speaking, America, New England. ... Some people coming towards me, children too. They are warning me, agitated. 'The Magistrate is coming for you!' I turn around. Men from the village gather, with the magistrate. I freeze, afraid. Now I'm just standing. What to do? Running away would say I'm guilty?! They want to arrest me. My Faith or beliefs are wrong! Witch! What?! I take stock... I've no family as such. I live with another family. I feel alone, especially now. They grab me; take me, tying my hands, pulling me along. All of this is like a whirlwind. Suddenly there is a gray courtroom. 'What have I done?' I am confused.

They are Puritans. I was born Catholic. My foster parents, my guardians, my Master and Mistress, now come into the cold wooden room. She didn't like me so much, and declares in a loud voice, pointing, 'I knew it!' He however is on my side. = Oh, this is my husband today, Willard.

She is jealous. Is this Hildegarde, Willard's ex-wife? No, it's Kitti, a cousin. We've disliked each other since childhood. Even four years ago she caused problems in my school, where I was teaching her nephew. ...

Marie has been with them since childhood. They are not that happy. Oh, I see ... there is attraction to him. More than that, we are secret lovers. (smiles) This makes so much sense. ... Kitti was accusing me of things I haven't done. But things were done in *that* life! But I know something,... she, my mistress, is not the right partner for Matthew/ Willard. I'm much better for him.

I stop smiling. There is a man who holds some position – a priest or bishop, who is a friend of my Mistress. What are they saying?

But I go to church, to their Puritan church! I'm honest. They think I don't have the right faith. 'Not sincere' comes to mind. My Mistress spoke against me. Her anger and jealousy has brought this charge. There is a heresy trial. My Master/lover is upset. He loves me. However his wife may prevail. I hear the words, the truth, … 'She has reason to be jealous.' But he and I love each other. There is more … I'm pregnant; I just discovered this and haven't told him yet. Oh, what a mess.

… They are going to hang me. I feel so sorry about this unborn child. It has every right to live. A dilemma, which could make more problems. I can't say this in front of everybody.

The bishop is happy I will hang = he is my current boss, Frank. That explains him! He still judges me. (Back story, this boss softened during and after Geneva's breast cancer. Did this touch his old memory of ordering her execution?)

I am jailed. Waiting. My Master bribes some guards in order to speak with me. I tell him I'm pregnant. His eyes are full of tears. He grabs my hands and buries his head in them. He doesn't know if he is strong enough to see me hanging, pregnant with his child. …

Marie is caught in this dilemma. She cannot plead for mercy due to the child, for then her lover would be exposed. He knows this – she is sacrificing her life for him. He approaches the council, pleads for her life. Suspend judgment! Please!

– They don't agree. Witchcraft is a serious accusation.
I have to die. …

They put a rope around my neck. I am hung. (Geneva hates today constrictions on her throat or neck, no scarves or tight clothing there.)
It all went quite fast. … now I'm floating.

A crowd gathered. Noises and even cheering. My old Mistress cheering the loudest. – It would have been worse had she known about the pregnancy. Oh, my Master is there too, at the edge of the crowd, aloof, sad., heartbroken actually. Guilty. We are both guilty.

He feels such doubt and guilt. He did not talk of our love, and our secret, an unborn child. I want to touch him, tell him I'm fine.

... He doesn't feel it.

I now feel the pull. – Going up. Fast. Lighter.

Laughs, laughter now – I'm meeting souls, friends, including Willard ... but I just left him! He's on Earth! I then remember, yes, *a part of us is always in Spirit.*

I, she, tells him of her sadness about the child. 'It is all right,' he says. I know this is true. They hug. He is more transparent, dull. A part of him is on earth.

Conrad is here, my wise friend. I feel his strong energy. He has been here for a while. He wraps me in a light blanket. Warm. He is bluish. He has such a glow, it feels wonderful. Can Conrad be my spirit guide?! ... Yes, he is my spirit guide! (and incarnated with her on earth; this is rare.) 'Leylo' is his spirit name.

'You should have taken it easier, slower,' he tells me. She, Marie, was too strong, impatient. Blunt, forthright yes, but too sure in her own ideas. Somewhat cavalier in what others thought. *It was not the plan* to die young. She was too careless with love and faith. Too honest. Can that be? She didn't integrate enough.

Lessons for Geneva: Faith and religion were important, they have played their roles. Geneva today was born Protestant and converted to Catholicism, and later gave up all systems. She grew beyond them. She studied metaphysics, astrology, mysticism. ...

Unborn children were themes in her current life – there were several miscarriages. These failed births have been great sorrows. Her Master then, called Matthew, shares with Leylo another part of the plan. They could have had a life together in that Puritan life, later. Kitti/the Mistress was going to die soon. A pity. ... However, neither of us could hold back our feelings. Impatience, love and desire were so strong. This will be met in a future life. ... My guide Leylo takes me to the planning area, for Geneva:

We are sitting in a sort of room with screens for viewing. There is a counter/table in this circular room. We observe the future life of

Geneva. Hmm. 'This seems difficult, with sickness and unhappiness. I'm not sure if I really want this,' I say."

"How about if I incarnate with you?" offers Leylo.

"Hmm. This is such a good offer. How can I disagree? I will be Geneva. This incarnation will be important. There will be problems, I know. I'm not happy with the body choice." (Scoliosis, various illnesses, operations).

Leylo: You cannot be "so careless" in Geneva's body.

"Marie in New England was physically strong, and fearless. Although problematic, Geneva will express a zest for life, impetuous and sensuous. – The purpose is to give and receive love. To nurture herself and others. See beyond romantic love, expand it. Cooking for others, for example. To learn through relationships. To bring up her daughter, appreciating a child more after miscarriages. *Geneva is willful. These miscarriages taught her that she cannot control things. There are forces beyond her. The willful earth personality must recognize this unseen power, and to let things happen, to release, and let God.*

Willard is a soulmate. *There is no contract, however.* They got together when she was 44. Before that, Geneva was not ready for the relationship with him. There were to be lessons with other men. Karma, experiences and growth.

Hmm, Willard seems to be drifting. His purpose is to serve others, to be there for Alicia and others. Is teaching a good fit for him? (They dislike public schools, but it is their careers.)

I need to show others about food, nourishment and serving. Willard could assist me in this.

… I get more on and for Willard. (We were blocked in our sessions with him, so nice that she can get info for him.) Willard's mother was too strong for him. Geneva is sometimes like his mother. She sees the hurt child in him who can't express himself. His father is unknown, and his mother is secretive about that. His father went back to Aruba."

SP: Send Willard love & healing.

"Hmm, hard to get through! Like a shield. This is more than protection. It blocks out everything! It comes from another life. Can't see it. (Tries hard, squinting eyes) Battlefield? Injury, spears? An Asian country. Mongolia, long ago. What a death.

Conrad/ Leylo my spirit guide can help him. He is a modern shaman. Please Heal those old wounds. Drop the shield!"

Advice from Leylo for Geneva: Stay true to yourself. Be happy with what you've got, have achieved and are now doing. Counsel, nurture – in school or out. This is healing. ...

SP: Astrology or psychic readings are also interests and skills of Geneva. Might she offer them professionally? This can help others.

"She has many tools. She can use Conrad's house in Florida. Classes, and retreats can be offered."

SP: Geneva had breast cancer. Why?

"Negativity is all around. She absorbed it into her bosom. Heart. She has to protect herself. Geneva knows how to protect herself, so she should do it. Her Soul name – Alara – the one that is shining! ... Geneva, you are once again with your soulmate. Enjoy your later years together."

...

So Geneva found her soul family again, and her love. They had various past lives and adventures together – it was not always easy. Some lives were blessed, and some were blessed only for a short while. One gets an overview perspective from Geneva's past lives and why she would be deprived of love and intimacy in several lives. We discovered that she was too willful and impetuous in love. She needed some time out; balance and patience were necessary. This made sense to her, ultimately.

Other souls incarnated upon this Earth are also finding periods of light and dark, close ties and broken chains. This is not only about love and luck. Time is of the essence.

Soul Partners – not always happy endings

In volume one I described many types of relationships, according to soul perspectives and groupings. Ah yes, love! Here we are, upon God's good Earth, with billions of individuals going about their business. Many want happiness, love, family, children and the good life. How many achieve that? Is happiness a given? It begs the question: Does our soul, spirit guide and the Spirit Council (the wise ones who have the grand perspective) want us to be happy? You aren't going to like this, but my researches into hundreds of past lives and much reading and collecting of stories is No.

Spirit, and the souls who align with It, are interested in growth and evolution. Love is very much a factor in all this, but it doesn't have to be romantic love. A mother's love, a general love of children, the love of a niece or nephew could be the main draw, karmically. And romance? Not so fast. Some people are surprised just who their soulmate is. In one session it came to light that my client's baby sister is her soulmate! They will always be in each other's lives, and their souls chose a different relationship this time. Why? They had been romantic partners in their most recent incarnation. They are learning other things this time around. They both found other partners who they love, but that extraordinary feeling is not there. Yes, says Spirit, there are other things to face right now.

I asked a soul why she died during childbirth at the young age of 19. It was a nice relationship with much promise, and now a baby. Her soul told me, matter of factly, "My task was done." The child had to grow up without her, and her husband's challenge was to carry on after a loss. Those who are fine with Buddha roll with it all. Those who appreciate the theatrical qualities of life down here go with the role. Others rage against the fading of the light. There are many reactions to life plans, and changes. When we learn the back story, understanding – and eventually acceptance – seeps in to our consciousness. There is a design. There are also scripts, with opportunities to ad-lib.

∞

I had a client who enjoyed an affair in ancient Greece that turned tragic. He was an orator and quite convincing in that life. He met a young woman on a voyage over the Mediterranean on the way to Rome. She was promised to a man and was on her way to meet and marry this stranger, her betrothed. But first she had to cross the waters. The orator smooth-talked her into bed and enjoyed a night of pleasure. The next day she was ashamed and distraught. Crying, she jumped into the sea and drowned. The orator was shamed and humbled. Fast forward to today. In this lifetime he's a shy musician, and met a woman who was traveling around the US. His town was but one stop on her planned trip. They connected, fell in love, and she moved in with him. A year later the woman had a strong urge to continue her journey and ended up in California, where she met a new man and fell for him. The musician was heart-broken -- and the orator of Greece was to blame – there was karma to pay. The new man? I don't know for sure, but perhaps he was the promised one from ancient Rome. They did have a child together, so it was important.

Ω

Nick was a bad boy in past lives…and in Spirit! In our session, he was going to be facing relationship Karma. He is an avid skier, which is a love, a metaphor, and a means of moving – in life and in trance! Nick started skiing at 14, in Canada. Tall, healthy looking, long dark hair past his shoulders, some gray. He came from a diplomat family, and lived abroad. Thailand was an important stop. He is probably the black sheep of his family; he hated the boarding school and did not follow the intellectual life of his parents. He had been eight years in Switzerland at the time of our session. Nick is a busy technician, doing electrical work. Life seems good. He has not been too happy in love, however; in fact, he has had difficult relationships with women. This was one of the main reasons that he had come to me, although he didn't know that. He did know that he had experienced many rejections and tough lessons in his present life, and he was frustrated. He is a proud Leo, an athlete, and good with his hands. We shall see that he remembered two sex scenes from past lives - rather unusual. He brought his Questions, and received answers:

- What is my life purpose?

Balance out an aggressive past.

- I want to understand issues, traumas with women and those various interactions.

We got lots of info on this subject!

- I want to understand circumstances I have struggled with, like education, authority, conflicts.

Okay, let us explore all of this. Nick is a good subject, and we quickly get to a comfortable trance, then he is outside, in the Alps ...

"Ah, I'm now on a snow covered ridge. The Sun is shining, nice and clear. This is relaxing, and yet invigorating! Here is my ski equipment, my outfit, a yellow jacket. Black ski pants. (Ha! Skiing in trance, his ideal!)

I look about the same age and size as Nick. I feel there are others – not clearly defined. Now I move … skiing down into a steep valley, fast. There is a jump. … to a black space. Not clear, but the sun is shining. Then there are images. … Still in my ski suit. A seaside, rather distant.

Another place… This place is rather unfamiliar. What? Now I'm getting an impression of hanging, with a hood – seems quite scary. Seems to be a crowd – yelling, throwing stuff." (His body/ belly twitching, suddenly in pain.)

SP: Breathe and release. Go up. You are freed… See this from a distance, float above it.

"… It looks like an execution, an angry crowd. - deep breaths -

Now I get a separate image, in a court, a sentencing! Accused of rape, debauchery, murder?!

I'm quite young; possibly ... seeing a body of a victim. Hearing Dutch?"

SP: Where and who are you? Go back... a bit further.

"Inside I would say. Looks like childhood, a number of women around. I'm 7 years old. I am called Damien. This is not his family, an orphan? ... No, not an orphan. Or not sure? Parents left his education to others. Sent away... to uncaring strangers. Oh great, this is a damned boarding school.

When? Several centuries ago? No. Not so long ago. This place is large ... It's quite palatial, or used to be.

One female is tall, with a long flowing dress. She's 40 I guess, but she looks very old to me, a boy. Severe, stocky – she is snoopy, poking into stuff. I don't think I like her; we're not related here at the school. Oh, but now = she is my mother today. (Who is caring, assertive, and emotional, thank goodness. She sent Nick to boarding school, however. She was obviously fine with that, as she ran one in her own past life.)

She appears angry, beckons me to come with her. I go down a long palatial corridor... (heart beating fast, he told me later)

It looks like a strap tied around my neck. I don't like it. Punishment. There are similar looking women in the background. I've got a costume, with a ruffled collar. She's trying to teach me some kind of lesson.

I think my parents abandoned me. (Or it felt like it, but they are wealthy and passed him on. Tradition.)

... I'm in school, being fairly boisterous, throwing stuff around. I'm not angry; this is my nature, a nuisance,.... I enjoy doing it, really. Now I'm 14 years old. They want me to stop. I should *Behave*.

This is England. 1866. Nathan is here with me (friend today). The leather strap is around my neck again.

… Another scene – a woman, writhing. I'm having sex with her, but I don't think she wants it. She seems to be a younger woman. We met in an inn. I'm 28, still a nuisance, yes, and more! … I'm rather well-to-do and 'forced' her to come with me. Actually I just told her to come with me and she went along. She struggled during sex. Oh my goodness, she = is my sister today. (He described his sister as relaxed, organized, and grounded. They are not so close.)

- quiet -

Damn. Nathan denounced me. Tension there. We are in a lot of conflict. He turned me in. He is my brother (of Damien). There were several women I raped/ pushed into sex. Now I get the court scene again.

My brother says 'You had to be stopped.'

I thought I would get out of this situation. I got out of others. This gal had an important father. Now I will die.

- hung -

I'm regretting it more – after death. I hear, 'Don't exploit people.' I was supposed to learn self-esteem (in that life). … a voice comes, with advice: 'Learn, and lighten up a bit, Nick.'

I,… it still seems to be a lack of self-esteem." (We have a healing, a lightening up as it were.)

SP: Good, things will improve. Did Damien meet his victims after death?

"Yes. There is a reconciliation with my sister. This is somewhat relieving, even relaxing. … There were five or six more women. *I'm afraid Nick has met them, including three of his significant relationships!* I feel regret. There were tensions. I see Sue, who I loved a lot. *The victims did not forgive Damien.*

(I do a "counseling" negotiation here. He got a forgiving hug from Sue, a former girlfriend, plus an awareness of the dynamics of his relationships.)

Healing and blessing, easing... a voice says to Nick, who is awkward around women, not knowing how to act, 'Don't take it all so seriously.'" (I learn later that Nick unconsciously feels the old guilt and regret from his past selves. We orchestrate a healing, offering a perspective: Nick did not commit those crimes, his past self Damien did. Don't confuse the two.)

"Oh, that's better." - deep breaths -

SP: Great. This healing shall continue in the next weeks and months. Let us now go to the next significant past life.

"Outside. Daytime. ... Further in time. Two different war scenes...

A battlefield, looks like I died in the battle – a woman is mourning over me. She's young and attractive. I see her wearing a long flowing white dress. We weren't married – I feel love, and a great loss."

SP: Let us go back, before the death.

"Carefree, happy and engaged. We're watching something, out in the open; I'm giving her flowers. She is familiar. Oh, I see = my friend Julie today. (He knows her as a friend, but she may want more than he thought.)

I'm Rafael; perhaps too carefree. I've been rather reckless up until now. France? 16th Century. There are actually charges against me. Insolence, disrespect and more. I'm being told I'm joining the military. There I am, before some tribunal. This is similar to the court scene. I balk. I'm not going along with the plans that were made for me. (And his father today has plans.)

OK, either military or prison. I'm not keen, but I'll go along with it.

...

I'm proposing to this woman, out in a garden. She looks at me adoringly and declares, 'Rafael, I love you.' She's the one I want to marry. I'm not in the military at this time. The scene is interrupted... I feel pain in my chest. A crowd appears; I'm being carted off! Some people don't want us to marry. I'm not of a sufficiently high station. (Hmm, the makings of a Leo, hurt pride?)

... I'm in the military. The battleground – in France somewhere. My friends Pete and Nathan are here too.

They lived through it. Rafael had a chest wound. ... I die. - quiet -

... She's mourning, Pete and Nathan there, observing, at the funeral. I feel the sense of loss. I am there, a specter. I want to tell her I love her. I did not tell her when I could. I hear *'Don't take things for granted.'*

In Spirit I get advice: Try a bit harder.

There was an element of giving up from Rafael – there is also a wounded heart and thus the chest pains."

We draw things to an end, I orchestrate another release, giving positive suggestions of ease and relief for the chest pains. Good for today, we will meet tomorrow.

Session two – Nick told me more about his life as a skier. To be out there, on the slopes, in the mountain air ... how exhilarating, a feeling of freedom. He had a dream of counterfeit money deals. What might this mean, symbolically? Honesty? Faking things? We then begin the journey...

"... I get purple flashes – now a mountain ridge and a seaside. Overcast, cold, snow. Alone – my ski suit again. Ha. I'm on a ridge. Going down the slope. Nice. (and off he goes!)

Thailand, this seems familiar. (Nick lived there as a boy.)

Outside, in the open. I'm with a woman with long silky dark hair, oriental, quite attractive. A lover. I'm quite short, wearing ... just shorts. An attitude. I have an attitude. Young and cocky. 17 years old? So young? Kanu, also oriental. I am a good swimmer, aggressive, strong. We're having sex on the beach. Strange, I get 'I think she hates me.' I sense manipulation here; she wants some sort of supremacy, and I want to be on top. I will have her. A conflict. ...

A new scene, not far from the shore, where I make my living. A wedding ceremony. Now age 27, with another woman – a bride, my bride. She's attractive, in a traditional wedding dress, but not happy –

she has cold feet. Why? I'm still aggressive, self-centered. …
Something about children – and the number two. Hmm. I have
children. I can have more than one wife; this will be my 2nd wife. My
#1 wife is with the children, some animosity here. She is the same
woman as on the beach.

Early 20th century? No, earlier. The 1st marriage had something to
do with money; she is … (Now recalling a memory from his present
time…) I was in Thailand when I was 8. – not good feelings. There
was an unpleasant experience. I was still wetting my bed. The maid
walked into the room and was laughing at me. I was ashamed. Now I
see that she, this maid, was the first wife.

And now this 2nd bride… seems to be my mother. (Who is probably
part of his soul family; she incarnates often with him.)

…

Outside, alone, diving for pearls, for treasure. Now 37, not so
successful these days; no longer strong enough. Dying in water – a
crocodile? Or some other creature. - quiet -

I am now on an operating table, I'm not sure. Some people trying to
save me. Too late. Ghastly wounds everywhere. I was found on the
shore. A lot of pain.

…

I am now free. I left that body.

It seems there's a judgment …

– from myself. Reproach, a self-loathing. And more …

I seem to hate women. Hmm. I had more women, (plus 2 wives) and
3 children, treated them badly, as Kanu. - quiet - Now a purple
space… Others flying around. Foggy too. Not much there,
something's on the edge – I can't make them out. Am I confined? …
800 or 1800 days there… in some sort of recovery place." - quiet -

SP: While you are there, I will ask questions. What do you sense,
what did you learn?

"I'm in a purple space, ... Not feeling differently. I get glimpses. ... I'm looking at my parents in Canada, 1959, before I was born. I have chosen them; they are expecting me. They seem happy. - quiet -

With this life I will get an opportunity to travel, and the boarding school."

SP: What did you wish to get from this school?

"I'll get self-awareness, and humiliation – karma. It is about self control, or controlling my impulses.

... I am meeting my spirit guide now – There is a purple space. Then an old man with a white robe and beard appears. We greet warmly. It feels *wonderful.* - quiet - 'Try harder' he urges."

SP: What was learned as Kanu?

"Issues of self-esteem and rejection. Kanu knew that these women did not like him. This pissed him off, and he treated them even worse. An ugly cycle of anger. And did this influence Nick? Yes, rejection, and uncertainty. Nick asked himself, periodically, Was he liked, really?"

SP: Can we heal, and help Nick today?

"Yes.... there was a cutting of the cord to Kanu. ...

Oh man, what a Relief! He was so stubborn. My spirit guide seems to be saying, ... *Now you can be free.* My spirit guide's name is Jacob. He ascends and disappears. I gaze around me. I'm free floating and adventurous.

- smiling - ... I'm meeting different characters. My pals and ski buddies! ... Pete, Nathan, Katie, Colin. Ha, we're slapping hands. Twenty souls here. My Soul group! There are attributes and themes we share: 'adventure, self–esteem, and depression.'" (Such emotions in Spirit? This was new to me.)

SP: Please use a mirror here in Spirit. How do you appear, soul?

"I seem to be aggressive and arrogant... a certain defiance, a reaction to many conflicts. My brother Mikel, and my friend Pete are also similar to me. (Interesting. "Negative" traits in the soul group. All is not perfect in Spirit, and souls are evolving.)

Colin is the leader (not on list). He's happy, the bubbliest of the group. His advice: Relax, be more open.

I get a picture of me skiing. *Skiing represents adventure, freedom. Nick derives aliveness, and self-esteem from it.* Also the word 'Competitive' comes to me. High spirits too. Our group ... seems to be laughing and enjoying ourselves. - smiles -

I get another piece of information about me, in my present life. From here about 30% of the soul energy was used for Nick. But I feel that *That wasn't enough. Insufficient resources for the tasks at hand!* I only realized that later."

SP: I have a question: if you had sent more energy, would aggression have been an issue?

"Yes, you got it. - reflects, quiet -

... with maturity I can get more resources. Then I hear, 'Direct your energies more efficiently. Refocus your attention in some respects.'"

SP: Jacob, dear spirit guide, is there more to add, advise?

"Now it is just him and me, alone, ... He's the same as me somehow but bigger, 'more energetic and active.' I see my life purpose: Overcoming rejection."

SP: And the aggressive past lives?

"Effectively balancing emotions over several lifetimes. Intimacy seems to be a tough ride, but had to be experienced."

SP: Is there a soul in his group who has volunteered to be his next partner?

"I haven't met that person yet. I feel relaxed about this though."

SP: Anything else?

Jacob: He can always contact me.

SP: Will you be with him also on the ski slopes?

"Oh, yes! One more thing ... Nick's soul name: Jonas, the climber."

Nick: I do like to climb, in various ways. However, I'm finding it hard here on earth... but I'm overcoming obstacles gradually."

Yes indeed. Bit by bit, step by step. Slope by slope.

Ω

I was in Vienna, Austria, one of my favorite cities. I set up shop there for a few months and saw some interesting clients who had intriguing stories of the past. One particular woman brought in a particularly complex tale. Sophie has dreams, premonitions, – a real 6th sense. She is definitely empathic, sensing the pain and discomfort of others; so it wasn't surprising that she was a good subject. Things started "amping up" for Sophie since her daughter was born three and a half years before. Soon after that birth she had strange déjà-vu feelings, odd dreams, and negative attitudes about her daughter. All this brought anxieties and worries. To my way of thinking, little Lois,

Sophie's daughter, seemed to have opened up psychic and reincarnation topics. Lois was testing her in many ways, and seemed wise beyond her years. Sophie said that this small girl "bears the weight of the world on her shoulders," but can also be extremely whiny. What was unnerving was when Lois "stared" at Sophie from birth. Eerie. One day little Lois woke up from a nap, looked at Sophie angrily and said "Mommy hurt me." Soon after that Lois had nightmares, and once she yelled, "*My children! My children!*" Sophie also noted that Lois is afraid of water on her face and hair. She saw a well one day and said "We had one. Lois fell in. Hurt face." Of course I was wondering about their past lives together. Obviously they are together again, and the unconscious dynamics are stewing. By the way, Sophie thought she would go deeper in our sessions. Expectations! With her *super-natural* abilities, she's already connected! We go to a past life ...

"I'm a little girl, next to a Christmas tree. I see a living room, an open fire, a modern house – something you might see today. 1970s? (Sophie was born in 1983, so we could be talking about a short life. We will see.) There is a big green couch, dark green. I've brown hair, wavy. I'm 4 years old? Sitting on the floor, coloring with crayons and paper. Mom calls me for dinner. I have to wash my hands. I hear my name – Annie. - tears -

This is America. The east coast. It gets cold in the winter. New England. Right now the fireplace is warm. Here I am, a dress to my knees, wearing tights. My dress has a white collar. I have an older brother. He's 10 or 11, at a friend's house, playing. Josh? Joshua?

Father is still at work, and should be home any time. He has a brown briefcase. Regular work I guess.

Mother is really strict, but loves me. It is hard for her, with my curiosity and messes. She is slow, somewhat picky, neat, and orderly. She wants a nice house. She is a perfectionist. (Obviously this is an adult with a good vocabulary viewing her life as a four year old. Many times when one regresses to a younger age the language matches the younger world view and expression.)

Dad's at work – when he comes home I run to the door. He's a nice guy who takes time with me, plays with me.

…

It is now summer, we're at the lake house, with a dock. There are trees, big ones, and lots of mosquitoes. It is a little cabin in Vermont. I see a little blue boat. Dad likes to go fishing with it. I'm 8 now, and small. I like my dolls. I play on the dock. Not into fishing, but nature. I like to be outside. I like being here. My brother is out somewhere doing boy stuff, finding sticks for spears, finding bugs to throw at me. Sometimes he goes fishing with dad. I wait for them to get back.

So I'm outside, playing on the dock, with my dolls. Mom is making dinner. She's always busy.

- whispers, tears - I fall in the water. … I can't swim. I try to tell my mom. She can't hear me. No one can hear me. I'm drowning.

- tears -

She hears my scream. Too late. … Now they're screaming… my name. Annie! Annie!

Dad runs out, jumps in the water. He can't find me, it's too late. I see them. Frantic.

I can't leave. I'm still there.

It was so stupid. I fell over. Stupid doll – a hat on the doll fell into the water. I tried to grab it, fell in. *So stupid.* " (Self-critical today, with a critical dad. … With her words, "I'm still there," I need to help her to move on – even though she was reincarnated, a part was left behind, in that lake in Vermont.)

SP: Let us invite a Light. It is time. Are you ready to go, Annie?

(She takes some time, breaths) "Yes. – It's okay. … I'm not upset anymore. Others are now near … orbs or lights, there is no one there that I know though. Now there is a light figure. I can't see the face.

I sense a hand out – and a soft hello. My Guide? He says *I have to fix this later.* ... I will. I can't fix it in that life anymore."

SP: Yes, that life is finished. We can fix this now, however. We need to cut the cords; please release Sophie, and her fears of water, of suffocation.

- tears - "This story is coming home. Now I understand … little Annie's mom = is now Lois my young daughter!, … She lost her daughter and died of a broken heart. She was very hard on herself, – she blamed herself. Her perfectionism, cleanliness, 'doing things right', was her focus, not her family, daughter, or special moments, blah, blah. So what!? My children, that's what. Then she took pills. - cries - … killed herself. Couldn't handle the pain." - tears -

SP: Please invite this sad mom to meet in Spirit with Annie. A reunion of mother and daughter. Please, help her to let go of her guilt. It wasn't her fault that that happened!

- waves of relief, then a voice comes -

The early death of Annie was planned. What was to be learned? It was for the mother … it was this – *One has to be in the present.* Don't waste time. Don't get lost in "activities and to-do lists" when one could love. *Live and love now.*

This mother didn't get the lesson. She actually lost two children."

- tears -

SP: … and Annie was a lake ghost for years. What can we now do, souls?

"Lois/Annie's Mom needs to stop worrying about me; and I need to stop worrying too."

SP: Yes. Release, let go of worries, and guilt. Little Annie is safe in Heaven, sending love and warmth.

- deep breath - "… I feel at ease. Something left me just now – it had to leave. It is light now."

SP: Bravo. I hear that the mother cried for two children, so her son died early too?

"Yes, Rocky was my brother (of Annie). Ha, of course he threw bugs at me! He is now my husband. (A real guy, a professional athlete who has had many hurts and cuts, and trips to the hospital.) He still likes to get dirty. He went to war in that life. Then he was wounded, shot here – in the chest, and upper shoulder. (gestures) He died quickly. This is exactly where "Rocky" has a scar today; he had surgery for a sports injury. This was another sorrow for mother. The last straw. Then she found some pills."

...

And this sad mother was born today as Sophie's daughter, with something very heavy to work out. We worked on it, freeing layers of guilt and grief, sorting out the issues and guilt. *That mother's children are now her parents!* I wonder if this will be a bossy child. Ha. On a higher note, I hope and trust our healing during these and other sessions will aid that hurt from long ago. And may Sophie and Lois learn to love the water again.

Θ

I am conducting another "simulcast," or a duo-session for Elaine and Johnny, who are both excellent subjects. Today we are exploring the subject of relationships. They are both easy to work with, intuitive, and they describe their images and experiences with great clarity. We are underway ...

She: Trees, evergreens, sky, clouds. A meadow. I feel a lightness. It is summer, and I am on this meadow, a warm day. I watch a bird circling in the sky.

He: It is a high plateau, a mountain meadow. Flowers scattered sparsely over this meadow.

She: Wild flowers, not like us at home, smaller ones. Pretty.

He: A smaller girl runs around, around 4 years old, ... she seems happy, playful, wearing a bright dress, I see dark hair.

She: I'm wearing pants, but older. I'm 50... an older man. (Not the first time that she has been a man in a past life.) I see a shirt, and wooden shoes, linen clothing. I've a beard. Ha. This feels funny. I'm aware of this girl...

He: I'm 30 yards away. Just playing. Soon we will be going home, or somewhere like home, or is it that we are supposed to go home?

She: She is my granddaughter. Yes, we must go home. We're going to a village, below. There ... a small path... houses. I take her hand...

He: I am Maria. I don't want to go. Please, no.

She: I am Paulo, Maria's grandfather. In southern Switzerland? Here are the mountains, the Alps. 1766 ...

Maria: I don't want to go down there. I am afraid something bad may happen.

Paulo: I have a bad feeling too, but nevertheless...we must go. Come on. (The genders are now switched, and this "couple" are holding hands, and descending.)

Maria: ... There are soldiers in the village.

Paulo: I see people running, yelling. Chaos. People forced out of their homes. Fire! No! Someone takes my girl from me, hits me! I want to help my granddaughter, but I can't. Oww. All is black!

Maria: All is dark,... why are these men here? This is not good. They are bad men. ... It is dark.

Paulo: I float above. All is burning. ... I hold my granddaughter's hand. I tell her "It is all going to be fine now. I have you, I have your hand. All is well."

Maria (emotional, quiet): A very bright light. A gate before me. Bright and white. But ... I don't want to go away. I feel heavy. No pain though. ... It is bright. I sense another... My grandma and mother are there. They hold me tight. It was so scary. Grampa will go on... on his own... (Hmm. Is little Maria angry with Grampa?)

Paulo: I see your papa too. They, we all died that day.

Maria: Others are there too. From our village. ...

SP: Enjoy the reunion, and the nurturing. Orient and attune. What was learned in that life?

Maria: I should not have gone down there. We should have listened to our feelings. (Of course, Grampa was in charge, as the adult. The child knew ...)

Paulo: I am so sad that I led her down there. She cried on the way. She didn't complain. I should have protected her, listened. ... I'm so sorry. This hurt me too. It feels So bad. - both emotional -

(Elaine, the Grampa then, feels to this day a protective feeling for Johnny, wants to care for him, pay for things.)

SP: Was all this planned? Ask the souls...

Maria: yes.

SP: Paulo, can you forgive yourself now?

Paulo: Yeah, but it is hard. I was not listening to my feelings and ... I did not show my feelings. I loved my granddaughter but didn't really say it. I remember,...she pulled away from me when I had her on my lap. But she returned. It was awkward.

Maria: I looked for something. Squirmed. (Trying to make it better for past personality Paulo? Sweet and kind!) ... I feel a lot of energy.

Paulo: I tried to be soft but... I tried. For example, I picked little flowers for her. She was delighted. I didn't want to show how this gave me joy. I didn't show it. She was my favorite in all the world. ... She had pretty blue eyes.

SP: Blessings to you both. Feel the love.

Good for today. They both lay there quietly, taking in the whole story, and the Inter-life resolution and understanding just accomplished. Pieces of their lives' puzzles fall into place, explaining habits and tendencies. There is a sort of purring. Love is in the air. I leave them there to enjoy the buzz, and the re-entry. I think to myself, "This work is so satisfying; what a blessing it is to do this."

As for this theme of relationships and soul partners, they are soulmates, and they are enjoying their partnership today. In that life in Switzerland they were opposite sexes and grandparent/grandchild. Yet another case of soul-mates choosing to play different roles. Since Time is of the essence, Spirit knows there is a lot of time to enjoy the highs of a close romantic partnership, but the individual souls have other tasks to accomplish.

In our next chapter we shall peer more closely on the ideal that Spirit/ God is Love. God is also Life, and life isn't always nice.

~ **9** ~

Hands Off and Far Away
Free Will and Distanced Perspectives

Prediction is very difficult, especially if it's about the future.

- Niels Bohr (7 Oct 1885 – 1962) Danish physicist

We are being watched from above. This sounds comforting, but don't jump to conclusions. Let's get a greater view. I am reminded of my client, Anne, who experienced several profound regressions with me. Later she described further details, in an email to me, of her life as a young male teacher being burned for teaching heretical ideas, like individuality and thinking things through. This sincere, and shocked, young man was on a pyre, and suffered. Just as she needed some time to gather her images and write to me, I sometimes need time to sort things out. During the intensity of such a session as Anne's, there is little time for me, the therapist, to contemplate the other stories, travails and tears from many clients who had similar horrors, but through the years it is a relevant and soul-searching confrontation. So comes the questions: why all the suffering and brutality, especially if we are being watched from above by advanced beings of love? We all know that there are earthly challenges in living on this material plane, and I am aware of the triple whammies of Earthlings which I had described in volume one: bodies with their own inclinations, programming coming from various sources, and authorities and con-artists who would love to lead us to their own benefit. Our instinctual bodies and manipulative conditioning can overpower our good intentions. Sadly, so much of the pain and sufferings here upon the

Earth is caused by humans. In the last chapters I have described troubled personalities to angry souls, murderers and torturers. There is a lot of pain and suffering. Some divine intervention would be welcome! It seems to me that too often we are left to our own devices. Oh God, why have thou forsaken us? Looking at the big picture, however, could we be perceiving some sort of Cosmic Tough Love; caring spirit parents who let their children learn their own lessons the hard way? I do believe this is part of the dynamic. We are here to learn, even by our mistakes, failures and tears. This is Life, as in the Law of Nature or law of the wild. We fall we bruise, we cut we bleed. We kill and are killed. Karma and Free Will are part of the elements of Life here too. This is indeed a tough place to live.

Now something rather unsavory ...

Surprisingly, there seems to be a certain callousness on the part of some spirit guides and soul planners partly due to distance, specifically to the strong emotions and body sensations (intense or damaging stimuli for starters) we must endure here on the earth plane. At times it seems like theory to those without bodies, and a "game plan" or mission can overrule the compassion and sensitivity needed for particularly difficult lives. Are cosmic directors following scripts like theater scenes? Are things planned too abstractly? Are earth emotions forgotten or minimized on this immaterial plane of divine essence living close to eternity? Life is fleeting. What is one life? – perhaps an afternoon walk to those who reside in timelessness. Do some souls watch our earth tragedies like we enjoy a good horror flick? I hope not. I have observed this, however: Beings not living in emotional bodies that sense deprivation and pain are planning lives which will include famine, suffering, abuse, torture and ugly deaths. This is hard to swallow.

Carl Jung, the innovative psychotherapist and philosopher, described the dark side of dreams. Read his quote below, and imagine that something similar can be said about Spirit too. You may glean from the last chapter (8) on Soul-mates and Soul Companions that there are not always happy endings. In love and life, romance and "forever," our guardian angels are not necessarily making sure we will remain secure and happy. There are other agendas, there are other goals. It is ultimately more important, for instance, to learn a lesson than to live happily ever after. Here is Jung:

"... dreams may sometimes announce certain situations long before they actually happen. This is not necessarily a miracle or a form of precognition. Many crises in our lives have a long unconscious history. We move toward them step by step, unaware of the dangers that are accumulating. But what we consciously fail to see is frequently perceived by our unconscious, which can pass the information on through dreams.

Dreams may often warn us in this way; but just as often, it seems, they do not. Therefore, any assumption of a benevolent hand restraining us in time is dubious. Or, to state it more positively, it seems that a benevolent agency is sometimes at work and sometimes not. The mysterious hand may even point the way to perdition; dreams sometimes prove to be traps, or appear to be so. They sometimes behave like the Delphic oracle that told King Croesus that if he crossed the Halys River he would destroy a large kingdom. It was only after he had been completely defeated in battle after the crossing that he discovered that the kingdom meant by the oracle was his own.

One cannot afford to be naive in dealing with dreams. They originate in a spirit that is not quite human, but is rather a breath of nature – a spirit of the beautiful and generous as well as of the cruel goddess. If we want to characterize this spirit, we shall certainly get closer to it in the sphere of ancient mythologies, or the fables of the primeval forest, than in the consciousness of modern man. ..."

  - Carl Jung, Man and his Symbols [17]

---

[17] Man and his Symbols, edited by Carl G. Jung; Aldus Books Limited, 1964. Doubleday & Company edition 1979; pages 51, 52.

There are many reasons why Providence or Spirit does not seem to be "on our side." Karma, pay-back, cause and effect, experiencing being the perpetrator *and* victim; even curiosity – a soul in the Spirit world not believing that an innocent person could be treated in such unjust ways. Oh yeah? Guess what!? True ... I have met many souls who, in heaven, felt that a good, upstanding and caring person could not be a victim on Earth. Not in their equation was other negative personalities who didn't give a shit what they naively believed. You have met some in these pages. Thus, Karma can be "manufactured" not only by deeds but by thoughts and desires. So I tell my clients from time to time, Beware of what you ask for, for you just might get it – even from Spirit!

We know of the "school of hard knocks" and we recognize that some people learn, unfortunately, when they are laid low, or kicked in the butt. People change their lifestyles only after hurts and heart attacks. Counselors for alcoholics and addicts are familiar with those who *hit bottom* before they get it together and change their ways. Psychics giving readings in Spiritualist Churches understand that just because uncle Ted died and is on the other side does not mean that suddenly he is all wise. We have already met individuals in their soul families who experience self-esteem issues and even depression. After difficult deaths, some flaws and failings follow us into the bardo, weighing us down. Meanwhile, on the earth there are predators and prey, in the animal kingdom and in the human jungle. There are cowards and heroes, selfish and selfless individuals all around. Some brave souls become martyrs, sacrificing their lives so that others will learn. Over the years I have heard all of these stories.

מ

Dr Marion, recalling a life as a caveman, had this positive life with some close connections, something she lacked in other past lives. She had some interesting lessons on the themes of Oaths and

Promises from chapter two. Here, in this recollection immediately after death, the soul is talking, referring to the body and personality just left behind. Within seconds of leaving that person, the soul distanced itself. –

"I now feel a lightness. I have moved on. ... He is behind me; not important.

I'm without form. Moving slowly... I enjoy this." ...

Wow. Finished. The earth personality is no more. "Not important." Move on. Hmm ... This distancing, this "drop the laundry off at the cleaners" attitude is not uncommon. Yes, there are those souls who love and cherish and admire their past selves, but I have come across this seemingly cold attitude many times. We may be discussing a young soul, of course. There is certainly more compassion and empathy with more advanced souls. In the Spirit World, there are junior guides leading, and learning from their mistakes. Are they allowed to make mistakes in their apprenticeship? "Sorry about that cannibal thing. My bad." There are seasoned soul guides who naturally take a "hands off" approach, allowing their charges to learn on their own. "Bus stop! School of Hard Knocks. Get off." Or maybe it is more like observing things from a far distance. One can get philosophical and opine whether we here on the earth are like ants to an advanced eternal soul. Hybrid and alien souls sometimes show less empathy, treating some lives like science experiments. We have Free Will and so we are allowed to make such decisions, and lives. Time is relative too. One can understand that this short, brief and brutish life [18] is not much in the greater scheme of things. Indeed, a single life could be but a brief strut across the stage.

---

[18] I am paraphrasing Thomas Hobbes' "Leviathan," from 1651. Hobbes (5 April 1588 – 1679) described the natural state of mankind (before a good government) this way: ...man has "no account of Time; no Arts; no Letters; no Society; and which is worst of all, continuall feare, and danger of violent death; And the life of man, solitary, poore, nasty, brutish, and short." Life can be pretty miserable down here on the earth, and there is a lot of evidence to prove it.

We do have the age-old question confronting us here: how can we have all of this misery when there are loving, wise and spiritual Beings watching over us?

"City of Angels" is a 1998 film starring Nicolas Cage and Meg Ryan. In this film, angels do not quite understand humans and their issues, worries and even pleasures. An angel played by Nicolas Cage gets a chance to be human and is confronted by the rough reality of earth life, including robbery, hurt and loss. From my experience, this plot – and distance – is not far from the truth. City of Angels was inspired by a German film, "Wings of Desire" (German: Der Himmel über Berlin, released in 1987) in which the world of angels is shown in sepia tones while the world of humans is in color. This part I would not agree with; the world of angels and souls is multi-sensory, inter-dimensional and rich. The sepia tone angelic perspective symbolically represents this distance, however; a different frequency. A subplot in "Wings of Desire" involves Peter Falk, who was once an angel and had grown tired of always observing and never experiencing, and so he renounced his immortality to become a living participant in the sensual world. Only then did he understand the human condition. German director Wim Wenders then did a sequel in 1993 titled "Faraway, So Close!" (German: In weiter Ferne, so nah!). The plot gets more complex, but the angels still hear the thoughts, fears and worries of humans and console and comfort them as best as they can. Another angel wishes to feel life as a human, as did his friend in the first film. However, he is the new kid on the block and gets thrown off track with alcohol, sensuality and a lying con-man. As I have described in previous chapters, even a high being with good intentions can get off track – via temptation and naïveté. Thank goodness that there is understanding and forgiveness, eventually! All in all, these are fine and thoughtful films and good tales, with some pieces of truth.

"How wonderful that we have met with a paradox.

Now we have some hope of making progress."

- Niels Bohr, pioneering scientist

Some of my clients made soul contracts, then forgot them as earth personalities and reacted. I related the story of a farm woman in Kansas during the Depression who lost a child – she reacted, became hurt and angry, and she cut herself off from God, ... and lost a bit of self. Part of my task was to play the negotiator in a kiss and make up scene with her soul guide. Once she went back to the point of recalling/agreeing to that contract – that death of her child on earth, she could begin to cool down and take responsibility for the drama ... not without some grumbling I might say. She did not like the earth drama, and wanted to re-write the script. I was certainly sympathetic to her cause. I am also reminded of Geneva, who we accompanied in chapter 8 on Soul-mates and Soul Companions. There she was, in tune with her soul, feeling good in a meadow, and sort of floating. She had a basket with a bottle in it, a magic elixir. Then came a woman in a gray habit who wanted that bottle, that drink. The soul flew up, No, you can't have it! She was glad that that grey woman didn't get it. In our session we discovered that the woman in gray was an unhappy nun from her own past, and it was planned that no, she would not drink from that elixir of love and intimacy. Once we understood the story and the plan, the now compassionate soul gave the poor past self a drink ... however, the initial meeting still seemed cruel. A poor nun, a lonely girl, wanted to taste the good liquid of pleasure, and the soul flew up and deprived her of it. Cold and aloof, or just part of the plan, the contract?

On a similar note, you may recall the torture victim in prison from chapter six, on Angry Souls. Sandra in her past life was an older man in the same dungeon with her now son, who was young and vulnerable in that miserable past life. The older man had found his peace in Nature and was able to withstand the pain better; however the poor young man in his cell was suffering. The old man wished for death so that he could comfort the young man as a soul. He did die first, and then …

"… But I didn't help after I died. I was curious. Detached. Happy with the peace, relieved to be out of there. I went back to nature."

The old man, so focused and passionate in life, selflessly wanting to aid the young man, promptly forgot about earthly woes when he left the body. The soul detached, and went his way.

There seems to be a chasm between the ethereal and the earthly. Spirit is indeed far away. No wonder that millions of people, skeptics and atheists, don't believe – or they can't wrap their minds around the dichotomies and inconsistencies. In the meantime, those who sincerely believe may be praying for relief, and waiting and waiting. Some people are really on their own. They do need to pray. We need to pray.

Achala is a fan of Edgar Cayce, she believes in humanity, reincarnation, karma and the unseen world. She is an Indian from Hyderabad, with a Hindu upbringing. Short stature, nice figure, dark hair and complexion. She is drawn to Europe and presently works in Stockholm – her Swedish is okay but her German is better. English quite good of course. She has a busy work life – crazy actually, with an abusive slave atmosphere at a major tech company! Things are so tense there that Achala is overworked, stressed, and close to burn-out. The managers in Munich do not care. I thought this was against the law? She is the classic overworking manager of her department, "on salary" working long hours; she is long suffering, and a Capricorn, fancy that. She tells me, "I have been loaded with work and over-stressed, and have frequent body pain, headaches, and chest aches. I get very emotional and depressed. What to do?" My immediate thought is to tell her to quit this job, but I bite my tongue. We'll see what her soul advises. She has vivid dreams and possesses a good intuition when she is not exhausted. She did well with the suggestibility tests; when I suggested outstanding hearing in the intake, she heard an elephant! Ha. Echoes from her native India. Off we go ...

"Green waves – very soft and healing, seem to be touching my face.

- moved - There are mountains, green fields. People are happy there in this calming atmosphere. Springtime. - smiling -

Not alone, there are other people, far away. There is a playful flow beneath me, moving... Everything around me, revolving, this is odd, and I'm somewhat dizzy. – Mountains, it is autumn.

Everything is jet black now. Nighttime. Revolving ... A kaleidoscopic whirl. Things get quieter. I'm alone. Outside. Somewhat cool. Alone. (whispering)

I'm a man. There is misery everywhere. I'm clinging to a lamppost, – ready to go. I am around 35. I'm dying. People around me are dead. My head is spinning. I don't know! War? Europe.

Pascal is my name.

My chest hurts, I'm coughing. War? 1945? '47?"

SP: Please go to a time, earlier, in Pascal's life.

"... Outside, younger. I'm standing next to a car, with my hand on the roof. Proud, and laughing. ...

There are others. Neighbors here. A good friend too, he is near. We are in front of a small shop? I'm 18. This is my car! Mine! - smiling -

We're speaking English. A sunny day. I'm just talking to people. Happy. I got a job, and money. Yeah. I bought this car with my money. I'm sharing it with the people around me. I'm with my friends. My best friend is here. I've family in the same town, but we're not close. I prefer my friends.

- earlier -

I'm a little boy. 8 or 9. A picket fence. A very small house. I'm trying to paint the picket fence. I have a baby sister, 2 years old. I see my mother, far away. Distant? I can't see my father. The connection is not so great. ... I try to protect my sister from him. She's by the country road. But I am also painting the fence white. I'm doing my job. (Capricorn! Hmm. Parents working their 9 years old, like present bosses?)

Back to first scene... Holding on to a light post. I'm trying to awaken someone, but he doesn't respond. He is my best friend. I look around ... a lot of misery. Blood everywhere. The lights on, the streetlights. Night. I'm clinging. I'm coughing. It's painful. British. ... I was just walking by. Suddenly a man... a German was here? Shot us? ... My clothes are very shabby. The war tore them away.

...

Very heavy. Dark. I'm on the other side ... I see the gray light from the sun (?!). ...

Now it's bright all of a sudden. I see a figure coming towards me. Very abstract – not a human figure. It is very tall, tan. Can that be? It's smiling. It is a stranger. – Now familiar? A lady. Not human. A smiling face, with her arms out. A greeting. I don't know who she is.

I still feel heavy. I have been ... a ghost for four years.

This lady takes me... to a place that is bright, – an orange color. She's pointing the way to something. I don't know where. She's pointing to the way to go - a direction; she fetched me. That is all. She leaves. I float in that direction. ...I'm just floating.

Water below me. A large heavy fountain. I'm floating on top of the fountain. Just floating. The water is very cold. Refreshing. ... I'm feeling lighter. (A slow transition in bardo, the recovery place)

... I see a white light. A being...We greet with a smile. She is feminine too. She is happy to see me. She's wearing a white gown, and a halo around her head. She is happy, welcoming. ... She's trying to make me fly with her. – I do so. Very nice. Nothing beneath me. Over the clouds."

SP: Great, enjoy the flight, the higher perspective. What did you learn as Pascal?

"Let people be in misery. (Huh?)

... I didn't want to see people in misery and pain but I couldn't do anything to save them. Let them be.

I died hungry. (She is plumper now; cause and effect?) There is a boundary, a limit, to helping others."

SP: Yes, there are many people in need and we cannot help them all. We can help those near us, however. Pascal, will you help release Achala? She feels some of your pains.

"*I will not release Achala.* She needs to feel the pain. – *She needs to feel the pain.*

... My spirit guide does not agree."

SP: Okay, spirit guide, can we bring Pascal to the circle?

"No (!) I cannot let Achala let go of the pain. She needs to feel the pain."

SP: Why? What's to learn?

"I don't know. (Wait a minute, the guide always knows, so this is *not* her spirit guide; perhaps past life personality Pascal? I don't think so, for Pascal was a positive person. I suggest we follow this voice back...)

... "I'm in Hyderabad, India. Home. Floating above my house. The lady with the halo is still there, holding my hand. I see myself as a baby ... *bringing the karma.*

... Pascal was good. He wanted to help people, but he couldn't do anything. My spirit guide says I need to help people. And my present job at the tech company is not helping people. (Good point. Quit that job!)

There is an opportunity coming. In Europe.

The name of my spirit guide = Maria (not Indian). She offers advice: *Just face it.* – Achala knows what that means."

SP: Good to know. Now, if you don't mind, let us assist Achala.

"Yes. Healing... I feel vibrations over my whole body. It comes and goes. Triangular waves. This is good....

Sanji (Her fiancé) was Pascal's best friend. He was there with the new car. They died on the same day. Somewhere in Europe.

My mission: *Learn to be happy, regardless of good or bad times.* And Remember to help."

...

We end the session. She is somewhat spacey. I bring up a few details and ideas, and she says, "That was lovely. I really enjoyed that... but my body is heavy. I feel a bit dizzy, and I don't remember anything." This was a sign of deep hypnosis, a somnambulism, and so I did a recap of what happened. The karma carrying past life brought the parcel, the heaviness from a past deed, from a past personality, to little Achala. This *baggage* became that voice, "I cannot let Achala let go of the pain. She needs to feel the pain." Someone from another belief might have thought that voice was a demon or even a belligerent ghost, wanting to make people suffer. Thank goodness her spirit guide was there; however, she/the guide was being passive, and the negative voice was front and center. The negative and even punishing voice was connected with some past life karma, not with the immediate past life Pascal nor with her present personality Achala. The disturbing thing is that this karma was probably connected to another past life, but it came from out of the blue as far as we were concerned. I had some work to do to circumvent that punishing attitude. We persevered, and aided her to separate from that negativity. Of course we still need to visit that particular past life and unravel the negativity, but that will have to wait for another day.

And so it is, with karma to work out, souls far away, and the seemingly harsh laws of cause and effect, and planning things before birth. Sometimes it seems like taking the medicine for a particular (karmic) ailment while downplaying the side effects. In the section, "Soul Partners – not always happy endings" in chapter eight, we described the short life of Annie, who drowned during a summer holiday. We learn in Spirit the purpose: "*The early death of Annie was planned.* What was to be learned? It was for the mother." ... Yes, the mother learned about the preciousness of living and loving *now*. However, this scared little girl became a ghost in that lake for decades, and the present personality is afraid of water. Excuse me for second guessing the divine plan, but one would think that either her past mother could have learned this lesson in other ways, or there could have been something like a loving angel immediately in the water to comfort that child and to wash away the fears. Yes, I periodically question the Plan.

Let us take the story now to the exit, to that point after death and into Spirit. I have also experienced very inhumane and even felonious past lives; we have already met some torturers and a cannibal. Once these predators and killers died and they were reunited with their soul guides and spirit families, all was forgiven. Some religious past personalities *thought* that they would be punished for their sins, but they weren't. Quite a few times I heard something like, "There, there, that is now over. Let it go." But they were brutal criminals! They harmed many people! - That's okay, lessons learned. Let's move on. – I mutter to myself, "unbelievable". Much more can be said on this thorny topic, touching upon ethics, morality, destiny and philosophy,... and souls planning lives from far away. Fascinating and sometimes disturbing food for thought.

I believe that it comes down to this: there are those who declare that God is Love. Yes, one can also say that Love is a positive *attribute* of divinity. Greater than that, however, is this ... *God is Life*. And Life in the universe, and on Earth, has order, physical laws – unemotional dynamics and rules. Supernovae and black holes. Evolution and Darwinism. Harsh winters, earthquakes and forest fires. In the Old Testament of the Bible the believers *feared* the Lord. Is this a poor translation of some other meaning? A psychologist friend of mine had a vivid dream, a lucid vision, of meeting God; a peek of the Divine Essence, just for an instant. He was shocked and surprised to be confronted with the terrible face of this raw God, some awesome power of creation. His hair stood on end, and he balked. It may have been a confrontation with the thermo-nuclear explosions of a fiery sun. Primal. Frightening indeed. Yes, life pushing down like an avalanche. Run! Sometimes I look at it this way ... One could yell at gravity when one falls, or be upset with momentum, or blaming a tornado for destroying homes. Acts of God. Yes, there are the laws of physics, and of metaphysics, such as hurricanes and karma. I can get that, but I do not follow a simple blind faith. When I come across distant or theoretical souls, making their difficult plans on this third dimension, I find myself as an advocate for my Earthling. *Hey now! Come on and help us here!* I have found myself time and again petitioning or negotiating for a "lighter sentence" or a re-consideration of what seems like a certain fate. This is why I have developed some healing techniques, specifically trance-personal journeys, coming next chapter.

~ **10** ~

Healing & Transformation:

Transpersonal Journeys (TPJ) Revisited

> "Know that there is within self all healing that may be accomplished for the body. For, all healing must come from the Divine. For who healeth thy diseases?
> The source of the Universal supply."
> - Edgar Cayce reading 4021-1

Trance-personal journeys (TPJ) are formed of many techniques that I have developed over the years. I devoted a chapter to this in volume one. Let's go deeper. We begin with aiding the clients to move to those trance states, ready for a past life exploration, but then their soul indicates that we need to resolve something else first. It may seem like a block, or stuck in a floating place, with colors. What's up? Something is left undone. These spiritual journeys involve exploration, perspective and very often, releasing and healing. This can unfold like a therapy session, doing inner child work or reorienting sub-personalities with the client in a good trance, and it can be totally orchestrated on the Spirit level.

I recall Jean, who had a miserable childhood with an alcoholic mother. This was not Jean's first unhappy life, for in her past life she was the lonely Annabel, who died at 40. She may have starved to death. This famishment helps explain the unconscious cravings of Jean today, who also experienced deprivation and hunger pangs. Once Annabel died, her beloved dog came to her in the inter-life:

"Kara is here, happy. She accompanies me. We are above the ground. It is white and yellow all around us. Lovely, like full summer."

SP: Great. Do you sense your Spirit Guide too?

"Yeah... I am now in a ... room? Shimmering... Blue, violet colors. There is a feminine presence. She says 'Come to your peace.'

(This is my cue. I invite Annabel to a healing, a TPJ – surrounded by souls, etc.)

Such a beautiful light... All around me! Beaming lights! ... I feel tingling in my hands and belly. - smiling - Oh, there are so many here, and it seems that I am important for many. My father is here too, supportive, in the background. (feeling the healing vibrations) This energy is so pleasant, I feel like I could jump and spring like a child! No cares! Annabel smiles now. What a relief."

SP: Glorious. What was learned in that life?

"Patience. I endured a lot, so endurance. These are useful lessons. However, she was not 'living' or feeling. She was so shut down. I do not want to live like that. I want more lightness."

Excellent. Great insights and advice. Our journey in Spirit continues. Andre was Jean's first great love, that youthful love that a teen knows. He developed cancer and died before she was 20. When she met him he seemed full of life, then he quickly deteriorated. Was she a jinx? She felt that he was infected by her sick dysfunctional family and so felt a lot of guilt. She still thinks of him, even though he died twenty-one years ago. Here we are now, and we have just sent away several attachments, or entities – this release is often a component of a TPJ. Ah, a sigh of relief. Then we continue our session:

"I feel that Andre is here. - emotional -

He is not one of the entities, he is here to visit me in Spirit. ...

Jean feels the old guilt, then asks him: *'Why this stupid concern?!*

So many in my family were sick. Sick people!'

... I felt I had infected him or he took the blow for me. Jean cries out, '*My family affected, infected you Andre!*' - tears -

... He says that is not true."

(Relief begins, after so many years.)

SP: With the help of higher beings, let us now remove the false conclusions, and the guilt. Release, let it go and find your peace.

"I still feel the pressure... overall, or in general, I take on many burdens, responsibilities. (I get a sense of "take me, not them" so it is time to remove this "noble" negative influence, starting with her alcoholic mom. Is she nearby?)

Margaret (Mom) is still clinging, even now after her death. I feel it. I feel her. There are cords, nails – 10 fingers – in me. She was afraid I would go, that I would leave her like my Dad did. She had no self–trust, and passed that on with me."

SP: It is time to remove those fingers, to cut or dissolve the cords. Spirit divine, help us now!

- she takes some time, and after three breaths -

"Yes, my father is helping me with this. He knew how to handle her. ... Ah. Finally. Done...

There was applause. (Yeah!) Kara my dog licks me. He He.

I hear 'Now you can live'." - smiles -

We get on to the next layers of this family, with the siblings, and the father. A spider's web of intrigues. She recalls the cold hazel eyes of her Grandfather. He was mean, cruel, and her mother suffered... and then passed on the suffering and coldness to her own kids. Mom was a liar. What was the truth with her? It was rather convoluted. Jean, earlier, told me of the near molestation by her step-father. We continue the release, protect the inner child. We cut the invisible cords of connection, removing some family influences. This is a rich trance-personal journey on the Spirit level.

SP: *Are you ready to let go of this family?*

"Yes. I have to separate from them. But not from my father. He is fine, and healthy. He can help me to separate from the older siblings."

"See," he says, "I can be of service!" Ha. We are both smiling.

Jean: How nice. Many light–spheres, orbs, around me, all smiling, without faces. One cannot make out distinctions or persons. All are loving though. George, my husband, belongs here in this group. He is as warm–hearted as my father. He is my great support. I know this. Also Andre (1st love). When George and I are arm in arm, we have amazing power. United!" - smiling -

…

Amen and thank you for those soul allies! This transpersonal journey was complex, for it involved many members of her family, as well as entities who had attached themselves to this dear woman, who was prone to taking in stray cats and dogs. A successful transpersonal journey (TPJ) calls upon our souls to venture outside of time and space to request aid from past lives and far away souls to help us here today. Most of the time our soul friends and guides are very willing to help. Caring, love, kindness, forgiveness, sympathy and more are all positive traits and attitudes that can aid the healing journey. Amen.

◇

If we begin to forgive others, the law reacts with forgiveness for us. And, best of all, if we forget the misuse or abuse by others, then ours is forgotten, too. … What we give, we receive. The law is filled with latent grace waiting to be released. Do we seek forgiveness? Then, we must give forgiveness. Seek understanding? Then, give understanding to another. If we want our sins forgotten in the Mind of the All-Knowing, then we need to forget what others have done to us. Let it go; release it. Stop holding onto little spites, hurts, and bitterness. They weigh us down, limiting our ability to grow closer to heavenly consciousness.

- John Van Auken [19]

---

[19] "Karma & Grace", an article by John Van Auken - www.edgarcayce.org/ps2/soul_life_karma_grace.html

We are again with Jasa, who we last met in the chapter (6) on Angry Souls. Now she is looking back at Mary's life. This past life Mary grew up with a violent father. Even before she was a teen in that life she was so traumatized that she vowed not to talk to nor trust anyone again. She kept that vow and died lonely, and remorseful. In Spirit she discovers a surprise. ...

"*I chose to be alone... when I was born.* I feel I need to understand this better. ...

I go to the time right after I, Mary, died. I'm feeling pulled... I feel my present daughter, we are all in Spirit. Oh God. She's so warm! Protective and warm! Like she's my mother. So strong and good. My sister is here too. Loving... I'm happy, and not alone. Oh, there are so many souls around me. It's amazing. (This is just what poor lonely Mary needed!)

... but I'm very strong. I see that now. There is a lot of light.

- smiles, musing -

I am not alone. Not at all. ... I've experienced this before – but not so intense. My Spirit guide is near – John... I don't like this name. Too common. Ha. I think I'm going to meet him."

SP: Excellent. Many souls have gathered. Let us create a healing circle for poor Mary. Call upon the spirit team.

"Yes, Mary, in the middle, ... She is so scared. Distrusting. Now a light, and something touches her. ... something divine. Then she cried, then opened. She is so relieved.... and in turn Mary releases Jasa, me today. - smiles -

I hear my mother say, 'She's a very warm person.' So loving, and now freed. So nice."

...

Excellent. A trance-personal healing orchestrated, in Spirit! I just witnessed it unfold. I didn't have to intervene or lead, I just watched and learned. Thanks, souls. I am grateful.

☼

The energetic healings conducted in Spirit can be very profound. All in all I call this type of work *Soul Level Healing*. The object is that layers of issues, from a variety of triggers and sources, can be understood, integrated and even melt or sent away. Psychology as normally practiced is more focused on the mind and personality, and much can be done there. As we take this up higher, however, we expand the options and possibilities, alleviating issues and pains way beyond the subconscious. Spirit is involved, which can work wonders.

I am now with my very intuitive client Sophie, who has suffered from anxieties for years. When we were in Spirit, I thought it would be useful to get a higher perspective about her condition and issues:

SP: Shall we meet your spirit guide?

"I feel anxious, tense, even panicked. (Hmm, with one's guide?) I don't hear a message. This feels difficult."

SP: Please go back, follow these emotions to the origin or source.

(agitated, uncomfortable) "I feel trapped, almost buried. I can't move. A panic, but I cannot do anything. It is dark, I'm scared of the darkness! Like I'm in a coffin! Or under something!

... I am a female. Margie. I'm 19. I think I'm in England.

(This trapped place is not a good starting point, so I suggest we go with Margie sometime earlier.)

I think we're at war. 1943, in a big city, Manchester? I hear sirens, planes, bombs. WWII. They tell us to go inside. I don't want to, I don't think this is a good idea. I have a bad feeling. The people in our building, complex, all go down to the basement. There we are supposed to sit it out. I don't like it. ...

Oh, my Grandma (Margie's) is here = she is one of my sisters today. There seems to be lots of people, huddling, waiting. – This will not go well. The house will collapse. That's why I don't want to go down there. Margie, I, sense things, intuition. This is not the first time I've had hunches. ... Yes, the building was bombed, and it did collapse. I knew it. ... We were directed to go down there, for our safety. I feel regret and frustration ... I knew what to do, and just followed the crowd. I was there three days, trapped under the building. Can't move, waves of panic and despair. Dirt and dust. Pinned down. After that… *I stay close to the body. I still feel it. It is hard to shake these anxious feelings, dread…*"

SP: We may have found a major source for your anxieties. Margie still feels it, and perhaps she is passing on these fearful emotions to you. Angel, please bring Margie home!

"Lights from above, even before you said that. Movement. A relief. … I feel or hear laughter; however, the anxiety is so deep inside, it creeps in again."

SP: Let us invite poor Margie now to the circle in Spirit; it is time for healing, and releasing. We increase the divine energy.

"We're in an expansive, airy place. They're all there, the others. Like a big family. They smile, try to comfort me."

SP: Let us reinforce this deep release, healing...

"… I feel lighter. I think the fear has left."

SP: Excellent. We take this deeper. Allow the removing or cutting of cords, those from Margie to Sophie today.

"Yes. (breath, then a nice smile) *I feel I found what I was looking for!* (Yea!) I don't see anyone, I just hear, 'I'm okay for now. I have to continue with my life.'

Okay … it is good for now. My spirit guide was there. He nods at me, from a green light. He knew I needed to do this; that's why I got scared when he came. The memories of that entrapment, buried alive were … just on the other side of meeting him. He is content now. He tells me, 'Make sure you use what you learned. Live and help other to live too.' Yes. *My mission is clearer now. Coaching, helping others. Being a Light in others' lives. Essentially to help them to help themselves.*"

Sophie pipes up: "I did everything I could."

"At this moment my spirit guide nods. He is being patient with me. Okay. I feel like a child coming up with an excuse. He sees through it, gazes at me, silently. He is strict. I'm a little scared of him. He says, 'It's time to get to work.' Ha. I will do that, yes."

And so we return. We discuss, debrief, which is a conscious reinforcement to integrate, to imprint that which was just received and resolved. Sophie is impressed, thoughtful. I give her my Reveries. [20] I tell her to "Listen to either of these two 30 minute guided imagery recording to deepen and to refresh things." After some weeks, she listens again to the recordings we just made. She is pleased, and writes me, "Everything makes sense; it all fits. I understand myself and my family better. Thanks for everything. I hope we meet again." Me too.

A

Gina used to live on the border of Austria - Czechoslovakia, and now lives on the German - Luxembourg border. This *on the border* thing might be symbolic. Her partner Jerry is also from Austria. She has created a patchwork family with him, her two daughters and Jerry's girl – all harmonious it seems. Gina is an inspired painter, sometimes painting angels. I am pleased to learn that Gina comes from functional, loving parents (Yes, it is unusual to see this word without the dys- prefix, unfortunately.) Their good traits were passed on to Gina, who is consistently caring and kind, plus she is an animal lover and activist. Her beloved dog Bear is listed. Her sister's dog Shiva is on her list too; the dog died one week after this sister died. There will be some past life connections from the animal kingdom! Gina is afraid of water, specifically rivers. She is in nursing home work, and she knows first-hand that "death happens." Her mother recently died at age 75, then her papa, and she was by her sister's side when she passed away. Her 1st husband Tim killed himself; he was normally a cheerful, fun guy but could not handle the pressure of the family business and difficult finances. He died in 1999. She dreamt of Tim last night, before our session. This means to me that his soul is

---

[20] I created Winter & Summer Reveries some years ago. Soothing music and my guidance. Don't listen and drive! - www.transpersonal.us/reveries.html

probably near and wants to communicate. Then, just before our appointment something rather eerie happened. She met an older man yesterday as she was walking around the city. Out of the blue he says "Perhaps we'll meet in Heaven." Okay, we will pay attention. She is intuitive, a good subject. Tissues ready, we go for a journey...

"A light feeling... and some lights, not a bright light. I'm in a meadow with colorful flowers, wild flowers; it is summer, I hear birds. (tears, emotions) My mother is here. She is wearing white. She touches me...'Be careful' she says."

Gina: "Are you with your mother and my sister?" - cries -

Mother: Yes, my mother and Melissa (= sister) are here.

"So nice to hear. I feel their love. ... My mother has dark hair, like years before. She looks healthy now. My sister too. We kiss, we walk together... and then my dog comes! - tears - Well, it used to be my sister's dog. So sweet. And my papa too... We have our little reunion, then my grandmother leaves. She seems fine.

I orient myself. I sense my mother and sister, by my side, in a garden, watching and waiting. Waiting for what, or for whom? ... Oh yes! My Great-great great Grandpa is coming! He had the Bible with the names of the family autographed. Their signatures, my heritage, the men of the book. He brings that thick old Bible. I have it now, it is in my possession. He approaches, waves. He has a beard, he is a preacher, Phillip. Our patriarch. - cries -

I ask him, are you incarnated? ... He doesn't answer.

Our family tradition – it goes back to him; this is why I have the Bible at home. Grandpa's grandfather, my multi-great grandpa, it goes back – all the men were entrusted with it. And now I carry the Book: Martin Luther's Bible. I am moved.

A mist comes.... Me, my mother and sister are now on a meadow. We go... to an old street, an old alley.

Mother is gone, I see old Phillip, with a pull-wagon and the Bible. A fog blows in. 'Where am I?' It is cold... I'm barefoot, with the Bible.

On cold stone…Oh it's cold! Stone buildings left and right. I trudge on. I am Phillip with the Bible. Oh heck! What is this?! I am he?!

My knees are heavy… I'm wearing a long jacket or coat. I have a gray beard…

It looks like they said – family stories, but this feels more like memories. Stone buildings, a cobble-stone road. The road… now twilight time. No one is outside, they're all inside, these townspeople. They look at me, distrustful, behind shutters. Uneasy feelings. … I've been here before as Phillip. (emotional, red nose, hand on forehead) They shut me out. No people. Am I shunned? …

Some cats come out. I feed them, and an old dog, hungry and lean. The poor thing; I give him my bread. - cries -

I take the Bible out and put the dog in my wooden wagon. … The dog came out and now he is with me; he's not so big, doesn't need much room. (Phillip carries the heavy Bible) He's happy to lay in the wagon.

… I don't know where I am at… I'm outside, by a gate, I go by a city gate… a castle? A walled castle, with the dog. … I've seen this before…but where?

It is daytime, a courtyard in this castle. I'm alone, with my wagon, here. That can't be! Huh?"

Sophie: "My Grandpa comes out, Phillip's grandson,… and gets the dog. Grandpa is old, however, older than Phillip. How can that be? Am I mixing things up? He was a sheepherder when younger. And this is a sheepdog. (Hmm. Legacy? Symbolic? She saw Grandpa as an old man, as *she* remembered him.)

There is this old sheepdog, now, given to my Grandpa – a heritage left for me. … I have the Bible in the wagon. Oh, I see. *The sheepdog is from my Grandpa! Not my sister. This is Shiva. This dog-soul has been with my family a long time. He's doing well. He's reincarnated! He's been with our family for generations.*"

Phillip: "I go on. No bad conscience. I leave the dog and go. I go out the gate, on my way. (left hand gestures) There … two children come to me, and a woman. … I am younger, with my Bible."

Sophie and her soul continue: "I look at the two children and I think about *my* daughters (Sophie's). Is it them today, returned? Maybe so.

Now I'm back home. So here are Phillip's children, and there is his, my wife. – Who is this woman (today)? They greet me, somewhat formal. I was gone a while. Nice to see them, I feel. A good connection. (Or so he believes.) I put away my wagon, go in the cabin. No animals here at home. It is a simple place,… I am given bread, I drink something. I look at these humble furnishings, the warm fire.

I won't stay long. - tears -

It is nice here but… My wife knows I will leave again. She doesn't look me in the eye. A silent reproach.

… I shave my beard off… What?? I look like my father, Horst. Tall, and slender. We are definitely from the same family. Ah, also I see … Phillip's wife is = my mother today.

…

Oh, strange. Now I'm in Luxembourg, where I live today. An old town is here, and nearby is an old convent wall. It is springtime in Luxembourg. (Bear, her dog, brought Gina to these old walls. A pleasant find, a place to poke around.)

I am Phillip, in a place that I know. I'm still alone, I don't have my wagon anymore, but I do have my Bible. (Gina brought it there.)

I look around. The wall... things are overgrown. I don't sense much... *I should leave, but I stay. ... Phillip doesn't seem to want to leave. ...* A feeling of waiting, by these old walls."

SP: I am getting a strong sense... is Phillip a ghost?! Is he still wandering, stuck there?

"Yes. Roaming around there. Gina moved here with his precious Bible. I look around. I am in the convent grounds,... in the 1700s it was closed. The wagon is now here, he's there. Waiting. But … there is nothing more to do."

SP: Interesting indeed, but it is time to rise up in spirit – Angel, please, escort Phillip to the Light!

"He prays, raises his hands. He was devout. A mist rises.... He is gone. (As that past personality, but the same soul is reincarnated as Gina today! Phillip is a soul piece that was left – for a few hundred years! A spiritual integration. Now I will expect a more whole and unified Gina!)

Only the Bible is there. ... Now I know why I had to go to Luxembourg. It was familiar, it felt like home from the beginning."

SP: Did Phillip die there?

Gina: I don't know.

...

We don't have enough time today to dig deeper. We debrief after this session. Gina was dizzy for ten minutes afterwards. She felt that he was gone, released from that place, and the old Luther Bible. I get more details, like information about her holding on tightly to this Bible. Gina would never sell it, although it is valuable. I ask her, Now that Phillip is gone, would she sell it? No, she says. We opine if he wandered down to Luxembourg in his lifetime, or after he died. Since her family is still using the Bible, I'd say he died at home, passed on the book to the family, and went to Luxembourg, following Gina and the precious Bible. She is pleased. Phillip has been released. I feel she just completed one of her assignments! We'll meet tomorrow.

Session #2 with Gina.

She got lost, even though she was here yesterday, and called me from four blocks away. Symbolic of course; we will pay closer attention to the path, the journey, today. She and her husband Jerry are camping nearby with the RV and the dogs. They all like it there. Jerry was told in her session that he had a healing touch, so he laid hands on Bear the old dog. He had hot hands, and Bear, with his poor hips, was rejuvenated. So then Jerry went to Gina's shoulders. Good and rejuvenating, she admitted. I get more background information. Her mother (The wife of Phillip back then) suggested several times to visit Luxembourg. Why? This mother Kathy had a young teen romance from there. Ha. Gina's mother, at 48, was hit with a strange illness; this was followed by a misdiagnosis and wrong medication. Then she died, within weeks of Gina finding a new home there in Luxembourg. Mission accomplished! Jerry found and organized everything. He is probably in the past story. Gina feels lighter today, excited. Pieces of the puzzle are coming together, like her longing to leave Austria those many years ago. And, from our release yesterday, now that Bible can be set aside! Off we go to another past life...

"I'm by a river, water. A horse and buggy, it is daytime. There are children here, my children. No bridge, but we have to cross it. I'm a woman. - emotional - I have to cross the river! And the children!

I'm anxious.

I'm 30, Eleanor, with two young ones, girls, and a baby boy. We are in Scotland, and the weather turned bad. I have to cross a creek that is becoming a river. - upset -

We have two horses pull our wagon – but one horse falls over, tipping the carriage. The children... I hold on! The current is strong. I can't do it! I'm there ... - tears -

I believe no one lives? Panic. No, not true ... my girls made it, but my baby is swept away. I lost my son!

Such sadness.

A cemetery... a grave and a tombstone. I'm sad, but I must be strong for my children. My partner is stoic, persevering. Oh,...

Eleanor's husband = is now my Jerry! We are together again! - cries -

He protects me and the girls. I have to be as strong too. As I look at my husband, I see a leather shirt, see a smithy. A court blacksmith, shoeing horses. 1800s? The girls... are they incarnated today? I see that my Terry (step-daughter) is the older girl. The younger one is Angela (Gina's 2nd daughter)? Not sure. (emotional, feeling the love)

I see so many connections from the higher Light, after that life. Much is now understood and integrated... one more thing: the sea, water...

I love the water, but I am also afraid. I was confronted with floods too, as well as from the past life as Eleanor. I live now by a river.

There are periodic floods, and high and low waters. I am frightened of the gray moving river."

SP: Very well. Time for a healing for Eleanor *and* for Gina; a loving circle. Soul family, please help.

"I hear *dauntless*... I feel lighter, relieved. ... It is good now.

There is a movement, a new place. Now I'm in West Austria, or perhaps I am seeing it from above. The home of my youth? Not exactly, but where me and Jerry lived, near there. Where my mother died. I'm there... My mother Kathy had to die there. This is the town of Julbach,... Tim lived near. (emotional, her 1st husband who killed himself) ... He is now here with me in Spirit. He's sorry. - cries - He left us, and the children. He couldn't do it anymore. Sorry, he says. I'm so sorry."

SP: Feel the grace, and forgiveness. Tim, did you live in the time of Phillip the preacher?

"Yeah..... There were not only two girls, but a boy. I get the picture of Phillip leaving. The boy hid himself. He didn't come out; he was afraid." - Gina cries -

SP: Let us work on understanding, forgiveness – Phillip was not there for his son, and Tim left Gina and her kids. The cycle turns full circle.

"Yes, a full turn. Gina forgives him /Phillip for not being around. I believe I am a better parent for this.

... Wait, ... Tim is in the shadows. *Tim is a ghost.* Stuck. He is sad and sorry ... and sort of frozen." - cries -

SP: We call upon an Angel, a loving soul, please help with the release ... please aid Tim.

"It is light.... *Oh, my sister comes to fetch him.* (She recently passed away, helping her on the other side.) Thank you. ... He is gone."

SP: While we're on this theme, I sense that there is a lot of background noise, so I ask ... are there lost souls too near? – entities or attachments?

"There are 7 entities – (No surprise to me, for the preacher may have been doing some missionary work; and she is a caregiver, taking in stray dogs and people.)

That number ... There are also 6 entries in the Bible. I would be the 7th," (This was an aside, an association; She will write her name in it, as the first woman. A renewal, and a matriarchal change.)

SP: Send them home. We ask for an Angel escort. They should go to the great Light. Please, take them to the other shore.

"... Now I'm alone. Thank God. Oh my goodness, that was a whole troop! That was busy. ... I can breathe, feel me, more myself. I float a bit....

I'm back in Luxembourg, in my garden. A meadow, lovely, near my home there. I see the Cloister wall. Phillip was here. Now he's in the light. Gina is only here. (Yea, good confirmation!)

He left a message, a knowing. He wanted to show me... that there were women burnt there – accused of witchcraft. He tried to stop it... He argued against the Catholics there. Women, ... one of them I know..." - cries -

(another voice says) "He can't get to me. I wasn't burnt. The gates are closed."

"Oh, this is Silvia, my friend, who lives there too. She was accused but not burnt, she escaped. We started an animal shelter together there, two years ago. She was there, back then! When we met it was as if we knew each other forever."

SP: You both tried to save the herbalists, the "witches" then, and now saving others – caring, saving the animals. Good for you. ... let me ask about Jerry, your husband: Was he also in that life?

"Yes, he now comes, in Spirit. He approaches me. He comes as a priest, a monk, to me. This is interesting. ...

Phillip was Lutheran, a follower of Martin Luther. Devout and convinced. The monk is a Catholic. Most Catholics did not want anything to do with him, but this one, yes! They met, talked, shared views."

The monk speaks, referring to Phillip: "He was on my side. He cared, took my side.... We met in Bohemia, ... there is a castle nearby."

Gina interjects: "I know why the monk was interested ... Luther was not against priests marrying. The monk thought this good and just. He left the Catholic Church, later. He didn't join the Protestants however. He was free, went his own way."

SP: And as Phillip helped him to get free, now he is helping Phillip/Gina! Full circle.

Jerry: "I will not leave you. I'm not going away."

Gina: "I will stay by you too. I will not stray. I love you with my whole heart." ...

Then her soul communicates with Gina: "You mustn't fear. All is well."

"Yes, there was a fear, of being lost, of getting lost. This came from Phillip, who became a restless ghost. Phillip is now at peace. I'm not seeking, searching, anymore. *I'm not running away.*

... Now comes my spirit guide. – The color is ... gold. Oh! My angel! I've painted him. I've seen him! The great wings, enveloping.

- gestures - He is always with me. His name is Rafael? – Yes, protecting, and healing. Glorious!"

SP: Greetings Rafael, please tell us of the life purpose for Gina?

"Help the poor, aid the old and elderly. As you do now; to go to heaven, to the light, to be happy and to recharge. - and keep painting. You will sell them, and you can donate the money to animals, and to others."

"As good as I can," adds Gina.

Her angel smiles... "and please do not forget me. Take care."

SP: Outstanding. Thank you, dear souls. Could you please give us some advice for Jerry, her husband?

"Help him find peace in his thoughts. He's been restless, and has moved a lot. Now we have the RV, a good solution. Travel is good, like a mendicant monk, he has the same urges as old Phillip. Good.

I'm at home in Luxembourg. He can come and go. This is all good. Thank you, one and all."

...

Gina is very pleased, gave me a big hug. She could have gone to a past life regressionist in Austria, but happy with me, a wandering American. I will see her again. Blessed be! This was a complex and fascinating case, with twists and turns, missions and meaning. Gina is now the keeper of the family Bible, and her own past self started the family tradition. She will take time to listen to the recordings. We too need to listen to the divine messages.

"☾,☽"

The soul's dark cottage, batter'd and decay'd,
Lets in new light through chinks that Time has made;
Stronger by weakness, wiser, men become
As they draw near their eternal home.

- Edmund Waller (3 March 1606 – 1687) English poet and politician

Having quoted that, there are attachments, entities, oftentimes unknown, and visitations that could turn into long-term "guests." If that is the case, then I would suggest a prayer of protection. Here is one that came to me from my spirit guide:

Prayer for Psychic Self-Defense

We attune to spirit Divine!
Great Spirit, Mother-Father God:
I ask to be a pure channel of Light, Love,
Healing and Wisdom.
I am protected in a bubble of light;
surrounding my aura is a golden light of love
and protection.
That which is positive, I gladly accept.
That which is negative bounces off of my protective aura
and is sent to the Central Light, which transmutes it.
I am a pure channel of Light, Love, Healing and Wisdom.
May the Divine Power flow through me, not from me.
I am benefited by being of service, here and now.
I am blessed by my contributions and circle of friends.
I am centered in my faith and serenity.
And so it is. Amen.

- Stephen Poplin

Inner Journeys, Cosmic Sojourns

We have covered many themes thus far. It's story time. Basically this chapter puts many motifs together – love, karma, adventures, lessons, bleed-throughs, reactions and more; many themes that enrich the telling of soul journeys. Let us combine them first in the artful story of Audrey, who survived interesting, dramatic and ugly series of lives, with periods of insanity. What a saga; Audrey experienced a past life crime of passion – and then forgot about it. Audrey is an interesting, intuitive and perceptive woman who enjoys the I Ching and its symbology, dreams and signs. She is personable, shy and emotionally complex. Born poor Irish; she married well the second time around, or did she? We'll see. Audrey is petite, has a nice face and complexion; looks younger, but on the thin side. She downplays her looks, body; wait, … on our second day she wore tight revealing clothes. Oftentimes I was confronted with contrasts and dualities – she even argued with herself in the sessions. Audrey feels stuck in her marriage and now wants to break out and be on her own. As she enjoys gardens and homes, she has been contemplating a real estate career. We discovered that she owned a fine estate in more than one past life. Her son is her pride and joy, but unfortunately her second husband is jealous of him, and competitive.

She came to me with a seven page list of people, with many questions and a lot of details. Some e-mails leading up to our first meeting were dramatic and emotional. She had some stories too. Her first husband was Karl, also from Ireland. As a young man he was very nice, civil, and protective. They were eighteen years together. Over the years he became more and more aggressive, until Audrey feared for her life. Hers is another example of a person who fell in love with a lower, coarse earth-bound soul with the intent to lift his evolution – to show him a higher way. She was pulled down, however; maybe sideswiped is a better word. Her aim and intention was noble, but this "charity work" of ennoblement takes ages. There have been physical repercussions too; Audrey has been hard of hearing the last 10 years – when she was tired of listening to her ex!

Her father was a dynamic extrovert, social and popular. But he had a dark side from his own violent upbringing; as he was beaten, he passed on the beating ethic. Today perhaps he would have been diagnosed with PTSD (Post-Traumatic Stress Disorder) and maybe social services would have stepped in for her family. Basically, he wasn't so interested in domestic life. He was frequently aggressive with her mother, and hit Audrey often. He died at age 50 from a heart attack. He contributed to Audrey's inferiority complex and her codependent personality. Mother Iris played the role of the martyr, appearing to sacrifice herself but actually manipulating those near her. She loved to be the center of attention, and was critical and projecting. What a stew.

Audrey's second husband is Marvin. He appears to be a positive person; however, there is a tension within, and an emptiness, she told me. He is anxious and shy and, according to her, he went into the technical field, partly, not to communicate with people. Sitting at a desk for years, he complains of back-aches. She told me that two women had left him, and he shut down. As a result of these endings, he is suspicious, envious and angry. Marvin has an addictive personality with pornography, and a stocking fetish. She says that they both manipulate each other, and there is constant tension and unhappiness. I thought she was in an unhappy and even abusive relationship, but then she told me her side. She was quite jealous herself, and she could fly into blind rages. They have had some real physical fights, and she admitted to losing it and beating on him. What a contrast to the petite, polite woman who came to me for guidance. However, she confessed, it was through this difficult relationship that she began the self-awareness path: Audrey is in to self-help books, learning to control herself, and working on her jealousy and anger. She turned out to be an excellent subject, with vivid descriptions. Her narrative reads like a well-written story; and it should, for she wrote a lot in her past life, and now she is an avid reader and writer. I even have titles for this complex narrative....

A Scandinavian Landscape

Through our suggestibility tests I discovered that she can attain a deep trance in short order. Then the story begins ...

"... I feel a heavy arm, pulsing fingers. Yellow behind my eyes. I'm floating.

Now – a coastal land next to a sea; a path of sand and grass. I walk along this way, this path. ... It is so sweeping. The sea, peaceful and open, everything! I turn around, feel very open ... no hindrances, lots of air. Endless. On this day it is rather pleasant, not too cold due to the wind. Very good. ... I'm alone, wearing a crimson rain jacket. I'm wearing jeans, barefoot ... a yellow T-shirt. I appear to be about the same age as Audrey, but I'm a redhead (Audrey is a brunette).

I'm content. ... Something red against the wind. Far away is a cabin or hut. ... I feel the sand beneath my feet. It is not summer, the sand is cool. There comes a fog.

That hut. I feel my arms getting heavier ... my voice changes – strained. My lungs, chest – a pressure. I feel like crying. Some pressure. Strange. What is it? My arms. I shake. Why? I go along. (shaky voice and breathing)

My name is ... Barbette. I don't live in this hut. I see something red, that hut, a soiled cloth hanging on it. It is very small, a shack, not for living. – It is difficult to breathe. ... The shack is white or light blue painted, made of old wood. I keep my distance. I sit nearby, on the sand. There is some fear... of the unknown? Or something, I don't know, or don't want to know. (labored breath)

The Denmark coast? Maybe. Beginning of the 20th century ... 1927.

Behind me are trees. Some trees bent by the wind. Otherwise it is empty, barren. The hut or shack is shut up, locked. I leave.

I have a green dress, with yellow flowers. Now I'm in a house, inside, ... before a table, a wooden table. Barefoot, I feel the cold ceramic tile ... the cold floor. Where are my socks? There by me is a wooden table, I look down at my dress, then the ruddy floor. I'm dizzy. I feel bad, as before, on the beach. It just comes over me. I just experienced something, then suppressed it. ...

I don't feel anyone is here. Behind me is a big window, the sea and coast outside. A huge window.

Summer, my summer dress, and apron too ... it ties behind my neck.

My back is to the window, I look down, at the table. Something is off. It's wrong. I hold onto the table – hold tight.

The big window. What can one see out there? Is that the shack? The landscape is flat; sand, dunes, grass.

A very nice area. Quiet. There is a beach just before this house.

I have a family, a husband. He wears a blue shirt, wavy hair. He is a big man, slender. He's not here. ... I have a little girl, long red hair, thin. I see her in shorts, a shirt without arms; freckles, a nice smile, with dimples.

... but something happened. - hands nervous, moving -

A feeling, like... I'd like all of this to stop. A white fog before me. I hold onto the table. I feel faint. The white fog. What should I do...?

I go out, turn around. I go past the window, two steps outside. Three steps more. I'm on the sand.

What is it?

A man, with dark hair, sitting in the sand, white pants, socks. My husband? Why am I excited? Agitated? My mouth – I feel I will lie.

I don't want to say something.

I see a kitchen knife. I don't see blood. I don't want to lie.

My husband sits, looks at the sea, his back to me. Black shoes, white socks, cream pants ...

I saw a knife. A flash... I don't know. - starts blabbering -

Wha … oh, white fog, socks. Who? Huh? … I have gray eyes. I go on, glass balls. Gray glass balls.

I'm not there, behind the eyes.

Perhaps I use a knife ... in his shoulder – I go behind him … his jacket, a wind jacket. I don't see any blood.

The girl hid in the shed. With the red garment."

Audrey speaks: Perhaps I was insane?

"I now see blood on the jacket. Red. He falls over. A man. … Why? What did he do? - emotional, cries -

I'm wearing an apron, a bit of crimson, a slaughter dress?

Inside... behind me, it is dark. The furniture casts shadows, a cabinet with closed doors. I'm in this room, afraid. Night. … My husband is coming.

I don't know where my daughter is. Is she sleeping? No picture of her. I'm afraid. It is not good. Something happened. … He comes from the bathroom ... says something ... to put me down, to put me aside. – He is so arrogant, overbearing! He said something to me. He doesn't care about my feelings! He told me he wants to leave me. There is another woman. No. No!

I put on my stockings. Nylons? I wear sexy clothes to entice him, but he leaves. I feel so small. Barbette is humiliated. I'm old, wrinkles, in my 40s.

He's still good-looking. He found a young woman. He is so arrogant. He is leaving me. Quiet, he turns away. - tears -

I thought he loved me; I thought we were happy. But that was not so. I can't take it. - cries -

...

I put his body in the shack. I don't know if the daughter saw it.

Do I have a daughter? There is… a 10-year-old girl... I don't know her name.

Huh? I don't see his face. Do I know him? ...

218

Oh, there is that landscape, the sand ... a dark red sunset. Dark.

I have white hair. I look out across the sea, with my gray eyes. I sit on my stool. I looked at my weary hand, arms – very old. I'm tired, alone, and sad. – so sad, and tired. What happened on that day? It is all gone.

I'm in another house. Sit on a veranda. A wooden chair, ... staring out to the oblivious sea.

I don't feel regret, just tired, sad, old and depressed. No more feelings. I sit and wait.... It is evening, just after sunset; there is a reddish tint in the sky. I'm tired.

I die.

I'm sorry... *Sympathy calls,* pity ... I will go. ...

From above, I sense things, then ... I go. So sad ... just sadness. *I float up ... but not happy. Death was not a release. I was dead in life. I was dead already. There is no difference, except now I'm floating.*

I see the house, a small point – all below. ... I feel a peace ... it works its way in me.

I'm an empty room. There is nothing around me. I feel this sadness – my soul. I am the sadness. There is nothing else. ...

But then I hear, 'It is good as it is. Let it be. That was then.' – Who said that? ... There is a light, a shadow, something yellow and warm. ... I relax now. I'm being relaxed. Peaceful, quieter. The light comes like a cloud over me – not so big, ... pleasant.

It was expected, somehow. I feel I'm hugged by this cloud. I feel safe, but sad. The cloud allows this; I can be sad, – but I also feel love. I sense love.

I talk to the wind and say, 'It has come this far. It has come to this.'

- cries -

The cloud knows I'm sorry. It hurts. - I needed eight years of recovery here....

Now I feel my soul, ... mixed with sad, a pain ... stabbed deep. After the murder, I just left. I fled. I left it all. Ran. ... The scene at the end had a similar feeling, – quiet, sea, another hut, alone. I kept it within, I told no one.

... I sense my present man. My husband. Is he the same person? I saw his socks. (He with the foot and sock fetish.) Yes. He is the man.
 - cries -

I ask for forgiveness!! That was not right. I beg for forgiveness!

– his soul comes... (Audrey and her soul cry.) I don't feel him. I see his face, from today. Solemn."

Barbette: Please forgive me. I should not have done that! I'm so sorry! ... I don't think you can forgive me. How can you love me?

"... He looks at me. He can't forgive me. ... How can I make this good? - cries -

I'm so sorry. Forgive me, I pray. ...

– I feel the shower. Golden rays. A light. I stand in it.

His face is blue, cool. He is unreachable. – A blue red unemotional face. This makes me afraid.

Marvin has back pains, lower back. Stabbing pains. I did that.

I pray for forgiveness. I feel the cloud hugs me, and him. He is blue, like the blue shirt he wore that day. The same colors."

SP: He suffered, was hurt .... and the daughter?

"There was no daughter... just a wish. ... It was a failed birth. He did not want a child. I could not forgive him for that. (deep breath)

The warmth comes... He is no longer blue red. Now a nicer face, normal colors.... He likes me now. But he is also very sad. It has become better. There is a warmth. I know this feeling. Jesus is by me. I am thankful that he forgives me. He hugged me, and me him. I feel the love in his eyes. I sense his truth: God loves all who come. This is the great love that leaves no one out, not even sinners. Thank you."

...

Relieved, Audrey found her peace during this session. Whatever was left undone those many years ago had a chance to integrate, release and find solace. We spoke of old tapes or programs that run in the background of our minds. During the healing portion of our session I told her to allow them to release or dissolve on their own. We are good for today. I put down my notes. What a tale, what a story. We were *peering at insanity through the back door*. Both she, Audrey, and I were confused at times. Who did what? She was mad, insane, dissociating, in a past life. This tale, this case offered an unusual insight: what does insanity look like from the inside? This client could view this phenomenon from a certain distance, for it was not she who retreated into another world, but her past life personality. Food for thought from a ghostly memory, and a murderer.

Audrey is serious about her therapy with me, and she has many questions. It will be interesting how she will relate to her husband now. We soon met again. Audrey worked a lot with the material. She told me that she had many crazy scenes with Marvin over the years. She was jealous and attacked him several times with her claws, her nails. He, on his part, had experienced at 15 his father's suicide, and two women left him; so both she and Marvin were insecure. She feels she must leave him, but this would be yet another "failure" for them both. Nevertheless, she wants out. She wants to get a secure job first. She confesses that she dislikes her body; is this from the rejection in Denmark before she was born? Imprints are left from the past. She is hard of hearing the last 10 years. We will discover she did not want to hear some things. We continue our sojourn the next day. ...

A French Interlude

"... a tree, blooming. I'm in its shade. It is spring, nice. I am in a clearing, where nearby there are other trees. I sit there; before me is a path ... From the left on to the right is a meadow.

I'm wearing a light blue-white dress with rose flowers on it, white knee socks. White shoes.

I feel my feet don't come to the ground, ... I'm floating."

SP: Welcome soul. Would you like a guide today?

"... something ghostly comes from the woods. He is of concentrated light, sun-rays, see-through – masculine? It stands before me.

- smiles - I feel very good. I feel the good vibrations, and a new hue. Now It feels feminine – a soft, tender power, emanating. Nice. She looks like a fairy, very pretty. She has a wand, with a golden star on it. She smiles so pleasantly. She gives the wand to me. She is a good-natured being, very caring. I feel so happy and pleased. I'm surprised; I thought my spirit guide would be masculine – but I'm happy she is feminine. (Actually the spirit guide first appeared masculine; of course in Spirit there is no gender. There is probably a reason why he/it is now appearing feminine ... probably to help Audrey's femininity, plus her difficult experiences with men.)

- smiling -

I wish I can always feel this power and trust; I lack this trust in my life. She, my guide, gets clearer, still see-through, sort of condensed light, shimmering. It feels so good to be near her. She is like a good mother, a loving mother. Not a little fairy. ... She is big now, like a half circle, floating, here before me, a protection. She is a very good being. She shines, protects. Nothing wrong can happen around her. (In awe) She is so pretty, protective. She is a high being. ... Astel? Astera."

SP: Thank you, Astera, for being here. I know you love and protect Audrey. Perhaps you could use the wand to delete the mental viruses. Please banish the negativity and limitations. (We spoke of old tapes earlier, even mental programs.)

"It feels like I'm in a light-bath. ... I feel clarity, a clearing."

SP: Great. This shall continue. Shall we go to a relevant past life?

"... Astera takes my arm. - gestures -

I'm small, she is big. We fly ... over the forest. We left that place, we fly gently. I feel good. I see the earth; pretty landscapes, below. A river flows underneath us. She says we'll go there, to a hilly landscape. Nice. Pretty trees. – There is a presence here, a special feeling. Like the Loire Valley in France. I've seen this in pictures.

We come to earth, gently to the ground. There are great big trees ... next to the river. I walk along it. It is summer. ... I see the huge trees, next to this river.

Suddenly there are spots, foggy – a block or obstruction? Like yesterday. I feel the trees, though – calming.

I feel like a young girl, the dress is nice and durable. Blonde hair, two braids. How old? 10? 7, 8?

My nature – I'm so headstrong, willful. Ha. I'm not so shy as Audrey was as a child. No, I'm not shy; I feel full cheeks. Ha. I like it. ... This path continues, then darkness comes, on the right. On the left is a white fog. I go in this direction, right to the center.

I'm cheerful, curious. I live here in the area. This park or estate belongs to the house. There is an incline, and a waterfall, over there. The black is where I'm not supposed to go, but I'm curious. I want to go there anyway. I go on. It goes down. A waterfall is there. I'm curious, I'm not afraid ... I go on down. ... The light shines through the tree leaves. I'm happy, exploring. By the water is a path. Then a lake – a dark green color. Nice. I look in and see my face in the water ... a sweet face; fat cheeks, nice eyes, a space between my front teeth. Ha! I'm glad I came. It was forbidden. I did it and now I'm proud.

I'm Molly. It is short for something. Madeline?

I live up at that house. I have a big brother; brown hair, right now in checked pants. Interesting, he wears clothes from another time. 19th century. I look at my outfit. My dress, white and rose, patterns. Now this is stylish. (She remembers all of her outfits!)

He's not here in the woods. My mother has blonde hair; a fine lady, who plays cards. Her hair is styled up in a funny way. My father has a mustache. He is older, and portly. We live in a fine dwelling, a small palace. There are big trees, and large grounds, the estate. Here it is good. Very nice.

My mother plays cards with her friends. My brother plays, explores meadows and things. We all do our own thing. ... There, about the house, a man is there, heavy ... father. He is a full man. I like him.

... coaches with horses come and go. It is peaceful here; I like it. We live well here.

...

Now I'm bigger, in front of the mirror... I'm not so satisfied. This face was sweet as a girl, but now it is not so pretty. Too full. I don't let that on; I'm self-assertive, I project that. But I am uncertain, insecure, on the inside. – Women should be appealing.

My hair is up, I put on a nice dress, but... I'm not slender, I'm more like my father. I'm not big, but not pretty. Alas. There is a party tonight, and I'd like to be pretty. I'm around 20. I feel I won't marry because I'm not so nice-looking. This is my life. ... It is still nice, but I'm a bit bored here. I was more curious as a child, content. I'm not so happy now, like I was. I'm dissatisfied with myself."

SP: Check in with your wise soul or spirit guide; ask if this is really true, or a self-critical girl.

"Perhaps Molly is not so bad looking, but she compares herself. She wants to be elegant, but these clothes don't fit so well. Her body is not in vogue.

... She leaves the fine room, her dressing room, and goes out. She passes a window, the trees in the distance; one sees the woods. (I coax her back to the first person, aiding her to connect more fully with this past personality.)

I go down the wide staircase, for effect,... it is evening; the guests arrive slowly. It is summer, a garden party. ... I meet people, but I have no great pleasure. I smile, but I'm bored, uncomfortable. Introductions, I'd rather not...

However, there is someone, but he doesn't look at me. As kids we spent time together. He has grown, now a young man – he is cheerful, surrounded by young women, of course. Charming, alluring. He doesn't know how I feel; he isn't interested. I don't say anything, but it is painful. – The other young women enjoy his company, in my house. I'm sad that I must smile.

I'd rather take the dress off and relax; I hate these parties, so boring. My whole life is boring.

I see my life again as a child. Life was so nice, then. I was happy, strong, curious. I can hardly see her in this 20 year-old. ... I am rather sad, dissatisfied now. It won't get better, I feel. ... Maybe that is why I like to eat. It is so right, genuine.

This life is empty, without sense. It is all here, and yet so empty; each day is like the other.

France. 1892, perhaps. (hmm. Molly's date conflicts with Barbette's timeline – 1920s – in Denmark? Maybe, but the Danish Barbette was not in her right mind, and sort of outside of time.)

There is a hopelessness, a futility... almost a depression. Not only because I'm not attractive,... it is this whole charade. It doesn't seem real. These people... they don't say what they mean. It is all a theater. Pretend. Not honest nor happy.

...

I see a woman in black, but fat. Blonde hair, those cheeks – it must be me.

A funeral? I'm 35. I'm wearing black, a little hat.

I tread a path, to the far side. The family cemetery... I go home from there. I walk slowly. I live in the same house. My father died; the plump man with the mustache. I miss Père, father. I sat by the little cemetery, near our estate.

I never married. My mother and I live here now. My mother has her friends. I don't.

My brother left. Moved away.

... I'm even more depressed. I don't want to live. What for? No reason to live. No real activity or purpose... No friends, no one who loves me. I miss Papa. Nothing I like to do except food. I walk, gaze into the woods.

There are these parties... hmmm, I'm dissatisfied, totally. Everything is empty, absurd, dreadful. I don't love myself. I got so fat.

I want to die.

How can I get out of this boring life? It goes on and on. Nothing interests me; no joy. I'm depressed. A lump in my throat. Frustration. Why? As a child I was so happy.

Sad ...

I close the blinds. It is dusk. I cut my right veins, wrist – in my room, my boudoir. I'm wearing strange clothes. A basin, where my hand is... a razor. I look... the blood drains. Red. I'm without feeling. So slow. How long will this take? I don't regret it, but I find this boring too. Not fast enough.

Not much older. 40 to 35 … 36 or 37.

I see a lot of blood in the basin. I get dizzy, sit back in the chair. My hand drops, blood...

I'm still in my body... dizzy.

I sense a servant woman comes. Or do I imagine this?

- dies -

… a pressure in my throat; I feel that in my present life a lot, a pressure. (Will center, self-expression)

I float. What do I do now? … I hope my spirit guide comes. I wait.

I'm confused. This doesn't feel good. *The sadness came with me. It did not stay in the body. I wanted to leave it. It is not better.* I feel like a gray ball, floating. A dirty color, gray.

… Then Astera comes, my spirit guide, a golden light. I am pulled with her, – a great ball.

This pressure though. Such a pressure, my throat, and more.

She says, 'It will all be okay. It is now over.' Not in words; I feel it.

I'm still sad. She consoles me, wraps me in her essence. I feel good by her, but the sadness – my throat, and heart. … A light pain – from my neck. I stopped myself from sobbing, crying. I swallowed it.

Now I don't see the earth anymore. I'm floating. I feel the light from Astera – getting lighter.

In my chest the tension, pain … I need to rest.

– It took six years to recover."

SP: In this recovery place you probably contemplated, reviewed Molly's life. What lessons did you learn?

"*I should not have gone into my sadness. I should have looked for light and beauty and worth in the world.* I did not give it the effort. To do it over again … I would have done it differently. We had it all. Land, beauty all around, family, wealth – everything – and yet empty for me. I did not find anything worthwhile. I loved my mother and father and brother ... but the links were not cultivated or deepened.

I destroyed it. I believed in nothing.

It started so nice. Lively. ... I could not understand the sense of it later....

Audrey also feels depression at times. She feels, at times, no point to things, a senselessness. She feels an inability to find something ... to find that something."

Audrey speaks more quickly: "I have more faith, hope and resilience than Molly. There is an inability to find the resources at times, that inner Well. It is not so extreme. (As with Molly) I have many more ideas, hopes, and wishes than she. Molly could have done everything – she had the money and freedom. She tried riding, writing, hobbies, but with no passion. ... Now I have no hobbies, but I really love reading. I'm a housewife, and I read. I'm very curious."

SP: It is time for healing. Let us cut the cords, thank Molly ... and free Audrey.

"I feel a blue cord to Molly, on my right side, my waist. I'm thin, she was fat. She had nice dresses. I grew up poor. She wanted to be thin, as I am, but this does not make one happy. Look at me.

(We will see that Molly's life is a recovery reaction from another past life!)

So many issues. I pull the cord from my side. - right arm yanks -

There are roots on it. I see Molly has the cord too. Should I pull it out?"

SP: Ask Astera your guide.

"Yes. Uhh. I threw it away. But now ... I feel a hole, like something is missing there. This is around the right kidney. Astera fills the hole, heals it. The neck, there is a knot there. Pressure, willfulness."

SP: Astera will help there too.

"... It is good. She put her hand in my neck, pulled it out, whatever it was. I feel the pressure – my throat, my shoulders... especially the right one."

SP: Astera, what is this?

"I see the face of my husband, or both of them. Cords from my ex
… on my right shoulder, upper chest: my heart... a pressure, burden.
(Good, a healing – the first of several.) … It has become lighter. It is
good. I see the connections … Molly's father = is now my ex-husband
Karl. I loved him. He was big in Molly's life, loving but somewhat
distant. Then her mother? Hmmm. Not so strong. But Molly's brother
= is now my beloved son.

And the handsome charmer? My present husband? Yes. *So I did get
him after all!*

To Molly, all relationships were neutral, repressed. She went to her
father's grave. Here there was love.

I loved my first husband, and cried a lot when I left him. There is
still some pain. During this difficult second marriage I have cherished
the first marriage more. (Nostalgia has mixed with a false regret. He
was not nice.) Our first 10 years were great, happy. Why is he still so
angry with me?"

Audrey pipes in: "But my father hates me and I loved him. Perhaps I
did something in a past life? Old pains. My father broke my nose. ...
My hearing diminished with my first husband."

SP: Did your father, or Karl your ex, hit your ears?

"Ears? Astera looks at me sadly, doesn't say anything. I see the
house where we lived. I wanted to be there, in that house. He was
angry, in a rage, and I was to blame! He wanted to destroy me. 'Watch
out,' he said, 'or you will see, in the woods – one day …!'

- emotional, cries -

I was so shocked that someone, my own husband, would say such
terrible things! It started out so nice... Why couldn't it continue? It got
so bad... I had to leave. I couldn't hear it any more. I still am sorry.
Regrets... I should have stayed. It was so bad, however. But I ran
away. I tried; then I pulled away. He felt that. He said I was at fault. –
I was so afraid. He terrified me. – I'm sorry. He loved me. It should
not have ended that way! He drinks now. And he is still angry. Why?!
… I feel guilty because I left." (Hmmm. Back and forth, an inner
debate. She forgets she was terrified, threatened, or actually

remembers the fear and regret simultaneously! This feels like the prosecutor and defense lawyer both arguing her case!)

SP: I suggest we follow this back... there may be yet another life to explore.

...

Viking Roots

"Oh, my head and back, tense. I don't see anything, but my body feels strange. It is night time. I feel stuck, trapped. A cramp. I feel it. – No images. I feel my back, and shoulders tense. It is difficult to breathe.

(We back up a bit more in time – she relaxes.)

I lay in bed. I'm a woman. I see old homes. ... Medieval, old alleys, cobblestones. A small room, the ceiling is low, it is dim. I have dark hair, oily and uncombed. I lay there. I must be sick...

I'm ill. It's day and I'm in bed. A nightgown, blue, white stripes.

The bed is made of stuffed cloth on iron, cold. The window there, the street below. - gestures -

I hear the noise. It is warm, damp, and muggy. There is a wooden floor. I have to spit blood ... by my bed... I hold onto a pail.

I'm not young, but not old. I feel 50, but I'm 40, maybe 38. Dark hair, just a few gray hairs. Green eyes. I spit blood. Pains, I'm not well. I feel my shoulders, my lungs, as I cough.

Outside I see a bit of blue; there is another house in the way, but there is a piece of blue. It is hot, sticky.

Raja is my name. It means hope, but I have little.

In northern Europe. Finland? That's not right, but up north.

I have a husband, and a small son. Next to me, on my left, is a door.

- gestures - Someone can walk through there.

… I will die."

SP: Okay, let us go back, before the illness, with Raja.

"I'm a pretty, a young woman … with long dark-blond hair, green eyes. 25 … tall, slender, nice figure. I've a leather skirt, a simple leather top. … and something of another cloth too.

I sit on a chair, with my son, a handsome boy; light brown hair. I love him so.

I sense an early sickness, or a threat of one. We are home. An open fire ... the kitchen, I'm cooking. It is dark, just a little window. I put my son down, I must cook, and in a hurry! I have a bad feeling. I must cook a good meal, - emotional - or my husband will hit me. When he comes home, he expects all to be done. ... Is everything right? Or will I get beaten? This is sickening.

My boy cries. I'm tense, agitated. I must do it right.

I cook ... not good enough! ... He complains a lot. He opens the door. A big man, like a Viking. Huge, coarse; like a storm, he comes in and wants to eat."

Audrey: He can't be a Viking though, can he?

"Our son cries. I'm so scared. I serve him. I put the boy on my lap. Wait. He must be quiet or else. I soothe him, but he yells. Papa won't like that! I lay the boy in his makeshift bed. It moves, swings... a cradle.

My husband – he looks at us, angrily. He does not love us. He calls me to him. He says, 'You know you did something wrong! Not enough salt!' I look down. He gets up, flings the food. 'You can't cook! I work all day and I'm hungry! You have to feed me!' he yells, angrily. I get up, search. I get a bit of bread. Thump! My ears! He beats me! Beats me. - tears -

My ears ring ... my child cries, he looks at this shame! ... I lay on the floor, he kicks me then. I see my soul saying 'I cannot be here.' ...

Then it is over. Hurt, bleeding. The storm spent. - cries -

He leaves, slams the door. Slowly, I stand up, go to my child, still crying; I try to comfort him. Where shall I go? What to do? I don't know!? ... My child is my only consolation, but – I fear for him. I'm afraid! If something happens to me, what will happen to him? It hurts so. ... a pain in my shoulder. I'll stay until my boy can fend for himself.

Seasons, winters. He is in his teens – a strong lad.

I cough, catch my breath. It was dark. I close my eyes.... my deathbed is stained crimson. My eyes closed. ...

Astera holds me. 'There, there, Raja. It is over.'

I'm not a ball, but a woman. She takes me away, far away. ... Many white clouds – we float through them. I am so weak. We go on. I feel good, safe, now.

Now I see my Viking husband = Karl, my first husband. What a beast. But – how could I love him? I felt fear from the beginning, this I remember."

SP: Did your soul want to help his soul to evolve? At some point perhaps you decided to sacrifice your self to show him something softer, kinder, more loving. Is this true?

"Yes... but... Karl changed. He even looks different today. My son saw the changes too. He developed somehow a bigger jaw, a belly. Odd. He looked, eventually, like the Viking. He is not the same man. It was frightful to see. (Her other voice, and perhaps a vow, adds ...) If only I had stuck it out, perhaps he could have changed. I gave up too soon. It was good in the beginning. I was egotistical. I left him, and he is still angry! If only ..."

SP: Listen to this question: Had Raja loved the Viking more, would he still have beaten her?

"That is ridiculous. It was his nature. He was crude and violent."

Point made. By this time she was going on again, arguing about why she was a failure and left him. Her love could have changed him, etc. I have to do some convincing and coaching, with Astera's help. What happened, when we step back and get the big picture? The Viking became Molly's father, and he was corpulent and easy-going. He did protect her as the father. Audrey met and fell in love with that part of Karl, but later, the Viking emerged. Bleed-through times two!... We eventually cut the cords and saw how the different lives created a perfect storm cycle: Raja was beautiful, and attracted the Viking, who beat her. The unconscious message: beauty attracts savagery, so keep away from that. Best not to be pretty. Her next life was Molly, who was recovering, fat and unattractive, hiding – safe, but overly protected and lonely. The Viking, perhaps regretting his cruel treatment of his wife, took on the role of the protective father of Molly, who found him warm and caring. She had detached from all the joys possible, however, and killed herself. Then came the insecure Barbette, who lost it when her husband decided to leave her for a younger woman. The old Viking rage and revenge blew like a volcano and she killed him. She fled, escaping her deed, and her mind – never fully recovering. Lonely... by the churning sea. Now comes Audrey, who had a brutal father, wanted to escape to the agreeable Karl, who was Molly's nice father ... but this husband slowly showed his ugly Viking viciousness that tortured poor Raja. Audrey left him, with her son, and went to Marvin, who she killed – and owed – from Barbette's life. She still feels unattractive, but this is not true. Marvin stays with her, but he must vaguely know that he died by going for another woman. So now he remains with her and lasciviously watches other women via pornography (It is a bit safer). This still pushes Audrey's buttons, and she has flown into jealous rages....

Can this story end happily? In Spirit we orient, release, let go, forgive, and understand. At the end, she is sitting on a park bench, with Astera, and Jesus is before her. She warms in their presence. She feels levels of liberation, and discernment. This soul has experienced many tumultuous and dramatic lives and lessons. In her present life Audrey is striving for balance and independence. She loves to read; she is feeding her mind, and finding her peace; – a complex and fascinating soul and persona. I wish her well.

As this case illustrates, there are struggling personalities and wayward souls making their way through various lives and lessons. Thank Heaven there are comforters and wise helpers to the rescue. Astera and Jesus are aiding Audrey; and Audrey volunteered to be a helper to Karl. A hierarchy of helpers, of guides and caregivers. When lost or in need, remember: Each of us has a guardian spirit. We need only ask.

We continue this cosmic study of love and relating from a higher perspective. We also have soul families, companions and colleagues. We do not have to do this journey alone. Yes, we have so many types of relationships here upon the earth, and our soul family and companions in Spirit all play their parts. As we take the vibration up a notch, we will discover other beings. These special souls have higher missions, and we are in their care.

˜ **12** ˜

Watchers and Guides – Incarnated or Not

John Van Auken, a Cayce expert, tells us that "Some souls did not always incarnate with their group, choosing instead to skip a cycle or enter with another group, though they usually rejoined their original group eventually. Others, though cycling into the Earth-plane with their group, did not actually incarnate, i.e., did not enter into a body; rather they stayed in the spirit and helped from a higher vantage point while the others incarnated. One example of this comes from an Edgar Cayce reading for a woman who wanted to know why she hadn't been given an incarnation during the Palestine era in which her present son and husband had incarnated. She was told that she was there, but not in the flesh. She was, as some of us would term it today, a "guardian angel" for her present son while he lived and worked in that period." [21]

So often past personalities, bruised and beaten, leave the earth plane and meet with their soul guides, seeking solace, compassion and love. Recovery and rejuvenation are important, especially if it was a heavy or difficult life. I have also heard from departed uncles or aunts who stayed close to their loved ones on Earth. Some of them are guides, and they still want to be of service. Luckily, many wise and loving souls *are* incarnated. There are "angels" among us. In Spirit there are also higher perspectives, and loving beings. Elaine, the animal lover and musician, who we last met in the chapter on soul-

---

[21] "Past Lives & Present Relationships" an article by John Van Auken, www.edgarcayce.org/ps2/soul_life_past_lives.html

mates, is now delighted in our session. She has just left an earth body and needed to rest. Now she is quite happy in Spirit. What is she up to? ...

"I see a little butterfly. I take it carefully in my left hand, like this. (gestures) I believe I should take it with me. I explore this place some more. ... A waterfall, a pond below it, a lot of green, a meadow. ... I lay there, a chance to recover, and stretch out. The butterfly is here; it doesn't fly away. (In one of our sessions her guide appeared as a butterfly.) Not far is a bridge, over the pond. Suddenly, many dogs run over it, to me, happy, wagging their tales, or seem to. Ha. They kiss me, lick me. (Names five of her dogs, now in heaven.) Oh. My dogs! And others I don't know too! They are all here – and more! Oh, so happy. They are elated. I don't know why, but I feel a sort of *congratulations*, it seems. Or a gratitude. So loving.

I sense my butterfly again, and ...many points of light. (her right hand caresses solar plexus)

My feet tingle. Something special in the air. ... I see horses. Then the clip-clopping sounds. They trot over to me. Sweet. They nudge me with their muzzles. – I hold on to a mane, then I go with one very fine steed. I mount and off we go. Yuhuii! I'm riding in Heaven! We go to a very big space – with water? It seems like it, with splashing. There are spots, shining, like the sun. A lake, shimmering? We ride over the meadow, the one I saw yesterday in our session. We get closer ... this one, this lake, holds another life group, it is sentient, alive, sparkling.

Oh my, it is a huge mass of horse-souls, not a lake!

This is amazing. I get closer, dismount. ... I take a dark cloth from one, so ... it can beam? Yes, it had a coarse cloth. It was mistreated, poor thing. I help. I feel and send Love.

... I sit on a white ground, looking out to a pale sunset, with bright energy. A circle of animals around me. I sit in the middle. There are rabbits, snakes, horses, cows, dogs, birds – all here! So peaceful, mellow. A great Peace. I look down... a small golden heart on the ground; I pick it up – a happy feeling. A gift?

Then they, all of these animal beings, all go up, like a mass of butterflies. Dispersed and flying up and away! Beautiful. I'm in awe. … Five little lights come, like children of white light. They must be children, they are small and sweet. They take my hands. The blue butterfly is on my shoulder; we go to a table, which is shimmering. Everyone has a flower, a bud… I show them how to make it blossom. They are happy, laugh. I go to each one, place my hand over theirs – the flowers bloom. They are overjoyed.

I see Johnny (her partner) – he has three kids or young beings – He's teaching too? His butterfly is on his shoulder. The kids have bonsai shrubs. The leaves grow quickly. We watch. So nice. I notice the contrast; blossoming flowers with us, and no leaves.

I see a tree with many blossoms, or buds.

I think of someone I know who takes in blind cats. No one else wants them, so she does. She now has two blind cats. She cares, like us. She is here, bless her.

I go with Johnny, next to the tree, to see its branches. We hold hands and beam – the whole tree begins to blossom, leaves and all! Birds come to the branches. Lovely. On the ground, flowers blossom. We sit and relax, under the tree.… the little ones come again. We make a big circle. I see little white butterflies – each child gets one, and must take care of it, keep it alive; care for it.

… I see a horse; it puts its head near me. I hold his neck, caress him. It is Derek, who was one of my dogs! Ha. As a horse. Appropriate! I knew he was special even before he opened his puppy eyes. I believe he will be the last one to go. (Elaine has two old dogs, who soon transcended.) He has been a good companion.

(Her right hand has steadily, slowly, caressed her own solar plexus, her belly, like petting her dog/horse.)

… Ah, satisfied. So satisfied."

It was a sweet and gratifying trip for her, and a reminder for us here upon the earth that we have companions of all sorts in Spirit – and on Earth. In Heaven/Spirit we enjoy our soul families, guides and higher beings, and the glory of plants and animals have their heavenly correlation there above. Mother Nature smiles, puppies wag their little tails, and wood fairies prance in a glade. We are not alone, and humans are not the only game in town. I am reminded of animal companions, and pets as teachers. Sometimes it can be only a dog, a pet, that can get to a closed-down human, and melt a bruised heart.

"☾,☽"

Nancy got some sage advice in Spirit about her marriage. It was not as she expected, for her mundane mind was focused upon security. Her wise soul, and her soul entourage, gave her a wider view of it all. She continues her spiritual journey:

"I see mountains. Daytime. All this is clear, and vibrant. I'm alone. A man. A Thai monk. I sleep in a cave, and I live on donations or begging. A mendicant monk. I have to open my heart.

I'm old. I am here to… Be.

I learned … to experience this, an assignment of my choosing. To be alone and to open my heart.

I'm content. This is all rather vivid. I get a name… O…Osip.

Now it is brighter… I'm satisfied being alone. Peace and quiet. I meditate a lot. I've attended to Self.

Alone and at peace. Lights come. Wait, who is there too? At least two souls. Johanna my grandmother and my father. - emotional -

They accompany me in Thailand. They did not incarnate. I commune with them; they are like guardian angels.

…

Osip dies. He fell one day, he was weak. Hit his head. Then … he floats over the body… He 'stands up' and goes home. The body stays.

… There are many souls here, by him. His spirit is free. They come… to a brighter space. It was dark, … I move along. I know the way; now it is bright. Peaceful. …

Nancy inherited his intuition, and psychic abilities."

Osip offers advice: *"Keep your spirit attuned, to be free. Don't get distracted."*

"I feel my hand – this is intensive…what is that? Oh, a present, given to me, from him. - emotional -

Oh, my soul parts are returning. (Spontaneous soul retrieval. Cool.)

… I am now stronger, whole. Thank you, and Blessings to All living things!"

Audrey, who had such dramatic past lives – described in the 11th chapter on Inner Journeys, Cosmic Sojourns, is having her third session with me. She is dressed very feminine today, with a pink top, and a light thin printed skirt to her ankles. She tells me of new improvements with dealing with her truth, especially concerning her husband Marvin. She respects his wishes, feels her own needs, then makes her decision. A few times she prayed for Astera her guide to be there, and she quickly came. Audrey noticed a new reaction too. On a bike ride in the past she would lag behind and watch Marvin spying a look on a pretty woman. This time she rode in front, not caring where he would look. Freeing. Books have helped too. What will we discover today? She goes easily into trance. We countdown to an emotional healing. I use a very helpful tool for this cleansing opportunity; I suggest a magic hoola hoop with an invisible filter to catch the negative past and present life "residue" – it easily glides over her head to her hips – stays there for a bit... she takes a deep breath and describes her healing journey.

"I sense a hue, dark, and a bit of yellow. Ah, this is good. … I'm floating – it feels light. I sense no negative residue there. (the hoola hoop continues down her body, to her hips) Sexuality came to mind – something to cleanse; the things I have experienced, dealt with... the hoola hoop now by my knees – good. I had a knee pain yesterday, riding the bike. Now the hoola hoop passed my feet. – it is gone. Finished."

SP: Wonderful. Let us go to Astera, your wise and loving guide.

"Yes, she takes me to some woods, trees – a tunnel of trees, shaded, ... we go to a bridge, a pleasant area. She leaves me to go on my own. Many shades of green, lovely, a nice landscape. Woods and meadows. A little bird sings. I'm traveling...

There is a coach, I'm in it. I'm wearing white gloves, holding a fan; a pretty carriage. I'm alone, content. A light summer outfit, long and airy – not the old heavy dresses ... Rose and pastel, layers of fine cloth, light. I'm young, brown hair, styled up, not like Molly. (Her past life French lady, who was drab, plain.)

I drive through this landscape, content and happy. All is well. I reflect upon my life. ... I'm an important person? Wealthy. I'm in a good mood, and why not?! I'm a 23-year-old, or 25. A lovely area. I enjoy wealthy circumstances, like nice dresses and fancy shoes, – they are tied up; fine gloves, jewelry in my hair. I'm slender, pretty. Sybille.

I have recently accomplished something. Good.

This area ... similar to Molly's France ... it could be France. A large manor house, gray. I don't live there, do I? (Her modern and modest present self could not imagine such a thing.) I arrived. There is a statue, fountain, at the entrance – very pretty. Not a palace, but a villa, a manor, no towers. I ascend the wooden steps, and there is an elaborate interior, with a red carpet. Familiar ... all known somehow. I go upstairs, open a door, enter. My mother sits there, and greets me. She drinks tea, a porcelain service set with delicate flowers. I sit opposite her. We are in an elegant room, nicely decorated. I look around. French windows; below them are chairs, there is also a place for chairs in a circle. On the right, a bookcase. - gestures - There is another door to yet another room beyond; a reading room, lovely, with a view to a garden with flowers, nice trees... I'm cheerful, happy for some reason. ... I live here. I was somewhere, and my mother wants to know everything. I look around first, and now I sit by the window with her. We talk. ... my mother is also happy, pleased for me. She kisses my forehead, proud of me. – Why? I accomplished something. – A feeling I am free; or freed from something. There was an old promise of betrothal, and I couldn't go through with it. It wasn't right. I met with the gentleman. He was courteous, perhaps disappointed, but stoic. It was an important meeting, and a civil agreement. Good. I can now relax. I will now have the freedom to do what I want. I can read, these are my books.

My chest feels strange, however.

Some weeks later a new event. When? … beginning of the 20th century? Is this possible? The clothing is right. 1900s, early. I'm still young. I am told that a man in an elegant, tailored suit has arrived. He should come inside. ... He has come to see me, to talk to me. A young man, a gray outfit. I welcome, receive him. He has a staff in one hand, his hat in another; he's wearing gloves. Is he fidgeting? Could this be embarrassing? I don't know him so well. Perhaps he has a message? Yes. Let us go outside, I say. We go out together, through the door, off to the left, a park like space on our estate. He wants to tell me something. This must be important. I feel strange – in my body...

We do not walk. We're at the park entrance, stand before each other. What does he want to say? … Someone is sick. This person sent him, and wants me to visit. I have a bad feeling.… This is someone I know well, an important person. I'm worried. I will depart immediately. I leave the man, thank him, go to the house. I'm afraid … I call for my carriage and go. This person is dying. I go inside. - emotional, shaking -

I'm alone... with this news. - left-hand over heart -

I shake, go upstairs. Oh my God... what now. - tears -

I go to the dying woman … strange, motherly... the same woman? So familiar. No, this one has grey hair, not brown... she is in a poorer room. I feel she is a near relative,... I feel – she is like my real mother. She is poor, lives in modest circumstances, and I live in that fine home. What is going on? - still emotional -

I sit by her bed, take her hand. I love her … She is dying. - cries -

She tells me, and I believe... she *is* my real mother. And she worked in the big house. My father is the husband of the woman in the fine house. This poor woman ... gave me away. I grew up as the wealthy daughter. Their daughter. And this woman ... she was dear, so loving, pretended she was my nanny. She loved me so, that I know. I loved her the whole time. But now I know the truth.

Why did she tell me this? Now?! She says it was the best for me. She wanted a good life for me. She is dying and it is time to know... the truth. The lady of the house could not have children, but this woman could. She loved me as a mother. Our servant. I loved my nanny.

But it is all a lie!? How could this arrangement be? All lies.

Then she dies... now! Just as I know the truth.

She asked for my forgiveness. I belong to her, and to them. She wants me to know, she wants me to help the poor. Don't be like the other rich, the high and mighty. Think of the working class.

... Now I'm not so certain. I'm shaken. I love her. That was good. That was real. But... things are not as they seem. Appearances can deceive. This is good, ultimately. And now she is dying. She loved me so. And I her. She smiles. She has little pain; dying comfortably.

... It was an affair. And the 'lady of the house' decided to have or keep the child. She wanted one ... of her own. My mother, this mother, accepted it. It would be the best for me. My father belonged to the best class, a noble. My mother could never give me that.

... and so it was arranged.

...

I'm in the library, as before. I write - tears - this touched me so deeply. She loved me so much. This has awakened so many thoughts and feelings. I have to write it out. Express it. However, I can't share this with my milieu. They would not understand, perhaps even react or shun me, us.

There is so much injustice! Façades. Social classes! This society. Such pain, injustice! And we are born that way?! People don't deserve such fates. ... My mother did not deserve poverty, by birth! So many thoughts... I write.

I'm not angry with my parents, no. I'm clear, it all made sense. But the bigger picture – what injustice! ... that a woman would give away her baby, deny her role, so that her child would have a better life; pretending...

So, my eyes are now open! I see more of the false society. I have a piece of the truth. I want to change things – but I do not know what to do. ...

I like this life. I appreciate the things I have ... but I feel guilty somehow. My (noble) mother was a good and loving person. She raised me as her own, loved me.

I want to write this down, perhaps to awaken others. Possibly others will understand. My mother, my poor mother, is a part of me. Society has erected barriers, fences, and there are the haves and the have-nots.

...

Many men are interested ... I'm waiting for a great love, the right man. I want more. I'm popular in my society. I believe the right one has not appeared. I know, at my age others have already married. I do not have the need or worry that I must marry. The right one will come. –

...

I am pregnant. I have a big belly. Happy, I'm so happy. I'm 30, not so young, in the same garden. Huh? I didn't leave? No, I am visiting.

I found my peace. A nice man is by my side. We love each other. He's a bit older. He's 40, I'm 30. He understands me. I told him everything. I feel a total acceptance. We live in trust. He understands me. This is good. And now I expect a child. Very nice, and fulfilling. What is also good: I write a lot. My husband supports this, stands by me. This man, my husband, is not so rich. Our home is not so big. Not so rich, but not poor. He has a career, a doctor or adviser. A good profession, earns well. We don't live like I used to. No receptions, nothing lavish, not aristocratic. We are not with the society people; not poor either. I am content. This is better than marrying someone from the upper class who is 'proper.' I am half-half after all. So it is good. ... I decided I will not have a nanny. I will raise my own child.

My husband supports that. We live in a brick house with a red roof. A nice little garden. A good life. We are very happy. My first 'me' was rich; this is the now me. A new family – we three. This life is so good.

I visit my parents, walk in their fine garden. I guess at some point I will inherit my parents' property, probably; but I will do something different with the house and estate. My parents are fine and fit. We all get along well. We love each other and they are happy for me. No talk of inheritance now, for my parents are alive, healthy. ... Perhaps the house can be a hospital, or some other public building.

Our life is fine. We have everything we need. I don't need or miss the high society. I'm content.

...

I'm 50 or 55 ... one would say an elegant woman, still attractive. I have my man by my side. Two kids, a girl, actually a woman, and a son. They are grown. There is a garden, our place,... they visit us. ... Life is still good. We have such a harmonious life. I love him even more than before. I'm still cultured and good looking. We are proud of our children. They have studied, they are educated. My son has a good career. My daughter is studying still. ... a very nice life. Fulfilled. And now I lay down, tired or ill. A heaviness in my bones.

- dies -

At this point I know my client, Audrey, and how she comes up with reasons why she cannot succeed. She has argued in the past to stay small, both in her everyday life and even in trance, in Spirit. She has now recalled a fine life with a wise and level-headed woman, Sybille. In this next phase, after death and in the Spirit World we will have some opportunities to break this negative self-talk. The interesting thing here is that a companion and an advocate for her in Spirit will be this past life personality. How cool is that? We continue: ...

– after death –

"I feel fine. *Not sad like all the other deaths.*

My husband was there, at the end. It was peaceful... I float. I will meet my love again. I know this., so it is easy to go. There are – white clouds... I'm embedded in these clouds.... peaceful, happy. My spirit guide Astera is with me. She gives me a wand – a magic wand?"

(I suggest some good advice for Audrey at this important time. This wisdom comes from her soul and from past personality Sybille, with her guide Astera attending.)

Astera: Use your wand – you have the power. You need to integrate all of this. Integrate your past with your present.

Soul: "Things have changed externally. Once Sybille knew the truth, it all came together. Then she met her partner, had a family. ... The first part was nice. But with writing, truth, understanding, and clarification, it all unfolded. Audrey wants to write too."

Audrey: When I write, the world dissolves, I enjoy writing letters, narratives. But this as my career? I don't know. We both love books.

Soul: "Sybille was shaken, and then she grew in awareness. From her emotions she wrote. This part of me, Sybille – was so nice, cultured and harmonious. It was perfect. To be so happy! I as her was fulfilled – I was a friend, mother, daughter, and wife. Perfect."

"Oh, but perhaps too perfect? And far from me," Audrey opines.

SP: This is a wonderful opportunity to hug, meld, and allow Sybille's gifts and strengths to be passed on to Audrey. Will you accept that gift?

- cries, tears - "*She gave me her inkwell.* I am so touched, ... but I can't take it. No. She was happy. I am not her. This desire in me ... to be her or to have her fine qualities, her looks? I don't think I can. There are many lives, personalities. Who am I? Now I know the many faces a woman has. And how much luck plays into things."

SP: Sybille learned of her true mother – a poor woman. Now you Audrey can see your past self as Sybille, a type of "mother" to you too – an attractive wealthy one, as your heritage.... Will you accept this?

(After a little coaxing, the shy Audrey accepts.)

"Astera is here; we are under a tree that blossoms. On a bench, she hugs me. She says, 'Go your way, your path, with courage. This is the most important thing. Have courage.' She is by me. She says... her strength is my strength. - cries -

I should simply take the first step. She will accompany me. However, ... I must want this."

SP: Great, let her know that indeed you want this, and deserve it. From time to time you can reach out to your guide and reinforce this new compact. Perhaps your soul can give you a sign that you are on the right path?

"Yes. A light body sensation. A *floating* in my chest, a meditative relaxation, peaceful. A feeling that all is well. The wand is in my hand. 'Go and do your magic. You can do it!' she says.

She gave me confidence. I'm on a right path. I hear, 'Use the power and go. Let it flow on through me. Allow it.' Astera says, *'It doesn't matter which path you begin; you will eventually be on the right path. It is not important what you do, but how you do it. Do it with heart, with feeling, take those steps. Don't let the head worry. Take the first steps. Do it. Go!'*

She is wise. She can't magically do it for me, but she can give me the wand and I can use her energy. It is for me to do it. It depends on me."

Wow, what a Great pep talk, from her wise spirit guide, her past life personality, and invisible companions; all watchers and guides – incarnated or not. And a fulfilling end to so much cosmic, spiritual work over several lifetimes. Through reading, intention and prayer she has battled, and loved/accepted, her shadow jealous side this past year; now it is a minor irritation. I sense more of that Buddhist detachment and perspective. Audrey is reading and writing, studying for a new profession. She is on her way. Blessed be!

"☾,☽"

˜ 13 ˜

Spirit Guides & Angelic Help

My client is relaxed, smiling. It looks like a visit to someplace divine. ...

"It is so peaceful here. ... It looks like the Sun coming through the clouds – such a light! Almost blinding – like a mirror reflection of light. So bright. ... There is a crystal, dark blue and peaceful white... Looks like a cave but very small. A being too... It is flying left to right, moving. I match the pace, we fly, dart around. Fun.... We're playing tag. Ha!"

I wondered if this was her spirit guide, and it was. Oftentimes there are these lovely and inspired meetings with advanced souls, who are ready to play, or to show something significant, or to beam their love, light and wisdom. With other soul guides deep feelings come. Awe and inspiration. For instance, a male client had just left a simple life as a wood carver. He was taken in as an orphan in a past life by a kind old man. Now we are in Spirit, after death, and he just discovered that this old man reincarnated as his beloved brother Ron.

" ... Ron and I – we are in the same soul family, a group. ... Someone is missing though. ...Wait – a very bright one, beaming strongly; Pulling me in! I feel... Love! - cries -

It is so strong! My Spirit guide! - emotional -

He says, 'keep going'? No, 'Pass it on! *Pass on the Love.*' Yes. Now a beautiful rainbow forms. I get now the name of this spirit guide. Shiera = light or light body. *Feminine, also Venus.* Other words too... Shiera Venus. Behind her, there is light everywhere. Lovely. Lights … they shine on me like spotlights. It feels like they want to fill me with light. I don't see me, just the light coming to me. Other souls are here too. Another three. No names. They stay. They shine and smile. Three beaming souls. I hear a voice, 'Find yourself.'

A change – a shift is felt."

SP: Lovely. Please find a magic mirror – what does your soul look like?

"… very big. Turquoise, rainbow colors. Nice. … They build a circle. Others here too. - left fingers moving - Like a chain going down!? Many here. Nice, and yet a bit scary – there's so much energy. But it goes down… a chain hanging… A karmic chain connected down – somewhere below. A way through … it goes to the Earth. The chain remains, today. And there is a dome over it. Like a sacred covered well. The Source.

All is a part of the whole. All is connected, like links on this chain."

On one level, the goddess Venus, or was it one of her devotees or maidens, was manifest as a guide – a very high being. What a blessing. This earth personality had the privilege of seeing or perceiving the cosmic chain of life and coming to be. Marvelous. She held on to this lovely image in her meditations and reflections. It seemed to help her not only to stay grounded, but to "see" where our ultimate thoughts and deeds were going – strait up to heaven. She was connected!

₪

I worked with an interesting and intuitive woman named Sola. She surprised me when she was in Spirit, for she appeared as an old wise woman, an adviser. She was bit of a newbie on Earth, however. This did not fit into my experience. This exploration began because Sola is pulled to a land, a place in Europe, for some reason. Amsterdam. She wanted to know, Was she there in a past life? She is fascinated with Amsterdam, the Dutch – even her email is Amsterdam. So I ask her in trance about it …

"It was Home. My first life, and very pleasant. ... I get memories ... on a street, dusty, dirty. There are many children. I'm a child, a girl. I hear my name, Aagtje, ... I see blond curls. Small, slender, 6 years old. Neighborhood kids here. My sibling are yet too small. In a city. Amsterdam I believe.

...

Now I'm 16. Ball clothing, pretty. Better conditions it seems. Nice. I'm at a ball. Still very slender. Now I've long blond hair, it is up and styled. Blue eyes. A pretty woman. I'm fun, playful, with many friends and admirers. I'm interesting, and entertaining. Yes, popular. There are many young men here, but there's one I like a lot. ... He's tall, dark blond hair, ... nice eyes. A light beard. Wearing a uniform.

...

I'm having a baby. A girl.

I'm married to that same man. I'm 22. So happy. We're doing quite well. He is an officer. We live near my parents in Amsterdam. It is around 1660.

...

A long life. I'm old. Grandchildren in my life. Lots of people around me. Oh my goodness, it's my birthday! I'm 80. My husband is still alive. All in all a good, warm, pleasant life."

SP: Are there some people here reincarnated today? (From Aagtje's happy life.)

"Yes. One of Aagtje's sons = is Harold. (Best friend for the past 30 years.) How nice. And Aagtje's grandson = my Papa today. Well this explains a lot. Our roles seem reversed.

(then, after death) Foggy for some time... then I was Marisa, in Switzerland." (Cool, clear chronologies of past lives. A good subject indeed. Before we move on to that Swiss life I have her pause and reflect. In this in-between place we can get guidance. I look at her list of questions.)

SP: Any advice from the other side?

"You're on the right path. Doing things right. *You are a loving person, so next life it will be better.*"

(In Spirit she gets a blessing, reviews past lives, and experiences releasing of old issues.)

SP: Dear Spirit Guide, I would like to ask for a mirror; what does her soul look like?

I'm old. I have long gray hair, and wrinkles; a ready smile. Feminine.

(I'm surprised. Her 1st life was in the 17th Century, but here in Spirit she seems to be an old soul. So I ask about lives elsewhere.)

I've only incarnated here, on the earth. I believe I've incarnated only five or six times. (Hmm. An old soul, with no alien or hybrid lives! So this soul began incarnating when she was already advanced or matured. Unusual.)

The more I'm incarnated the more I'll remain in the Spirit world. I feel happier there. I am there for others. (In Spirit.) I'm an adviser. A counselor. My soul name is Lucia = peace and light."

SP: Any advice for Sola on the earth?

"Keep working. Gather your friends, resolve conflicts and fights. And strive for peace."

Good and wise. We return, integrate and discuss. She is a peacekeeper and confidante in her social group. She is the glue, and a quiet guide. She doesn't teach or preach, but she could. This was interesting and unique case, clear, and karmic. I find it reassuring that advanced souls are incarnating with us here "below." We certainly need these higher beings. I sometimes wish they would intervene more, but they are tuned into a bigger plan than I know about, which is humbling.

The following trance-personal journey unfolded on day two of our sessions. He was a good subject; he reacts especially well to the idea of our divine antenna aligning with our spinal cord. The session was fascinating, for it unfolded on several layers, with many spiritual beings aiding the process:

"… There are two new colors, and the violet from yesterday. Violet is in front of me, my soul guide. The bluish orbs are to the side; then there are one or two others. The violet soul has a white jacket, no feet – does not need them here… but floating. He smiles, a bit impish. Yet I feel a certain distance.

Now I feel a warm energy over my left hand, which is on my chest. Wow, the violet soul touched my hand, a warm greeting. … The blue soul is a supporter, like a manager, and masculine. I get a look of acknowledgment. (Hmm. A junior soul guide? That happens from time to time.)

I get an 'All is well. Take it easy.' … a protective feeling. My guide has a blue cape, and opens it to take me in. I feel warm and protected. Then another soul or light comes... a yellow-green, behind me; it is like yesterday. Mom. She and the other soul are in the background, like a choir. Friendly and supportive.

(His hands cover his heart. We have been doing inner child work today, going back to several ages that were difficult. I give suggestions for healing and integration, especially since we are in the presence of wise and spiritual beings.)

I sense that me, under this great cloak, is with the 4 year old, and the 10 and 14 year olds … various parts and pieces of me and my past. A team, together. These include those special moments, those difficult times – frozen, or as if they were particular people. Slices of me... held in moments of time. There are many – ten to twenty parts! … small kids, youth, adults, business experiences … they are becoming more transparent … Together they are building a new shell or form. At first the little boy became transparent, then the others, merging and becoming a great balloon, see-through colors, diffuse.

(Excellent! A soul-level integration session – much faster than earth therapy!)

The blue soul is in the shadows, watching and overseeing this; we are in his energy field. He is – like a mother, holding us all. So he's parental, masculine but with that softness and tenderness that mothers have. It seems this great mass, this balloon of an integration, is becoming more congealed, a structure or form, bluish. Now two blue souls – one light and the other dark blue, and I go – where am I? With them … but I see these two blue souls, one is closer to me. Am I the light blue soul? Another I? First I felt me, then the group, now a new I, more neutral. My 'I' identification is less. As if I observe all this from outside." (Ah, he is attuning to his soul self – this Buddhist like perspective often comes from an advanced soul.)

SP: Perhaps you can use a mirror here, to see your new integrated self, and your eternal soul.

"I sense two silhouettes. One shines with many colors. The other is a grayish shadow. At the beginning I thought I could go back and forth, between these two, in the mirror. .. seeing both. I do. The gray structure is a stylized person, a stick man. The other is colorfully impressive, a lapis lazuli with black, bright reddish, green – many colors, but blue is the dominant color. Like a picture, and not a statue. 20 – 30 cm wide, one meter high. I can look from one to the other, the bluish orb, and the gray stick man. ... I move or melt into the blue self. This gray man is a construct, a personality to conform. Then I look at the shadow man – we send this 'supposed to' social man away. I feel a pat on my back from the violet soul. - jerks -

I notice I changed just now. I felt it as if I had sent 'him' away, but it was a part of me! This is disconcerting! Like a jacket I took off, but closer. Visceral. There is a quiet transformation… The gray man becomes brighter – white now, and golden … now coming out from the violet cape. It is disappearing, or changing … Now I stand alone – a blue being. I am now longer and larger. The gray one is now round and white and gold, a ball of potential – a piece of energy, not standing alone. What can I do, make, with this? I feel like an artist. ... I will add something bluish to it."

SP: Fascinating, you can co-create your earth persona. With the violet and dark blue souls, perhaps you can be inspired about what to develop, to make?

"Yes. I am pulled to the two souls, plus the parents in the background ... I sense the violet in front, an authority. I feel a great respect. Blue is by my side, like a brother, more familiar, and more similar to me. I feel a friendship, like being free or freedom. 'We will do it together,' I hear,... a friendly support.

... I just received something white, from above, and to the right side of my head. It moves around, looking for an entrance into my being, through the head. (He now moves his head, which we had earlier described as part of his personal antenna.) Now it's coming. A connection ... from above. It is diffused, a milky white, bright energy.

The Violet light speaks: *Let it come into being, into development. Give it time.*

The gray man turned into potential energy, and now it is like a golden crystal, and a fine cloth, whatever; ready for use, in any way or form I choose. *I can create my life. I can form a successful persona* here upon the earth. Satisfying, and creative."

...

And he has. He integrated not only past lives but modern concepts and conditioning on how he should act and be in his society, not some construct or stick man. He was aided by souls on the other side. I knew I was in the presence of wise and adept souls, so I mostly kept notes and observed. When all is unfolding smoothly, I can "stand" on the side and appreciate the divine guidance and wisdom. I watch and learn. It was a pleasure to be a witness to this high level integration. I know he is going to do well in life. He has a lot of help on the other side.

You do too. Just ask.

~ **14** ~

Messages from the Other Side

> I am an old man, an ancient one, and I have been many things,
> lived and died many times, and loved as often as possible.
> And I tell you the gods exist within the limits of every thing
> — stone or vegetable, woman or man. Even the red clay the
> potter molds hides their essence. That a creature or thing
> exists makes it one with god. Blessed are we all.
>
> *Becoming One of the Ancients*, from "Awakening Osiris"
> - chapter 43, by Normandi Ellis

If you have followed this cosmic journey with me this long, you know that it is a grand, mystical, inspirational and multi-dimensional sojourn for souls experiencing, fumbling, learning, innovating, growing and evolving. This goes for groups and families incarnating, learning and sharing together, which form associations, communities, religions, societies and nations. We are all on this path. The Divine Order shines forth, and our own marching orders become known and expressed, mixing compassion, love and lessons that are foretold or promised in Spirit/Heaven. Those inventors and scientists who make breakthroughs in technologies and aid us to comprehend Order in the universe, and those visionaries who describe a better world are "remembering" (or maybe downloading) notions and innovations that can help us to advance. Beings who have lived in advanced civilizations then share their visions with us, again aiding progress on this blue sphere, Gaia. These lessons are intuited and passed along (via these individual journeys, mystical and near death experiences, and divine revelations), aiding us upon the earth to improve our lot, to help us to develop and to thrive. As we attune and heed, we are following our missions, listening to our voices, and passing along the inspired information. Thank goodness. Thank God.

Over the decades I have been privy to much wisdom and guidance channeling through my intrepid sojourners. Where shall I begin?

Major Messages from the Other Side:

- ❖ keep on the path
- ❖ do not fear; follow the Light
- ❖ all will be well, eventually
- ❖ trust in Spirit
- ❖ work together for the good - cooperate
- ❖ create the Field around you; expand it and include others
- ❖ ask for divine Help
- ❖ honor all sentient life
- ❖ follow the Golden Rule, or at least the Silver [22]

Great principles. How can we integrate the wisdom? How can we speed up the process? Each of us must set individual goals, our Ideals, and strive to bring them to fruition: what are our ideals about right and wrong, about marriage, truth, fairness, about family and society, about compromise and cooperation, about individuality and teamwork? What are our ideals on these various themes and subjects? As we set our ideals, we co-create our purpose upon this planet – and beyond. This creates positive karma. We need just to pray, attune, meditate and grow towards the greater good. This to remember – As above, so below.

May we listen, learn and evolve!

---

[22] The Silver Rule asks one to refrain from harming others. Confucius (551-479 B.C.), the wise Chinese philosopher, declared "What you do not wish yourself, do not unto others."

"Thy kingdom come, Thy will be done in earth, as it is in heaven."

The Bible, Matthew 6:10, King James Version

I've been listening in on inspired (and tranced) conversations for many decades. I've learned that it would be advantageous to pay heed to the wisdom from souls. My next question is this, however: Which souls? Not all disembodied beings are wise and loving souls. "By their fruits will you know them." (Bible, Matthew 7:16) Some young souls or unevolved people, once dead, may not have the answers that we may want. Conversely, some wayward and abrasive people down here, once transitioned into the spiritual world, are surprisingly clever. Some of my clients are astonished to meet friends and relatives in Spirit who have different personalities than their earthly ones. To their surprise, the spiritual selves or souls are often much smarter and loving than on Earth. Yes, things are clearer up there. My client Sophie, from the chapter on Healing, remembered another life as a mother who lost her knight husband. She was a country girl and through her marriage to him she came to know more about court life, which had some intrigues and petty theater. She tried to fit in, but it was not her style. We go to an emotional memory – now she is dying, and worried about leaving her young children:

"... I have a high fever – I can barely breathe. I'm 43... laying there. So weak. Oh, what will happen to my children? - dies -

I'm somewhere else... there seems to be lots of things around me. I can't see, but feel them. I'm floating... its brighter. I can breathe. How Free. Nice!

... One of my kids is now little Sarah, Lois's friend (her young daughter's friend). She is four years old. No wonder I feel so close. ... From here I learned that the kids will be fine.

I also learned – *It's okay to be who you are; do not try to be someone else. You don't have to fit in with the "fancy people." Life was good at the farm, and more honest.*

… Look, here comes my Dad, so happy and easy going. Ha, not like now! He is normally very critical. He tells me, I have to be myself. *Just enjoy life. If I'm happy, I'll attract others – and make them happy too.* Hmm. Funny that he is telling me this! He is so grumpy. He should take this advice too.

… Now my girl, Lois, is here – and she is really happy! She gives me a hug, smiling. She's happy to see me. Then she tells me something in earnest. *'We have to be in this life together to do something - for others.'* I intuitively know she is right. We have chosen to be of service."

◇

"Turn then to those things within. Know the law and then apply it daily. Not by some great thing. Smile often. Speak gently. Speak kindly. Go out of the way to do a kind deed, and ye will find that He will walk closer with thee, and thy life, thy purpose will become a glorious thing in this experience."

- Edgar Cayce 3376-2

₪

When someone comes to me with questions about money, investments and real estate, I can almost guarantee that Spirit is not much interested in such things. Mercifully, most people don't ask about worldly things, probably because they intuitively know that there are other priorities in Heaven. Over the years I have learned that there are *other* reasons for material questions. I recall a lady, in trance, floating in Spirit. Sola is somewhat fixated on her home; worried that something might happen to it. When she thinks of her parents, who have both died, she gets emotional. She inherited the house from them, and so there may be some sentimental reasons. In trance I had the opportunity to ask her higher self about it....

SP: Why the periodic worry about the loss of your home?

"This comes from a past life. A house was burnt, so there is a fear of sudden loss, and a helplessness. The fire ... this was the parents' home of my past life as Deborah, who became a ghost. Her parents died in that fire, and she was shocked, shaken."

SP: Let us invite Deborah to the circle for this healing and release.

"I see Lights around her, a vortex. Slowly things lift, like a cleansing... Deborah smiles, then waves."

SP: Great. These are signs that we got through. Is there some advice from Deborah?

"Do not worry about the house. Deborah learned... *It was worse to lose her parents. One can always build a house again. She learned to appreciate people and connections.* Yes, there was certainly fear about losing the home, and a fear of fires; but *people we love are more important.*"

Yes indeed.

Carol sometimes isolates herself, then gets lonely. She is contrary, and works against herself. She gets insights, and then doubts her inspirations. She has a creative intellect, but she can over-think things. I now aid her to slow down the mind. She is in trance ...

"I don't see too many people. I see two... One feels like a teacher – a person of wisdom. One feels like a friend, who winks at me. Huh? It's Kim, my best friend. Am I making this up? We have something in common – we question things. We laugh. Nice to see her as a soul buddy."

- voice changes – her soul guide speaks -

Questioning is good. Carol does this. She will not follow, and then she feels isolated. This aids her in the universe, but not on the earth.

This pattern is rather confrontative for all concerned.

Carol: "This ... teacher is masculine. I feel I'm making this up, but okay. He's silver, gray, and he has purple skin. It or he glows. Wild, but colorful. He's very calm. This is a contrast, – some teachers are joking. ... He is broad-minded, expansive, he possesses a knowing. No jokes however. He is a rock; an anchor who steadies. He lets me do my own work – he's mostly 'hands off'. He has stepped in, however, from time to time, in Carol's life. He will send ideas... and then, suddenly, I get thoughts and inspirations! I'm feeling highly tingly right now.... He is laughing at me!"

SP: A physical sign; you're not making this up!

"Ha! – That's true. ... He is huge, letting me get bigger next to him. He holds me like a teenager who had done something well. This is not patronizing. He talks to me. '*Be gentle with yourself. Be kind, and patient. You have time; You are loved. You have much to offer. You have much to give.* It is okay that it is *a quiet giving.*' Carol feels it should be bigger, more obvious or seen. Then she gets images and impulses, memories. She passes people on the street, for instance, offering wishes and prayers for them – peace, good, and plenty. Quiet blessings. So ... she doesn't have to change the world. She offers these prayers. ... But she wants something 'Seen, demonstrative.' - Once this idea comes there is an answer. *Trust that it's there!*

My Spirit Guide's name – Yamm. Ya- mm, – which means peace & joy, and shades of other qualities."

SP (recognizing she is in touch with a higher source): Ya-mm, can you address Carol's loneliness?

"This may not leave her. She asks questions that very few people understand. She has 'opinions'."

Then Carol adds, "Yeah, Hippies are too 'spiritual', for instance. Not my style."

Spirit Guide: When she accepts, really accepts, then she will be at peace. However, her 'community' may not be fulfilled, at least as she expects it. This sense of belonging may not come from others, ... Peace however *can* come. *The more she comes to herself, the more she can be with the All,* and then she will be connected... ultimately.

SP: Could you please address her physical pains?

"As Carol grows more peaceful within, so shall she BE peaceful within (her body). Thoughts affect her nerves, and health. Her body is strained, and damaged. We couldn't give her a 'fit' body. She is too quick, flies too fast. So *we 'slow her down', so that she can smell the roses.*"

SP: Interesting. Good for her to know. Can you advise Carol about her children? She worries about them.

"Their handicaps will balance out. They came to earth with issues. All this is necessary for their journeys. They are experienced souls, and given obstacles to aid them. As a parent, this is very challenging, but *this* is good because it slows her down. She has to stop and think. They will be all right, when *they* wish it. *People do not come isolated to the world. Contracts are made. The past confronts.*

What they do, are choices. Their lessons are not of career, money and worldly things, but resilience, love,- in your daughter's case, self-love.

Carol is resisting me! (Ha, just like her, arguing with this wise soul.) ... Patience, let it be. These are choices made by your daughter. She may make choices that are not healthy. Right now your role as parents are not there as 'guides'. They have a different relationship with the world. It is good to let go, to let it be. Be patient. … Her daughter is rejecting the bond. This hurts, it's hard to watch. We know. Remember, *Patience and Acceptance.*

… Carol hates these answers. Think! It is not all doom and gloom! One can always choose. There is always choice. Her daughter can choose. Meanwhile, her son Freddy is choosing not to be Freddy.

Carol doesn't like these answers; she wants a breeze, a light wind. A magic wand. Sorry. *Those challenges are the reason to be here.* No one likes to hear that."

SP: She has chronic fatigue – what to do? Can this be counter-acted or resolved?

"Stop eating sugar. Yes, I know, she will smack me for this. She likes it. She thinks it gives her energy. This is all temporary, a quick fix. She needs to improve her sleep. *Sleep is critical to the human body. Furthermore, in sleep communications are given. Resolutions and inspirations come. So this is beyond biological.*

She has more energy than others who have chronic fatigue. She bikes, for example, and pushes it. – She doesn't like to hear that either. Ha. We're laughing. There is so much here that she doesn't like!

Just remember this: *We are loved. All of us. All of life. We are Love, and go back to Love.*

Whenever Carol feels negative emotions like deceit, doubt, criticism, etc., she leaves her path. She must strive to find her way back, to Who she is."

Her partner, also in Spirit, adds, "Much can be done later. Patience."

Guide: She must keep to the path, the Obelisk of Love. … She can gently come back. A little better, with gentle guidance.

Amen. Carol had to sift through the mental fog and contemplate the wisdom, but she also knew that all would be fine, in the end. Patience is part of the process. The wisdom for her spoke loud and clear; and so can it be for all of us, if only we would listen.

Donald, who has seen both the dark and the light, is in a trance, in Spirit, and there is a good connection to his higher self. From his questions I ask him, or his soul, for advice.

SP: Let's talk about the B&B and your work with your partner.

"I need to talk to another soul. I have my own ideas, you know. I need confirmation."

SP: Great. So, your spirit guide? (It takes a smart person to know when to ask someone wiser.)

- he places a hand over his heart -

"I feel more space in my chest. Breathing is very important. A reminder! Wow. There is so much inspiration ... I don't know where to start. So much. Now comes the autumn – and then the winter. My, our life is like a ship, a voyage. Winter is a good time to dock the ship. It is time to give it a tune-up. Make it strong – tsunami safe. This is an important rejuvenating time! Be very clear with the crew – those near and dear. Where is this boat heading? Reassess the commitment. You will find it right in the name, RejuveNation (Name of the B&B). Renew. Time for changing, rewiring. Ask for a commitment from the people in the house – and those around. In your home, your abode, your circle – there is no sect, and few rules. Tell those who are interested, 'We offer Freedom. Space to Be.' ...for this is the truth.

So, commitment is on another level. (He appears to go deeper.)

Blessings to you from us, and for the Souls on Earth. Patience. When my partner and I are together – people enjoy being around us. We do not have great teachings, really nothing new. Yes, she is a therapist, with ideas. We are a good couple. People like us. We dance, hug, care. Together we have awesome ideas – yes.

Timber, my partner, has special skills... In our circle couples are important. In service, for all – this is beautiful. Free love is okay; nothing against that. We however are a confirmed couple. Commitment is important to us. Together we create something special. This dynamic can be felt. ... I can get up and Go with this. I carry this idea – and sail with it. ... We need courage for the next steps. Security is in our thoughts, of course. That is how the game is played. I get money from a local job. I would like to be of service in a different way. Retirement is coming. Changes are in the air. I have to make things happen. ... We let imagination sink in. Imagine a new world – that attracts us! That certainly drives me: I came here to Earth to celebrate, experience and connect. – Something big is in the air. *Soon there will be a Celebration of a new human, an awakening.* ... Look at these so-called miracles. I think about serious illnesses, and then spontaneous remissions. It can happen. It does happen. Interventions happen. There is a point where this is needed. I fantasize about this change, and an image comes: God's hand comes from the galactic center! We are blessed. Renewed. Awakened! He/It speaks to us: 'Everything is okay. Be glad.' We are blessed. I also hear, 'You are forgiven.' So, as God does that for us, we can do that for each other. And so it can begin.

  – Then comes the party! And look, Jesus is at the table, the feast. ... We had previews in Atlantis. We're all here – gathered, again. Wonderful! When consciousness, every moment, is Blessed, we can awaken, then we get it! ... I get excited with this! Yahoo! The inner child is exuberant. Ah, I expand my lungs. Brahma is God manifesting his creation, which is an out-breath. We are at the point between the breaths; - the journey out, and in. What a wonderful moment! Here we are. – What a trip. I'm thankful."

Teresa was wealthy in a past life. She had good taste, organized parties and events. Today, in her restaurant, she is cooking and serving. Her clientele are happy and this establishment is thriving. In her development she is growing and evolving. Now she is floating ...

"My hands are hot. ... I'm in a tunnel. I'm traveling very fast. Stars move. White ones. I know where the Center is. I see a perspective from up high – 180 degrees wide. White ... some patterns. Beautiful stars. Up there *it is all One. You are part of it All.*

I am observing. I froze the picture. Then I look at it from different angles. I am using some old camera, gold colored. One can see through it. The device is symbolic. *Stop and focus. Perceive things from many angles.* Not so fast! And not so high up that you can't see the details! Perspective, and patience."

SP: Excellent. Any more advice, especially for the next phase?

"Be the light. Be the star. Be the Light. This life is yours."

"☾,☽"

It is always a pleasure and honor to be with wise souls. I have learned many things. There is a consistent message that comes through. As we view the big picture, we as souls are experiencing interplanetary sojourns *in-between* lives, and this goes way beyond the borders of this solar system. Our souls travel out to the stars and galaxies, as well as in other dimensions attuned and aligned in the great journey of life. Furthermore, as we grow in consciousness of this divine plan, we can bring the wisdom back to our daily living, and to our families, friends and communities. Listen to that still small voice. The wise and loving Order intuited in Spirit can be a model of how we interact here on the Earth, our dear Gaia. A living organism works as a whole, together. All lives matter, all lives here are *in* matter, and all lives will transform in death. And so we hold on to the paradox – honor life and not be afraid of death, which is but a transition. Things are in movement, flux. We all can live harmoniously upon this beautiful planet. It is possible to bring to

Earth a eutopian ideal of living together in vitality, diversity, peace and creativity.

As above, so below. This has great implications, and promise.

Be the vision!

"What a man can be, he must be.

This need we call self-actualization."

- Abraham Maslow (1 Apr 1908 – 1970) American psychologist

~ 15 ~

Advice for the Future

We may have all come on different ships,

but we're in the same boat now.

– Martin Luther King, Jr.

(born Michael King Jr., 15 Jan 1929 – 1968)

My client wonders why her children left home early and maintain minimal contact. She gets lonely. Yes, her daughter will hardly speak to her, and she doesn't exactly know why. We explored the roots. In a past life long ago my client was a poor, over-worked factory worker caring for her parents. However, she felt trapped in that past life in Belgium. She did something about it, freed herself – and left her parents; but was followed by the burden in her heart. In Spirit, her guide tells us that this lady "forgot her parents, abandoned them, and took off ... and did not look back. She lived for herself. ... Here we are now. Her children left her in turn. And so there are similarities today." I hope for resolution in our session, so I ask...

SP: It is time for healing, yes? Can you forgive yourself?

- cries ... a slow healing, letting go -

"It feels like a pressure has left. I feel I can breathe better now. There are happy orange streaks. Nice. (Hands over solar plexus, then relaxed, smiling like the Mona Lisa.)

SP: Advice for the future?

"Begin anew. Give love. *Do something lovely.* Be cheerful."

♥

"The soul is dyed the color of its thoughts.
Think only on those things that are in line with your principles
and can bear the light of day.
The content of your character is your choice.
Day by day, what you do is who you become.
Your integrity is your destiny
... it is the light that guides your way."

- Heraclitus of Ephesus, Greek philosopher (6th Cen. BCE)

A grand and important task that we have to grow into is the one lauded in ancient Greece – "To know thy self." That is one of our greater missions – to understand who we are. This was specifically described by Cayce in the following way: *to know ourselves, to accept what we find, and then to appreciate ourselves.* According to the Cayce Readings, it is said that very, very few people appreciate being with themselves. Poetically, Cayce declared that "the personality and the individuality do not cast the same shadow." Yes, some people are uncomfortable in their skins, and feel a dissonance. Many do not perceive themselves clearly. Some people are off purpose, not in sync with their goals and ideals. I am reminded again of one of the early definitions of "sin." = an axle that was out of, or off, center. Through setting our Ideals, we come into a personal cooperation, and this keeps us on our divine Purpose. I've interviewed hundreds of old souls and wise beings.

I took notes.

Teresa is an older soul who has experienced many lives. She appreciates life, nature and beauty. Right now she is tuned in, and tranced out. ...

"I am checking out the area. Such a beautiful sunset. There is a flat area before me, and it is a bit cloudy. I'm an energy, not a body or person. ... I'm in a new place – space, then... I'm back, as the monk,

on the mountain. People come for advice. ... He is multi-faceted, wise and revered. Simultaneously I watch him, from various views. He is at one with this moment. The sunset is glorious. It is perfect out here."
- deep breath -

SP: Excellent. (This sort of moment comes every now and then. I am in the presence of a past self with a lot of wisdom. I decide to ask direct questions of the past life Tibetan monk.) Thank you for your insights. Can you speak to us about this moment, here and now?

"There is always sun after rain. Enjoy the moment and let go.
The water flows out to the ocean.
Teach her not to follow. (Her finger pointing at herself!)
I heard the song 'Arm in arm and fancy free,
Strolling by the deep blue sea.'
Be the ocean. She should run her own course, not follow."

☼

I have learned many things from my own sessions as well as from my clients, including insights and advice for the future. We can all live harmoniously upon this beautiful planet, Gaia. It is actually possible to bring to Earth a eutopian ideal of living together in peace, development and creativity. What a great plan! This implies wise choices and will bring us collectively to some difficult ethical questions as a species. We will have to confront overpopulation, for instance. This overabundance of humans contributes to mass suffering, climate change, starvation, pollution, crime and dozens of other societal ills. As we have Free Will, we are free to have more children, even too many. Spirit stands back, as it were, and waits for us collectively to learn *that* lesson. Our collective *moral* connected with overpopulation could be this: we need to all learn to live with the larger picture in our awareness; we live on a small and beautiful planet with finite resources. Just because we can have sex does not mean that we should be having babies. This is about choices. We could have billions of souls live here on a "tight budget", with rations and frugality, and we could have fewer people living quite nicely on a bountiful planet – living harmoniously with other animals and wildlife. This could be a new Eden. It is our choice. Perhaps the countries that are producing fewer children in the world intuitively (unconsciously) know this. This brings us back to education, and awareness. Karma is not just something we are dealing with from past lives, we are creating karma now.

News flash from advanced planets: other civilizations have dealt with abundance and scarcity, overpopulation and finite resources. They advanced to the time of automatons, robots and technical aids. One of the modern worries of nations is that they are confronted with older populations and fewer young people to care for the elderly. Therefore, keep those kids coming. In other places and planets the answers came – technologies and social design came to their aid. For example, some civilizations left the abomination of slavery because machines did the work more efficiently; the machines did not tire, suffer nor complain. Thus, advancement is not only an arena of spirituality but of technology and development across the spectrum. There are some who believe that technology will take away jobs. Wise souls speaking through my sojourners are not worried about this. In fact, they declare that people don't want jobs, they want the security and material advantages that jobs/money bring. There are other ways, and means, to this end. Technology and automation can and will free us from drudge work, yes, but *we* can free ourselves from limited thinking. Citizens will first collectively organize education and healthcare for themselves, then they will go on to "granting" residences and food for themselves. Then they will recognize that money and finances were constructs, and real security was something that they would *grant upon themselves*, for are we not creating our realities? This may appear like pie in the sky. I've heard time and again, "Act as If". Are we not co-creating here? Do it. Act as if… we were grand manifestors. This will take some time, but Spirit is not limited by time. Wise souls in Spirit are patiently observing and waiting for us to "get it". Waiting.

On the Earth, however, it looks like we have a ways to go. A study of history is a sobering experience. There has been such needless pain and suffering, and for eons. Spirit again is waiting for us to get *that one* too. One day we will organize ourselves – think enlightened societies and political systems, and create just and efficient social unions, or governments. One fact we will have to confront: there are many *young* souls on this earth! Yes, somewhat like a huge board game on earth where the pieces and players are distributed, and the smart players wanting to win the game of life are waiting for their turn. Before we throw the dice, we will have to deal with the social paradox: we are all loved and respected by Spirit, *and* we all can't be captains of great ships nor leaders of large enterprises, or nations. The biggest issue is that the young souls, who don't know better, also have the aggressiveness and impulsiveness to push themselves into positions of power, where they can cause a lot of harm. No, little Donny, you can't drive the family car. No, you shouldn't run for president.

Jesus said that the meek shall inherit the earth; what I intuit from this is that the more humble and quieter old souls would and should inherit, or assume, the power and create through wise guidance the good and just society that we all have been craving since the earliest societies. When a social/political system is crafted that automatically allows, or invites, the more peaceful and circumspect older souls to assume positions of authority, then we will be seeing a better world.

I have received the following from several high beings:

Life is like theater, and we are actors. The audience is Life, other souls, and even God. Life is also like a focus/ study group, and we learn, strategize and plan the next steps in tandem with the troupe. We are confronted with a paradox: this life is indeed fleeting and one life is comparatively small ... but we need to take our roles seriously and do our best. It is said in theater that there are no small roles, only small actors. Do your best. When an opportunity arises in a social context, share your ideals, speak your truth. The world needs your kindness, your voice, and vision. This is the ideal that my team of social focused souls envisioned. Can you imagine?!

"Until one is committed, there is hesitancy, the chance to draw back, always ineffectiveness. Concerning all acts of initiative and creation, there is one elementary truth the ignorance of which kills countless ideas and splendid plans: that the moment one definitely commits oneself, then providence moves too. A whole stream of events issues from the decision, raising in one's favor all manner of unforeseen incidents, meetings and material assistance which no man could have dreamed would have come his way. Whatever you can do or dream you can, begin it. Boldness has genius, power and magic in it. Begin it now."

- Johann Wolfgang von Goethe (28 Aug 1749 – 1832)
German writer, philosopher

Through my clients, studies and work I have learned: It is always important to keep the bigger picture of *purpose* front and center. We need to keep our bearings, based upon our ideals. We are here to grow individually and collectively in consciousness, to evolve and to move towards a certain Unity in Consciousness. We are heading towards the One. We need to know this and to begin acting like *we* are this, and yet a unit of many. We are not alone. We are one united people on a relatively small planet. Let us not forget other sentient life here. Flora and fauna, plants and animals – life is all around us. Let us honor it all, and coexist with all Life.

In the meantime …

Surf the Now.

$$\approx \quad \infty \quad \approx$$

By focusing upon our common Spirit we can form bonds of identity and unity locally and internationally. For this we need a big vision, an alignment with something greater than ourselves. I find it useful to imagine the "body politic" – we as cells in a greater being. Cayce said that we are "as corpuscles in the body of God." Not only are we individuals living and striving in this world, we are individual cells in the body of God. We form groups with other cells and together we are the sinews, muscle, nerves, organs and systems – a larger form and organism is alive... Gaia. For this and other reasons, it is worthwhile to keep in contact with our Soul selves as well as with our other brother and sister cells. Indeed, as we contribute to these larger ideals we are edging ever closer to a harmonious world, a eutopia.

Some ways of keeping in contact with our eternal sparks are to create peaceful environments, get out in nature, enjoy serene or uplifting music and movement, nurturing touch like massage, friendly connections, humor and play, meditation and nature, art and creativity, etc. Acknowledge others, give and receive. Nurture that which needs to be fed. Find joy in children, pets, fun and nature.

Enjoy fulfilling work; express through arts and crafts, building and improving – leaving things, situations and people better than you found them. Group events, social bonding, and cultural creativity can all nurture a broader vision, and a sustainable future of hope and fulfillment. Along the way, Question things. See past the maya of illusion, cultural prejudices and assumptions. Make greater choices. Make up your own Mind, and feed it. Compare ideas given to you with the perennial philosophy, with thoughtful people and with the great visionaries of the past. Hang out with positive and kind brothers and sisters; from there one can get back to the "trenches" of everyday life and ephemeral politics with a feeling of unity, purpose and hope.

"Dance in the moment. Reach down and pull up song. Spin and chant and forget the sorrow that we are flesh on bone. I return to the rhythm of water, to the dark song I was in my mother's belly. We were gods then and we knew it. We are gods now dancing in whirling darkness, spitting flame like stars in the night."

Becoming the Child, from "Awakening Osiris" - chapter 45, by Normandi Ellis

It has been told to me via wise souls – Life is an Adventure. And so, what is this adventure about, and where are we going? We, as souls of the Creator, have had many past lives, and have lived in-between lives, referred by Cayce as interplanetary sojourns. We, as souls, travel to distance planets and dimensions. We journey to distant stars, through time and space. We are given deeds and contracts; we have missions to fulfill! We are born here to grow, experience, and to create. With our Free Wills, we have that power to create, to evolve. We have more power than we know, we are manifestors and co-creators. We are given assignments and tasks to do. These assignments come in many forms: a marriage, a familial relationship, a job or task, a skill to express, a community to connect with, to be of service, and so on. All the while, present-time Earthlings, remember that this third dimension includes patience!

According to Cayce, the general, or universal, aspects of our missions are: 1) to know ourselves, 2) to choose, daily, right and wrong, 3) to follow the pattern of the Christ, and the Golden Rule, as ideals or purpose, and 4) to evolve. With all of this on our cosmic plates, not only are we on the great adventure of Life, but we must be up and doing! An important constant in what we do is aligning with the God of Life and Love.

I hope I have given you a taste of what you already intuitively know: we all are divine beings living and learning here on earth. When we are not incarnating, we are continuing our interstellar lessons far away. We are experiencing cosmic sojourns in-between lives. We live, grow, bond, love, and age, we then die ... or *we think we do*. We actually transform, transcend and carry on – we return to Heaven, to Spirit, and to our loved ones. Free from the material world, our souls travel out to the stars and galaxies, attuned and aligned in the great journey of life. The travels continue, and the lessons. We then incorporate what we have learned and return, reincarnating into the earth. There are a million individual contributions for our living and thriving here on Gaia, the earth, but the basic idea is to bring consciousness into the everyday world and to grow, to evolve.

You are it!

Be good to yourself, to the world around you, and to others.

I wish you blessings on your journey.

Breathe. Be. Awaken.

"☾·☽"

Inner journeys, cosmic sojourns. You are in it. Make the most of it.

The journey for all of us continues...

I wish you blessings on *your* journey.

Goodbye, which is a contraction of "Go(o)d be with ye!"

Stephen

Stephen Russell Poplin, M.A., CHT

past life regressionist, LBL therapist, transpersonal counselor

website: **www.stephen-poplin.com**

~ ~ ~

PS: In the addenda I offer a public service announcement on keeping your thoughts untainted, some intriguing ideas on inter-planetary influences, plus continued reading and more ...

An Innerscape of Stephen Poplin
by Chris Arbo and James Yax

Addenda

Public Service Announcement

How wide is the scope of *hypnotic* suggestion? Let me count the ways. ... It is all around us, and affects everyone. Feel free to review the section titled *The Varieties of Hypnosis* or "The 9 doors of suggestion"... from chapter one. It is my belief that *the majority of the world is hypnotized the majority of the time.* Consider the many ways that "suggestions" can be implanted into our unconscious minds; the variety of entryways into the passive mind are numerous and surprising. Let's take this into the classroom, to the workplace, and to the voting booths...

First we need to understand the subtle mechanism itself. Essentially, when we relax our powers of discrimination, associated with our personal wills, and passively *allow* ideas and notions into our subconscious, we are open to suggestions or conditioning. This discriminating part of the mind is sometimes called the Gateway to the Unconscious. This open gateway happens naturally and is most apparent, and useful, in the way children can quickly learn and adapt to their surroundings. This is an automatic occurrence and part of the learning process. This dynamic of "taking in" our surroundings is not necessarily bad. Our cultures, languages and civilizations are passed on this way. It is fast and fluid and probably vital for the survival of our species to "learn" things rapidly. Children are like sponges, we are told. We are delighted by this open and vital acceptance and curiosity of the world displayed by children. Interestingly enough, adults who maintain this open sense of wonder are labeled naive and gullible. It is quite obvious, however, that, as children open their hearts and minds to their surroundings, sometimes erroneous or even damaging ideas are mixed in with good intentions and unexamined assumptions. Thus, this openness, sometimes termed the trusting mind (or naiveté), can be manipulated or programmed to unquestioningly follow the precepts of fairly narrow or negative people, families, groups, religions and nations.

In fairly well-adjusted adults, the faculty of the discriminating mind (the gateway) is better developed, through guidance and encouragement, so that they can make good choices in life. This whole learning process actually parallels physical growth and we should be able to *make our way in this world* by our late teens or early twenties. Correspondingly, it is during this time of life that young people voice their own views and seek the deeper answers in personal studies and exploration. They question, and perhaps rebel against, the assumptions which they grew up with in their families and communities. This too is part of the natural process of individuation and maturity. They are at the age when they are using, exercising, their perceptual gateways, their capabilities to choose for themselves. The path of conscious persons is to examine their personal truths and to determine for themselves what they will adhere to *and* what they dismiss. This truth will set us free -- and may also put us at odds with our family, communities, religions and nations.

Just to keep the record straight, I am an ordained minister from an interfaith church. I believe that all religions hold some truth and that if we eclectically choose the best ideas, practices and inspiration from these ideas, beliefs and philosophies, we will all benefit. There is a deeper complexity to religions of the world. Many belief systems that have grown into religious institutions started off with profound insights and clear perceptions of how life is and can be on this planet. There are times when these religions clash as to truth and interpretation, such as why God was chastising the USA with hurricane Katrina (yes, this was debated in the news the first decade of the 21st Century). Let the buyer beware ... We collectively get into problems when we set one way/one religion as the natural, superior, and right Belief System (BS).

As the ancient Chinese sage advised, "The thing all men should fear is that they will become obsessed by a small corner of truth and fail to comprehend its over-all principles." - Hsun Tzu (298 - 238 BC)

To understand the mechanisms of this learning process is to delve into the very routes and by-ways of education and enculturation themselves. The forging of characters, the development of personalities and the socialization of behaviors are all intertwined in complex but understandable ways in which we assimilate our surroundings, attitudes and beliefs. We can easily state that the *majority* of personal views are inherited, and each succeeding generation drops and adds (bits and pieces of) assumptions and popular truths in this very slow process of paradigm polishing, uh,... building. And this new input? – these new bits of information for our edification and progress? It would be great to state that we add bricks and boulders of new facts and truth. Nowadays however, we are bombarded with an overwhelming amount of news and information – and now the ubiquitous fake news and misinformation. It is easy to get confused in this fast-paced, hi-tech, Wi-Fi "modern" age. One of the resulting reactions to this speed and complexity is a dumbing down or simplification of things to make things palatable or easier to assimilate for the majority of people, which implies *with not much analysis nor reflection*. Examples of this are the omnipresent sound bites, or information bullets. A sound bite is, optimally, a clear summary of the larger context of a theme, but it can also be a particularly entertaining or cleverly worded (and quotable) statement that does *not* capture the essence of the issue but is manufactured to sell the idea – or to divert attention from the issue, or even to distort the truth. Sound bites are usually no more than 15 seconds, so they come quick and well packaged, – Under the radar screen. This is just one thing to be aware of when you sit down to check out the news, or listen, absent-mindedly (interesting word) to the radio or TV in the background. Catchy jingles, clever phrases, photo-ops and well-designed images and impressions are all part of the show. PR firms know this. Let the buyer/citizen be aware, or beware.

It would be better to spend time with thoughtful authors, well-researched documentaries, and great books, and to align with Nature, Light and Love. There is a divine consciousness, a great wisdom, that we all have access to – if we listen.

Turn off the noise, get thee in Nature, and attend the seminars of sunsets and rainbows, and the wonders of waterfalls and seasons. Peer out into the night sky and feel the enchantment. Be amazed.

Spiritual, Religious and Social Options

Modern voices ...

Although controversial, even to many Jews, the scholar, professor, and editor of Tikkun magazine, Michael Lerner (born 1943) has been an inspiration for modern Jewish activism. I first came across Rabbi Michael Lerner via his book "The Politics of Meaning" (1996) and especially his "Spirit Matters" (2000). I mention him here as a modern voice of spirituality and activism, which could inspire many to contemplate eutopian ideals. Lerner is a rabbi in ALEPH: Alliance for Jewish Renewal, a movement which he describes as "positive Judaism", rejects what he considers to be ethnocentric interpretations of the Torah. He has been outspoken against attacks on immigrant communities in the United States, and has attempted to build bridges with Christian, Buddhist and Muslim leaders around such issues.

Lerner writes: "This focus on money and power may do wonders in the marketplace, but it creates a tremendous crisis in our society. People who have spent all day learning how to sell themselves and to manipulate others are in no position to form lasting friendships or intimate relationships... Many Americans hunger for a different kind of society—one based on principles of caring, ethical and spiritual sensitivity, and communal solidarity. Their need for meaning is just as intense as their need for economic security."

https://en.wikipedia.org/wiki/Michael_Lerner_(rabbi)

In a similar vein, I would like to also mention the excellent book, "Spontaneous Evolution: Our Positive Future (And a Way to Get There from Here)" by biologist and author Bruce Lipton, and political philosopher and humorist Steve Bhaerman. Worth reading!

http://wikipolitiki.com/about-steve-bhaerman/

KARAMAH, Muslim Women Lawyers for Human Rights, is a U.S.-based non-profit organization that derives its name from the Arabic term "karamah", which means dignity. These women take us way beyond legal matters in their work. KARAMAH is founded on the fundamental principle that education, dialogue, and diligent action are the best tools to eradicate the dangerous and destructive effects of ignorance, silence and prejudice. Their vision is Dignity for All. KARAMAH envisions a world in which all human beings, regardless of gender or other differences, enjoy their God-given right of dignity.

"We believe that through education, women will be empowered to transform archaic, culture-based interpretations of women's status in Islam, to the betterment of themselves and their communities."

http://karamah.org/

The **Human Awareness Institute** offers workshops in intimacy, sexuality, community and more. From their website:

"For 50 years, the Human Awareness Institute (HAI) has dedicated itself to holding people in love, safety, and reverence as they walk the path of exploration of what it means to be fully human.

...

Inviting more love into your life opens a world of possibility and deep transformation. We are honored to accompany you on this powerful journey of transformation at all levels—physical, emotional, spiritual, and intellectual. This work can bring immense joy and freedom to your life, and it can also ask of you to address and heal old wounds and beliefs that no longer serve you.

At HAI, we take our commitment to walking with you on this journey seriously. Our workshop facilitators have years of training and expertise in holding a safe space for everyone to work at their own pace. While we encourage everyone to explore their edges, we honor choice and dignity above all else."

https://www1.hai.org/

Edgar Cayce and Planetary Influences

Edgar Cayce (18 Mar 1877 – 1945), the famous "sleeping prophet," gave very profound psychic readings the first half of the 20th century. Born and raised in Kentucky, USA, he discovered his intuitive abilities as a young man and then gave readings for the rest of his life. Mostly his readings were focused upon health and healing. The fact that Edgar Cayce gave information concerning astrology and reincarnation was a complete surprise to him, for he was a devout Christian and a Sunday school teacher. As people seemed to be positively influenced by these strange notions, however, Mr. Cayce relaxed and allowed more information of this sort to flow through him.

As a student of philosophy and esoterica, I have come across various proposals for the cosmological origins and purposes for our earthly existence – as well as explanations as to Why we are here at all. To me, no system or philosophy has felt *right* as much as that found in the Edgar Cayce readings. In fact, the legacy left by Cayce contribute to a larger world view that includes provocative and stimulating ideas on cosmology, purpose and soul lessons. The ideas found in the Edgar Cayce Readings form a greater picture that I call Cayce's Cosmology in the Adventure of Life.

Some of the fascinating concepts from the Readings include: interplanetary sojourns, reincarnation, astrological influences, karma, and the mission of spirits and souls. For instance, the "effects" of the planets, interpreted in astrology, are due to the intriguing idea that we have interplanetary sojourns upon these dimensional spheres in-between earthly lifetimes! Thus, astrology doesn't "work" because of precise calculations and figuring out one's birth signs and aspects between planets. No, we, as souls, had sojourns on these planets and stars and brought back the tendencies and lessons from these orbs. Now and again my clients inform me that they are on a foreign planet or a star, or inside a huge orb with thousands of lights – souls interacting and communing most probably on or *in* suns and stars. I intuitively understand where they are, thanks to Cayce.

In coming into the earth plane, we, as spirits, as souls, come in again and again into the physical manifestation of life. Spirit into the Flesh. The earth plane, or earth dimension, brings us lessons focused around the third dimension. As we have learned in school, the three dimensions are **length, width** and **depth**. Picture a cube type shape. That is what we learned in science class. Now forget it. That concept is more like a cube, and according to the Readings, this is called Space. Space, then, is one dimension. The 2nd dimension that we are experiencing here in the earth plane is Time. The third dimension, according to the readings, is Patience. Yes, Patience is a dimension of experience. Contemplate that.

When we, as spirits, come into the earth plane, the memories from our many past lives are remembered in our **emotional** centers, our senses and sensual memories. Thus, when we feel pleasure and pain, sensory delight, fear, hunger, securities, and insecurities, we are in tune with emotional memories of the earth, in this life and with those memories of past lives. We remember our past lives *emotionally*. When not in the earthly dimensions, we, according to the Readings, have interplanetary sojourns. We go, as spirits, as entities, to the dimensions of Mercury, of Jupiter, of Saturn, etc. Moreover, we have inter-planetary sojourns upon far away lights or stars like Sirius or Arcturus. These experiences of interplanetary sojourns are perceived as *mental urges*, or **mental** inclinations. And so, when we get those perspectives, or when we get those ideas, or flashes of inspiration, we are oftentimes recalling planetary memories that are felt as mental influences.

How does this cosmic picture fit together? The Creative Forces attuned the planets of our solar system for dimensional experiences and soul lessons. Let's get the story as Cayce described it [Reading 254-2, 19 March 1919]:

> (Q) Do the planets have anything to do with the ruling of the destiny of men? If so, what?
>
> (A) They do. In the beginning, as our own planet, Earth, was set in motion, the placing of other planets began the ruling of the destiny of all matter as created, just as the division of waters was and is ruled by the moon in its path about the Earth; just so as in the higher creation, as it began, is ruled by the action of the planets about the earth.
>
> The strongest power in the destiny of man is the Sun, first; then the closer planets, or those that are coming in ascendency at the time of the birth of the individual; but let it be understood here, no action of any planet or any of the phases of the Sun, Moon, or any of the heavenly bodies surpass the rule of Man's individual will power the power given by the Creator of man in the beginning, when he became a living soul, with the power of choosing for himself.
>
> The inclination of man is ruled by the planets under which he is born. In this far the destiny of man lies within the sphere or scope of the planets. With the given position of the Solar system at the time of the birth of an individual, it can be worked out, that is, the inclinations and actions without the will power taken into consideration.

The planets are vibratory centers that correspond to music, tones and color in a vast and orderly solar system and universe. We are aware of these orbs in our consciousness, much like recollections of our experiences or lessons in our memories. As we grow in consciousness, in awareness, it is necessary to pass through "the eight vibrations" or dimensions in our solar system, which are stages in development along our journeys to unite with the Creator. The following is a brief description of the planets and some of their effects. Be prepared for a few surprises!

Mercury is associated with high mental abilities. A mercurial soul is a gifted soul and needs to watch for self-aggrandizement or his abilities will be merely stumbling stones upon his path. Mercury brings understanding and communication, specifically the understanding of the other spheres, which means that inter-communication is key, and to understand others a talent. "Messages" are a part of life. Information please.

Mercury is connected to the pineal gland and the color indigo.

Venus is indeed the planet of love and affection. Sympathy, the alleviating of hardships, the seeking of love, esthetics and song are some Venusian influences. Beauty, either natural or man-made, will move these individuals; furthermore, there is a desire to beautify the home. Fairness is important, as well as balance. There is a strong attraction to the opposite sex. Charming and alluring.

Venus is associated with the thymus and the color green.

Mars may indicate anger, impulsiveness, and a temper. When focused, this is the stuff of heroes. Action and activity preclude any inclination to laziness. Accidents may occur. Stubbornness needs to be handled with patience and self-control. This entity may have an exalted opinion of himself, which is not necessarily bad. Mars on a higher level is courageous. Action!

Mars is connected with the adrenals and the color yellow.

Jupiter confers universality and ennoblement, turning one's attention to large groups of people or nations. It is expansive and may bless one with wealth, which includes a wealth of friends, a broad-mindedness, and the ability to consider others. Grand ideas and notions, but careful of exaggeration and over-commitment. Strength of character, jovial and humorous. Pack your bags.

Jupiter is associated with the pituitary and the color violet.

Saturn is the big surprise for astrologers. Far from indicating obstacles and restrictions, as many astrologers believe, Cayce says that it represents *changes*! These may be sudden or violent changes and represent testing periods of endurance and patience. Projects and associations are started, but follow-through may be a problem! Saturnians need to learn persistence, says Cayce! On the Saturnian dimension, an entity will meet constriction and the cosmic equivalent of a re-boot. A soul "banishes itself" to Saturn to begin anew, probably because the entity became stuck or fixed in some way. From here the entity was sent to Uranus, presumably to rebuild the will to make better future choices.

Saturn is connected to the gonads and the color red!

Uranus is the planet of extremes – and of the extremist! It gives an interest in psychic phenomena and the occult. "Moods and wonderments," says Cayce, "...when the entity is good, he can be very, very good, but when he is bad, he can be awful." A Uranian has times of smoothness and other times when "everything goes awry;" also, periods of ecstasy and depression. Thus, one's will and one's overall decisions to follow a path are important. Uranus seeks contrast and uniqueness. Group dynamics with hi-tech.

Uranus is associated with the thyroid and the color blue.

Neptune is the mystic planet. Neptune gives the urges to seek the unusual, the mystical, the "unseen" forces around us. Neptunians are drawn to water and liquids. This is a higher octave to the Moon. They may seem peculiar to others and could be misunderstood. A love of mysteries can indeed be spiritual, but it can also be "of the sleuth or detective nature." Watch for vagueness, confusion and hero worship! This is a good, kind soul who could positively affect others – if they overcome their reclusiveness and dreaminess. Envision and imagine!

Neptune is connected to the reproductive cells of Leydig, close to the sex glands, and the color orange.

Pluto was discussed by Cayce years before it was discovered! He had referred to Vulcan and Septimus – the seventh planet from the earth. When Pluto was discovered in 1930, Cayce affirmed that Vulcan, or Septimus, was the same planet. Regeneration and a growth in consciousness is indicated, but an affliction brings self-centeredness. Beware of wrath and grudges, warned the sleeping Cayce, "stay attuned to the love force." Pluto represents spiritual growth and development of the soul and its influence is just now developing in the destiny of humanity. What lies hidden?

Students of the Readings on astrology have noticed that Cayce mentioned all of the planets and their individual influences, but said little about the Sun, which is so important to us astrologers. Well he did say some unusual things about our central power source. First I will have you recall one of our spiritual admonitions – to know ourselves. A symbol of knowing ourselves is to look into the mirror, a sign of reflection. The Readings provoke and intrigue us here as we look at ourselves, and then look out into the sky, noting the bright Sun. In the Readings it was asked what are the sun spots? And it was answered that sun spots are those turmoils and difficulties *reflected upon the face of the Sun* which are the sins of man. Time and time again Cayce said that "we are continually meeting ourselves." So how do we collectively appear? As a blot upon the sun? And so he asks, "how does a cross word effect ye? As a blot?" Does that mark you? Are you marked, or darkened, because of an angry word or a cross thought? And in that sense who are you also? Are you a light unto others? And so our lights – and darks – are cast or reflected upon even the face of the sun! [As an interesting point of contemplation here: as Sun spots have an 11 year cycle of intensity (approximately following a Jupiter cycle), I wonder if our collective sins are cyclically washed or cleansed?]

This shows in a major way what a universal power and a duty we have – for our own development and even for the growth of our solar system. This is more of the adventure! What we do is reflected in the solar realms, and in the cosmos. And the stars are reflecting where we are at. Similar to what Cayce said of Septimus, or Pluto, that this particular planet was developing or growing, we can also say that it, and we, have not found our final form yet; we are growing! And so, in a profound sense (and this is an old astrological perspective which needs to be reinterpreted), *the stars do not rule us, we rule the stars!*

This cursory sketch is merely the beginning of a study of Edgar Cayce's contribution to astrology and cosmology. I hope it has piqued your curiosity enough to read further. A good place to begin is Margaret Gammon's *Astrology and the Edgar Cayce Readings.*

Official site: https://www.edgarcayce.org/

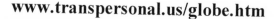

Stephen Poplin

> *Roaming somewhere in Europe or in North America, on planet Earth, like his guide suggested.*

Stephen's Travel and Lecture schedule:

www.transpersonal.us/globe.htm

Recommended Reading

The works inspired by Edgar Cayce, such as: "There is a River" by Thomas Sugrue; "Edgar Cayce's Story of the Origin and Destiny of Man", by Lytle Robinson, 1972; "Edgar Cayce on Reincarnation" by Noel Langley; "Reincarnation & Karma: Our Soul's Past-Life Influences" by John Van Auken; "Many Mansions: The Edgar Cayce Story of Reincarnation" by Gina Cerminara

"Life Between Life: Scientific Explorations into the Void Separating One Incarnation from the Next" 1987; by Dr Joel Whitton and Joe Fisher

"The Case for Reincarnation" by Joe Fisher

Dr professor Ian Stevenson, "Twenty Cases Suggestive of Reincarnation," 1974, and "Children Who Remember Previous Lives" (1987), "Where Reincarnation and Biology Intersect" (1997), "Reincarnation and Biology" (1997), and "European Cases of the Reincarnation Type" (2003)

"Inner Journeys, Cosmic Sojourns" - volume 1 by Stephen Poplin

Ursula Demarmels published the English translation of her German bestseller, "Spiritual Regression for Peace and Healing." 2015

Hans TenDam "Exploring Reincarnation"

Books on Life between Lives Integration - Michael Newton's books, "Journey of Souls" and "Destiny of Souls." "Memories of the Afterlife: Life-Between-Lives Stories of Personal Transformation" is a collection of stories and cases from The Newton Institute practitioners, including yours truly.

"The Present Power of Past Lives: The Experts Speak" and "Ending the Endless Conflict: Healing Narratives from Past-Life Regressions to the Civil War" by Joseph Mancini, Jr., Ph.D.

"Through Time into Healing" and other books by Brian Weiss, M.D.

"Reincarnation: The Cycle of Necessity" by Manly P. Hall

"Reincarnation: The Phoenix Fire Mystery" Compiled & edited by Sylvia Cranston

Books, continued …

Various books on reincarnation by Henry Leo Bolduc, including some free downloads. - www.henrybolduc.com/freebook.html

"Simple Spirituality: Finding Your Own Way" and "Opening the Aloha Mind: Healing Self, Healing the World With Ho'oponopono" by Jim Nourse, Ph.D., L.Ac.

M Scott Peck, psychiatrist, "The Road Less Traveled" 1978; "People of the Lie: The Hope for Healing Human Evil" 1983; "The Different Drum: Community Making and Peace" 1987

On Near-Death Experiences (NDE) - "Lessons from the Light" by Kenneth Ring; "Life After Life", and "Glimpses of Eternity" and other books by Raymond Moody

On astrology - "EcoAstrology: Finding Our Way Home" by Stephanie Austin; "The Exquisite Zodiac" by Rick DiClemente. An overview of how all of the astrology signs fit together. It shows how one moves and transforms into the next. After reading this book, one gets a completely new understanding of the archetypal bases that underlie this wonderful art/science.

"The Prophet" by Kahlil Gibran – for inspiration

There are many more …

Movies

Little Buddha with Chris Isaak, Bridget Fonda and Keanu Reeves

Siddhartha (1972) film based on the novel by Hermann Hesse, with Shashi Kapoor

Resurrection with Ellen Burstyn

What Dreams May Come with Robin Williams, Cuba Gooding, Jr. and Annabella Sciorra

Defending Your Life with Meryl Streep and Albert Brooks

The Adjustment Bureau with Matt Damon and Emily Blunt

Groundhog Day with Bill Murray and Andie MacDowell

Dead Again with Kenneth Branagh and Emma Thompson

Sixth Sense with Bruce Willis and Haley Joel Osment

Ghost with Demi Moore, Patrick Swayze, and Whoopi Goldberg

The Fountain with Hugh Jackman and Rachel Weisz

Cloud Atlas with Tom Hanks and Halle Berry

A Guy Named Joe (1943) with Spencer Tracy, Irene Dunne and Van Johnson … This was remade by Steven Spielberg in 1989 as …

Always with Richard Dreyfuss and Holly Hunter

Astral City: A Spiritual Journey (also known as Nosso Lar) is a 2010 Brazilian film inspired by psychics

Hereafter, directed by Clint Eastwood, with Matt Damon and Cécile de France

Dearly Departed directed by Darryl Anka, with Derek Partridge and Deborah Stewart and a large cast playing souls being "interviewed"

Made In Heaven with Timothy Hutton and Kelly McGillis

Just Like Heaven with Reese Witherspoon and Mark Ruffalo

Les jeux sont faits, known in English as *The Chips are Down*, a 1947 French film based on the screenplay by philosopher Jean-Paul Sartre.

City of Angels with Nicolas Cage and Meg Ryan

… and many more

˝C,Ɔ˝   ˝C,Ɔ˝

Index

˝☾,☽˝

About the Author

Stephen Poplin, M.A., CHT, spiritual hypnotherapist and transpersonal astrologer, has focused professionally upon personal and social improvement through self-awareness and spiritual understanding. His hypnotic specialties are past-life regressions, Life between Lives integration sessions, trance-personal journeys and talent enhancement. His social conclusion is that the majority of the world is hypnotized the majority of the time; we need to collectively wake up and take charge of our educational systems and policies.

After attending six universities in the U.S. and Europe, Stephen received his B.A. in philosophy and M.A. in Humanities (comparative religions focus) from Old Dominion University in Virginia. He has been a college instructor in several campuses from California to Virginia to Germany. He has studied history, psychology, drama therapy, astrology, Tarot, numerology and metaphysics. He moved to Virginia Beach, VA to study the Edgar Cayce readings. During his nine years there, he gave talks at the A.R.E. (Association for Research and Enlightenment). Stephen saw patients and taught courses at the *Center for Integrative Medicine* – a part of the George Washington University Medical Center, Washington DC (www.gwcim.com/). He trained with Dr. Michael Newton; Stephen is the former International Director of The Michael Newton Institute for Life Between Lives Hypnotherapy. He is a member of the International Association of Counselors and Therapists (IACT).

A globetrotter with previous abodes in Spain, Denmark, Austria and Germany, Stephen works with an international clientele. He attained the German state recognized Heilpraktiker für Psychotherapie and thus practices complementary modalities such as psycho-therapeutic hypnotherapy and counseling. Stephen travels frequently – conducting sessions, giving talks and leading seminars.

He wrote this book while in Story County, Iowa, USA. He divides his time between the USA and Europe, and the world beckons him farther afield. His hobbies are photography, hiking, biking, reading and exploring.

Inner Journeys, Cosmic Sojourns

by Stephen Poplin

Life transforming stories, adventures and messages

from a spiritual hypnotherapist's casebook

Volume 2

Story County, USA

◇

Web: www.transpersonal.us

If you enjoyed this book, don't forget to leave a review online,
and tell your friends!

I really appreciate your evaluations and recommendations,
and it only takes a few minutes to do.

Made in the USA
Middletown, DE
05 June 2019